"Make sure you are not going over the sea to find Utopia.
Utopia rarely lives up to expectations."

Richard Nelson Bolles

Second Edition - Complete and Unabridged

A Maverick Lifestyle Guide™

Published in the UK, USA & Europe by
Poisn Pixie Publishing
www.poisonpixie.com

ISBN 978-0-9571920-2-7

A catalogue record for this book is available from the British Library

CHUCKING IT ALL

HOW DOWNSHIFTING TO A WINDSWEPT SCOTTISH ISLAND DID NOTHING TO IMPROVE MY QUALITY OF LIFE

MAX SCRATCHMANN

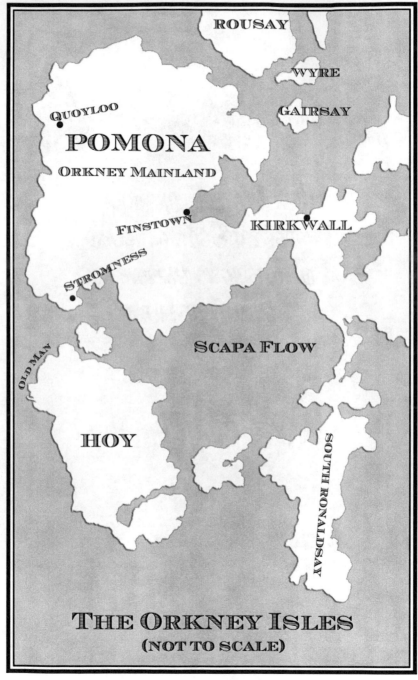

ROUSAY

WYRE

GAIRSAY

QUOYLOO

POMONA

ORKNEY MAINLAND

FINSTOWN

KIRKWALL

STROMNESS

OLD MAN

SCAPA FLOW

HOY

SOUTH RONALDSAY

THE ORKNEY ISLES
(NOT TO SCALE)

CHAPTER 1 – WHERE MY LONG-CHERISHED DREAM IS FINALLY REALISED PLUS I GET TO MEET A KANGAROO

I pull back the hastily tacked-up curtain on our new bedroom window and look out at the unbelievable vista of unending sea and sky before me. In the clear, painterly light of a cold April sun, I look down the hillside at a breathtaking panoramic landscape laid out in front of me like a camera obscura. Rugged sheep-grazing scrub quickly gives way to gently undulating fields which, in turn, flow down the placid slope of Snaba Hill like a river towards an ice-blue sea, where monochrome oyster catchers with bright orange bills dig patiently for sand worms on a narrow strip of pure white beach.

I can't believe it. After over six years on a drab Manchester inner-city housing estate, praying for a change, our goal has finally been realised and I am actually standing surveying an Orkney landscape. The lure of islands is, of course, as old as time itself, but most would-be downshifters dream of retreating to warm Mediterranean destinations when urban life gets to be too much. However, my own personal hankering has always been for the cold, clear light of the far North, and intoxicated from an early age by the razor-sharp lines and Arctic-colour-palette of post-impressionist painters like Stanley Cursiter, and later, the romantic writings of George MacKay Brown, my ultimate Utopia has always been the Orkney Islands, and here, now, this day, on a cold, clear morning in April 1999, we have finally arrived.

Suddenly, an irate snort jerks me out of my euphoric reverie, and I look around amidst the untidy piles of packing cases to a disgruntled hump on the bed that seems to be trying to communicate with me.

"Would you shut those bloody curtains, you're letting light in," the hump barks in a voice that sounds remarkably like my girlfriend, Chancery's. "It's far too early in the morning for daylight."

"But it's a fantastic morning and we're here, I mean, not just any old here, but *here*, here. You know, Orkney," I protest, but the hump is unswayable,

so I let the curtain drop again, plunging the room into darkness, and then quickly push my head under the drapes so that I can still see out of the window, frightened that my new El Dorado will be gone if I let it out of my sight for more than a couple of minutes.

However, the sky is still reassuringly ice blue and a stiff breeze is making some thin white clouds race southwards, and, as I try to breathe it all in, I remember just how long it has actually taken me to reach the stage in my life where I can finally call all this home.

I had, in fact, tried to make my first pilgrimage to the dark islands at the tender age of seventeen, when, having just obsessively devoured my Penguin Jack Kerouac Omnibus in the first week of the school summer holidays, I had decided to personally re-enact On the Road and hastily packed some watercolours and a change of underpants into my rucksack and hitchhiked up the old A9 to John O' Groats from my home town of Dundee, guided only by a sketchy map my mother had got free from saving tokens on the backs of Batchelor's soup packets.

Hell-bent on a pilgrimage round the isles, I nevertheless discovered that I had missed the last ferry and, with the impulsiveness of fickle youth, decided to hitchhike down to Land's End and the promise of Cornish nude beaches instead. But this morning, almost thirty years later, the urge for the Orkneys is still with me, and today is to be the first day of our new life in the isles, a land seemingly fairly close to home, being only some twenty miles from the north east tip of the Scottish mainland, yet so alien in geography and culture as to be on a different planet.

In fact, the whole place is so different from anything that I've ever encountered before that there's even a kangaroo on the grass in front of the house.

What?

I shake my head to clear my thought processes, muddied from the long journey north, but, no, it's a bit small but it's definitely a kangaroo. I look out, incredulous, and cautiously meet its eye and the kanga looks back.

Unblinking.

"What?" it seems to say.

I run quickly back into the room and shake the hump violently.

"Wake up, wake up, there's a kangaroo on the lawn!" I cry, and an incredulous face surfaces from beneath the duvet.

"We haven't got a lawn, and there certainly isn't a kangaroo on it," the face says very patiently. "Come back to bed."

"But there's a kangaroo..."

"Trust me, there are *no* kangaroos in Orkney. I've read all the guide books," the face mutters wearily, sliding back down to its warm place in the dark folds of bedding.

"Well, one of those little kangaroos things then..." I protest.

"Wallabies?" the face says, reappearing.

"Yes, that's it, a wallaby. There's a wallaby on the lawn," I cry emphatically, "you have got to come and see this. It's too fantastic to miss. And there are sheep and clouds and flying feathered things too."

Chancery sits up and eyes me coldly. "By 'flying feathered things' I suppose you mean birds?" she says carefully and I nod. "Listen, there are going to be lots of 'flying feathered things' here, so you'd better get used to it. I won't tolerate you waking me every time you see a seagull in a field."

"Ah, but what about the kanga?" I ask, playing my trump card. "Are there lots of *kangaroos* here too?"

Chancery, sleep murdered, gets up and staggers to the window, muttering, "If this is a joke..." as I triumphantly pull back the impromptu drapes and cry, "Ta-dah!"

The kanga looks up bad-temperedly and seems to mutter, "Fucking

tourists!" under his breath. Chancery looks at him and then at me.

"That's a hare, you prat," she says shortly. "Haven't you ever seen a hare before?"

"Oh yeah, of course, there are loads of hares in Manchester," I mutter into my socks. "They run hare food stores all over Rusholme for the itinerant leveret population. Talk sense, where would *I* have ever met a hare before? Except here, of course. Wow, there's a real actual live hare, right there, on our grass. Wow. This is going to be so cool!"

Chancery makes a disgusted noise like a cranky old cow with colic as she crawls back into bed, her last muttered words being, "God, it smells of cat pee in here," before she vanishes beneath the duvet.

*

It seems unthinkable that it is only slightly more than forty-eight hours since we set out on this epic quest, leaving Manchester, where we had washed up some six years previously, at half past six on a sunny morning in early April. Chancery, as is probably already obvious, is not a morning person at the best of times, and today she looks like an extra from I Walked With A Zombie; the cat is heavily sedated but fighting it manfully, and the cab is packed full of house plants and flowerpots, making us look a bit like a Triffids Roadshow tour bus. The rusty old truck we have hired from a small back-street firm is packed up to the roof, hates going up hill and literally eats diesel, but we make fairly good progress in cruising mode nevertheless, and at about ten, we cross the border into Scotland and stop for what must surely be poached haggis-bird eggs and toast, to judge by the price we are asked at a roadside franchise cafeteria outside Kilmarnock, where I avail myself of the opportunity to phone my Dad to report on our progress as I have been strictly instructed.

Now, my father is an anxious man who has been known to lie awake on summer nights fretting about what will happen to his daffodil bulbs when the frost finally comes in January, and he has been in a state of hyper-neurotic paranoia about our house move for the last two weeks, having firmly convinced himself that we will be unable to cover the distance in the time allocated, and has thus made up a detailed route schedule for us

to follow[1].

Dad answers my call a split second into the first ring and I can hear the beads of cold sweat from his brow hitting the receiver as he demands the details of our current location. Chancery makes insolent faces in the background while I give him our co-ordinates and he checks our position on the map, no doubt placing a little flag on the spot, but we appear to be making as close to satisfactory progress as his current frame of mind will allow and his anxiety is momentarily appeased.

"You're doing not bad, but don't get cocky. Keep the pace up," he says, apprehensively. "And watch out for broken glass on the roads. And don't go braking for any rabbits..."

*

We get as far as Perth, the 'Gateway to the Highlands', without mishap, but as we journey further north, and the gradients become steeper, our pace slows the further up the A9 we progress. I had last traversed this particular thoroughfare as a Kerouac-intoxicated teenager in the early seventies, hitchhiking all the way up to John O'Groats in the cabs of malodorous fish lorries and cattle trucks, and although fond memory paints the road as a narrow strip of tarmac fighting a losing battle through unforgiving mountains, I am nevertheless relieved to see, more than twenty-five years later, that the highway is now much improved, and dual carriageway for a large amount of its duration. But as we get into the Highlands proper, and the road cuts its way through dynamite-hewn gullies in ancient basalt, the going becomes almost as tough as it had been all those years ago.

However, chugging up hills and coasting back down, we finally make it to the junction for the trendy ski resort of Aviemore in the Cairngorms by about two in the afternoon, and although good sense tells us to press on while the fragile early spring light holds, Chancery has had her legs tightly crossed for the last thirty miles and is shifting restlessly from left buttock

---

1 - Unfortunately, here in Dadworld, the compiling of such a schedule is considered sufficient and my father has, of course, not thought to send us a copy so we have absolutely no idea if we are progressing along our route according to his timetable or not.

to right, so we take a quick detour off the main road and into the town for a lunch and pee break.

I park the truck in front of a rugged mountaineering-goods store housed, somewhat inappropriately, in a rather twee mock-Swiss wooden chalet that has a restaurant on the upper floor, and push my way through swarms of cherry-cheeked English teenagers with posh voices and obscenely hairy Fair Isle sweaters, while Chancery rushes off to relieve her overloaded bladder and I find a call box to phone my Dad again.

"You're where?" he cries, almost totally consumed by anxiety when I tell him that we've stopped in Aviemore for lunch. "No, no, no. You should at least be in Inverness by now. What the hell have you been playing at? I told you not to brake for bloody rabbits on the road, just run the buggers down. And you've no time to mess around with lunch, it'll be dark soon, just buy a sandwich and get the foot down."

I promise to oblige, but of course we stop and have a leisurely lunch anyway, figuring that what he doesn't know about won't hurt him, and we finally dawdle into Inverness about ninety minutes later and drive over the magnificent suspension bridge to the Black Isle and the official start of the Far North, just as the afternoon sky starts to display a faint tinge of pink. However, once we cross the spectacular valley where the laconic River Ness gives way to the tidal waters of the Moray Firth, the hills become considerably steeper, and the road quickly gets narrower and twists and turns more and more often, and I begin to heartily regret the Danish pastry and second pot of Rooibos as our optimistic five-in-the-evening estimated arrival time at the ferry port in Scrabster begins to recede rapidly into the ether.

However, all continues to go well, if slowly, until we reach a place called the Braes o' Berriedale, a natural white-knuckle ride situated in the middle of nowhere, halfway between the windswept coastal villages of Helmsdale and Dunbeath, if you're following this on the map. The road has been getting steeper and steeper and the old truck has been protesting, and I have dropped down to third gear, and then to second, as we reach the summit of a particularly tough incline. Suddenly a magnificent vista of dense pine forest stretching out to the sea is unveiled to us as the land falls away and a roller-coaster-style descent commences. The truck virtually

falls over the summit and then careers madly down the treacherously twisty road like something out of a cartoon, picking up momentum as a blur of twenty percent gradients signs flash by, indicating scary-looking emergency stop sandpits and imparting ominous subliminal messages of imminent death and destruction from faulty brakes.

I am down to first gear by now but gravity is still pushing the wobbly old truck downhill at a reckless pace. We can actually feel the load in the rear pressing into our backs as we rattle down the slope, and I have the brake pedal almost at the floor as we descend. However, it looks as though we're at the base of the slippery slope when, suddenly, a Zed-bend sign appears out of nowhere and the road takes a ninety-degree elbow-swing to the left and then starts to ascend just as steeply. The truck protests volubly as I try to coax it round the sharp corner, and the weight of the load makes the back wheels swing out as I brake too violently and the engine stalls, and, as we teeter on the foot of a one in five gradient slope, the heavy load in the rear begins to pull the van towards the edge of the road and a sheer six-hundred-foot drop to an angry sea beneath.

*

We've been sat now for a good four minutes, unable to move forward or back. We can feel the load inching cliffwards in the back of the truck and the handbrake is making protesting noises about having to keep such a heavy weight stable at this very precarious angle. The cat, having had enough of being tossed around in her basket and, totally unaware that she is supposed to be sedated, sets up a howling loud enough to wake the dead, while Chancery and I decide that it's the perfect moment to embark on a fierce domestic. I'm yelling that everything's under control; Chancery's yelling back that I should shut the fucking engine off and go and get assistance; the cat's screeching like a walled-up demon in an Edgar Allan Poe story, and the cab suddenly seems to be filled with a veritable jungle of dishevelled house plants that are all trying desperately to wrap themselves around my neck.

However, masculine supremacy asserts itself, and assuming control, I take a deep breath and start up the motor again, putting the truck into gear and attempting to move off. But the engine won't stand for it and stalls again. Determined to win this war of wills with gravity, I close my eyes and

transport myself back to being seventeen again and remember my old driving instructor teaching me how to do hill starts. The words "keep the handbrake on until the front of the bonnet starts to rise up and then ease off gently" float past my eyes and I restart the motor and gingerly put my foot on the accelerator. The engine starts to roar and I release the clutch fully as the nose of the old truck lifts slightly, thus allowing me to tentatively discharge the handbrake.

The back wheels spin on the spot, spitting dust and gravel, and there's a nasty over-heating smell that even an automotive ignoramus like me knows is the scent of a clutch plate burning out, but we don't move forward. Instead, the truck starts to slip backwards, the rear wheels scuffing the edge of the road with only a flimsy crash barrier between us and a six-hundred-foot drop to oblivion.

I try desperately to get the truck into motion but succeed only in stalling the motor again and we lurch back another six inches off the edge of the road and into the completely inadequate crash barrier as I hastily slam the handbrake on again, wincing as it groans in protest.

I can feel the strong gravitational pull on the whole vehicle, itching to pull it downwards to the sea. The cat is continuing to howl and Chancery starts yelling things about "bloody pig-headed morons with their bloody gonad-fuelled macho suicide attempts" and jumps out of the cab and storms off, returning purposefully a moment later for the cat and her cheese plant, which she installs at the side of the road, with arms tightly folded, like a furious refugee.

I, however, am still filled with this unaccustomed macho zeal to prove that I am, in fact, the master of this situation, but there's no way that I'm either going to win this argument or persuade the truck to perform a hill start at this gradient with the load it has on, and I have to admit to myself that each face-saving attempt is only taking me half a foot closer towards certain death.

Despite what my long-buried machismo would like to think, I have to face facts.

We are stuck.

*

Rescue comes in the form of a passing BT man. We have been sitting at the side of the deserted, wind-blown roadside, ostentatiously not speaking, complete with cheese plant and the cat still in her basket, looking like latter-day flotsam from the Oklahoma Dustbowl, hoping for someone to pass with a mobile phone so we can call out the breakdown service, when a British Telecom Transit Van comes up the hill and pulls up alongside us. We are overjoyed as he will surely have a cell phone in his cab but he laughs derisively at the suggestion.

"No signal up here, lad," he declares confidently in the strange Irish-sounding patois of Caithness and the far north east. "But dinnae worry, I'll get you going!"

He rummages in his tool box, a sort of yellow plastic technician's version of the Ark of the Covenant, and chucks a tatty blue nylon tow rope out to me, instructing me to fix it firmly to the front of my "wagon" while he skilfully attaches the other end to the tow bar at the rear of his own vehicle.

Wishing that I'd never thrown all those childhood tantrums and just gone to the bloody Boy Scouts like my mother had wanted, I follow his instructions apprehensively and affix the rope to the front of the truck in what I hope is a reasonably secure knot, trying desperately to excise images from my mind's eye of our overloaded vehicle pulling me and this friendly guy and his van over the edge of the precipice.

However, it appears that I won't be pulling anything anywhere, as the BT man glances at my feeble townie's attempt at a knot, tuts under his breath, deftly undoes it and ties it up again securely and seems finally satisfied.

"Okay," he announces cautiously, sniffing the acrid aroma of burnt clutch plate in the air. "Your clutch's taken a wee bit of a battering so don't start up until the rope starts to strain. You got that, laddie?"

From where I'm standing, I can now see just how unstable our truck is, and I'm so scared that I don't trust myself to reply in case I shriek like a girl, so I just nod dumbly, determined to prove to my still-blazing beloved that

I'm on top of this situation, and I get back gingerly into the precarious Cab of Terror, which, of course, whimpers protestingly at my added weight.

My rescuer motions at me to wind my window down and then gets into his van and starts up. The Transit's engine roars and it pulls forward, the tow rope going rigid as it is restrained by the weight of our truck, and I hear him going up a gear then see his arm motioning me from his window to start up. I turn the ignition key and tentatively put the truck into first and, experiencing a spontaneous conversion to Islamic Fundamentalism, I quickly say a silent Hail Mary just for luck, and release the handbrake.

The tow rope stays rigid, and there's a horrible metallic groaning sound, but nothing happens for an agonising second, then suddenly the BT van lurches forward like an energetic dog straining on the leash and starts to climb the hill, and to my astonishment, our marooned truck follows suit.

CHAPTER 2 - WHERE WE ARRIVE AND FALL PROMPTLY IN LOVE WITH THE DARK ISLANDS

We stand gripping the rail at the prow of the old MV St Ola, foam and spume splashing into the air as, after ninety uneventful minutes of unspectacular water and a couple of bedraggled seagulls, we suddenly behold the full majesty of the dramatic Old Man of Hoy, a natural four-hundred-and-fifty-foot rock stack that towers out of the water like a multi-story office block and marks the gateway to the Orkneys like the Statue of Liberty welcoming immigrants to New York harbour over a century ago.

The day has started bright and sunny, refilling us with the pioneering spirit of adventure that the fiasco of the previous afternoon had slightly dashed, and although we have slept late and completely ignored my father's strict instructions to be at the Scrabster ferry terminal for eight o'clock sharp to "get a good space on yon boat", we have joined the long crocodile of camper vans full of Easter-break tourists creeping slowly onto the ferry boat at half past eleven, and, at twelve noon precisely, embarked on our maiden voyage to the isles aboard the last in a long line of MV St Olas.

The battered old ferry boat has taken just under two hours to crawl cautiously across the Pentland Firth, a narrow strip of treacherous water just north of John o'Groats and a mere twenty miles of turbulent sea that has successfully defeated Norse invaders for thousands of years and, even with the benefits of modern nautical technology, is still often impassable during the long Orkney winters.

It has been a fairly quiet and subdued journey so far, but sighting the Old Man creates an air of fevered euphoria amongst the mobs of people who are now swiftly lining the rails of the upper deck, and the whole boat is suddenly awash with light as flashbulbs go off all over the place when scores of tame Scandinavian Twitchers produce cameras from their rucksacks and photograph each other against this phenomenal natural backdrop of water and rock. Fully caught up in the tourist thing, I grip Chancery's hand tightly and we share a moment of pure exhilaration, as we

stand awestruck by the huge monolith of red sandstone that towers above us, gulls circling it like Busby Berkeley dancers as spumy waves break around its craggy base.

The island bard George MacKay Brown, who has so influenced our decision to settle in this very remote place, has romantically described the newcomer's first sighting of the Orkneys as 'encountering a school of dark hump-backed whales in a storm-tossed sea', and with images from romantic tales of huddled crofters crowded around smoky peat fires while storms rage dancing before our eyes, we wait impatiently for the boat to dock and let us complete the final leg of our epic journey and find the new house that we have rented blindly, without either a photograph or floor plan.

The weather remains calm and sunny as the ship's master navigates the rusty old 'Ola confidently down the tranquil Hoy Sound, a centuries-old shipping channel that meanders slowly past the rocky shores and sheer cliffs of the mountainous island of Hoy to one side, and the green fields of the more arable Pomona or Orkney Mainland on the other. Then, after what seems like an age, the engines begin to slow, and the verdant slopes of Pomona's Brinkie's Brae give way to the ancient port town of Stromness, and we realise that we have finally arrived in our new home.

We quickly follow the stream of people 'in-the-know' heading down to the car deck and half an hour later sees us leaving Stromness and heading out into the open countryside. We have been expecting a grey and lowering vista dotted with grim Puritan churches and flaming Wicker Men, but instead the island landscape is lush, green and arable, with treeless gently-rolling hills dotted with little grey stone "longhouses" and mushrooming modern bungalows, and everywhere we look there are vast skyscapes and magnificent views. With no real clue of where we are going, we drive hesitantly along the island's 'main' road, passing quickly through cultivated green hills and then meeting the sea again as the picturesque Harray Loch meets up with the tidal Loch of Stenness. Despite the famous Orcadian inability to give comprehensible directions to strangers, and the total lack of signposts and house name plaques[2], we finally arrive at the

---

2 - These latter being considered a complete waste of time and effort as everybody knows who lives where anyway.

quaint grey-sandstone village of Finstown in the parish of Firth, with its collection of formerly turf-roofed long-houses and erratic stores – one in a derelict Methodist Chapel, the other a tiny little stone shoebox with a hand-cranked petrol pump outside – and vainly try to find the house we have rented sight unseen from Manchester via a classified ad in the Exchange and Mart.

Our new landlord is an eccentric little farmer called Tumshie John who has told us to find the house by turning left "where the dairy used to be doon the Grandon Road" at the village of Finstown, forgetting, of course, to mention that there will be no street sign and absolutely no indication of where that might be in the village, or even where the village itself might be located. However, with the aid of our map we eventually find the right yellow brick road on our third attempt, and I navigate the over-loaded truck cautiously down a narrow single track lane, scattering angry ducks left and right as we drive through what appears to be an old byre slap bang in the middle of somebody's farm.

A little woman on a moped squeezes herself grudgingly into a tight passing space to make way for us as we trundle down the dip at the other side, and the meagre track sweeps out of the village in a wide arc past a fine-looking derelict bere mill and a natural tidal lagoon called the Ouse, then back up along the base of the craggy Snaba Hill. The narrow single-track road is populated intermittently with old wood and stone long-houses which presently give way to sporadic harled modern bungalows, and we pass several possible places, none of which, of course, display house names, but we eventually arrive at a house that appears to match Tumshie John's description to the letter.

I'm frankly hesitant to believe that we can possibly be getting this house for the peppercorn rent that has been asked for it, the location being something like the Wise Old Necromancer's Cabin in an old Wagnerian expressionist opera set, and the quaint little bungalow sits midway up a steep hill on a large patch of coarse daisy-strewn grass, rugged sheep-grazing slopes behind and a fantastic panorama of farmland, sea and mountains in all other directions. There's an almost vertical dirt track leading up to the dwelling and I decide not to risk the truck on it – which is a mistake – until we have verified that this is, in fact, our new home, so parking cautiously at the foot of the trail, I go up to the house and knock tentatively on the

open wood-plank door.

"Hello!" shouts a distinct and very unexpected Lankie-twang, and a young guy with long blonde hair and a faded Happy Mondays tee-shirt appears in the hallway. This is definitely not an Orcadian farmer called Tumshie John, by any stretch of the imagination.

"You the new guy, like?" the latter-day-hippy asks in a strong Lancashire accent, flicking his flaxen locks out of his eyes as he drags me back to face a new confusion. This is getting surreal. Have I just dreamt the last two days? Am I still in Manchester, or even worse, Salford?

Pulling myself together I confirm that I am, in fact, "the new guy", and learn that this amateur Adonis is not the aforementioned John but Matthew, the previous tenant, and that he and his wife have moved up from Lancashire a year ago and are now relocating to a cottage in the village that's "closer to the bus stop".

"Sorry I'm still here," Matthew apologises, "but I've lost our Smokey. I'll be gone as soon as he gets in".

*

I have no clue, of course, who the fuck "our Smokey" is, but Matthew seems to think I do, so I leave him sticking his head into gorse bushes in search of God-knows-what while I go downhill to try to get the truck up the almost vertical incline to the house. But without any momentum behind it there's no way the old rust bucket's going to handle it and I'm terrified that I'll burn out the clutch before I can get it back to the hire company. Chancery, who can't drive, by the way, mutters something about my automotive skills that doesn't sound at all complimentary, and flounces off up to the house, taking the cat in her basket as she goes, and I'm standing in the middle of the road by the truck and scratching my head when an old Wallace and Gromit-style green van with a collie dog's head hanging out of the side
window, pulls up.

"Aye-aye, whit like? And you'll be Max, will ye no'?" says an already-familiar Orkney voice, and before I have time to shout "Fuck me! A talking

dog!" he continues bemusedly, "Why are you no' just going up to the hoose?"

Another shaggy head has appeared beside the dog's by now, and a florid face like a pink-iced chubby-cheeked Halloween cake peers out inquisitively at me.

This is our new landlord.

Tumshie John is what you might call a typical old-school islander, a little Hobbit-like sixty-something guy, about five feet tall and dressed in the obligatory check shirt and farmer's dungarees, with unkempt chicken-shit-streaked grey hair and stained, uneven teeth. He, in turn, sizes me up as a useless townie in a swift glance, mentally files his assessment for future use, looks at the truck and takes a sniff of the burnt clutch smell and quickly disappears back into his van.

"Aye, and you'll be needing to bring a new clutch home soon," he intones unintelligibly in what I assume must be the local patois. "We'll use me van tae get you home. Bide there a peedie[3] minute and I'll be back".

*

John returns a few minutes later in a muddy tractor with two mangy collie dogs, a coil of barbed wire and a couple of ancient fence posts crammed into the cab with him, and he throws a by now ubiquitous blue nylon tow rope out to me.

"Fix your motor onto the back," he shouts, "and I'll get you home."

Matthew, the former tenant of our very own Wildfell Hall, meanwhile, has been yelling, "Where are you, our Smokey!" and, "Gedd'eer now, our Smokey!" into every gorse bush on the slope, and his search of the surrounding undergrowth has reached the bottom of the incline, so he comes over to assist, and together we tie the truck to the tractor. But John merely tuts at our urbanite nancy-boy knots with withering world-weary farmer-patience, deftly reties them, and then effortlessly tows the laden

---

3 - **Peedie:** small, little, wee

truck to the top of the steep hill. He then formally introduces himself to us, informs me gravely that our deposit cheque has cleared, spends twenty minutes chatting up Chancery and finally gives us the house keys, but still seems in no hurry to leave.

Matthew is still wandering around the scrub yelling, "Here,Smooo-keeey!" like a lost extra from a Fellini movie, and we are all standing on the hillside looking out over the fantastic landscape of land and water that's spread out before us like a camera obscura, while Tumshie John proceeds to give us a panoramic tour of the locality, pointing out who lives in all the surrounding houses.

However, as the stocky little farmer gets fully into his stride, he launches into what proves to be a familiar theme for him, indicating newly built houses on plots of land which have previously belonged to his family and bemoaning the loss he has made on the transactions.

"You lost money?" I say and Matthew gives a little sigh.

"Oh aye," John replies sadly, "thoosands and thoosands..."

"What, you were cheated?" I exclaim with an outsider's naivety, unaware that I have just risen to the bait on a very well-worn trap, as Matthew groans deeply and disappears into undergrowth the with a desperate cry of, "Smokey, where *are* you?"

"Oh aye," John sighs, a small smile appearing on his face as he mentally congratulates himself on successfully luring yet another gullible foreigner into his trap. "I sold that land there for three thoosand pounds in 1973 and it's worth about sixteen thoosand noo. That's thirteen thoosand pounds I've been cheated oot of. And I only got eighteen hundred for that peedie bit doon there in 1982, and that's worth at least fifteen thoosand noo..."

*

Matthew is packed and ready to go by now but he is still scanning the hillside around us with anxious eyes. We wonder if this is some local departure ritual that he's picked up during his scant year in the Northern Latitudes, but eventually he confides that the aforementioned Smokey is

his grey marl cat who has been out all night and has not as yet returned. Relieved that some half-crazed junkie is not, in fact, going to murder us in our beds during the night, we assure him that we will keep a weather eye out for the errant feline, and once we take a phone number and a full description of the culprit the worried Matthew finally bids us a fond farewell.

Alone at last, we look around us in sheer culture-shocked disbelief. We are still, it is true, within the British Isles, but our surroundings are as foreign and unusual as any faraway land. The landscape that we survey from our large picture window looks like a rich and arable, but very alien planet in a classic episode of Star Trek, and the golden afternoon sun is slowly setting over the bay and casting long purple shadows over the lush green fields that sprawl lazily down the gentle hillside to the white sands of the unspoilt beach. The quiet feels more like something is missing, with no sounds of traffic, or the ever-present sirens of Manchester housing estates, and at every turn there are beautiful sea-and-landscapes where no-one is dealing drugs, bellowing at their kids, or having a screaming argument with their spouse, and the only sound we can hear is the cry of seabirds and the occasional baa of sheep in a neighbouring field.

After far too many stressful years of merely existing in some of the worst districts of the North West of England, we feel that, at last, we will be able to put down some roots and begin to live our dream in this beautiful tranquil place, and be able to grant our creativity the freedom that it has been craving for almost a decade.

Yes, we say smugly to each other, all the struggle and money that has been spent getting here has been more than worth it, we have *finally* downshifted and life is going to be just peachy from now on.

*

We spend the rest of the afternoon and early evening unloading the van, awestruck as a huge orange moon rises slowly up over the bay like something out of an animated Manga movie, and we go to bed, worn out, at about ten o'clock, experiencing a perverse sensory deprivation when we turn the light off for the first time and find ourselves engulfed in pitch blackness darker than any flotation tank.

The quiet is almost deafening and, ironically, this proves to be stressing and I find myself lying fretfully awake waiting for the Druidical Virgin Slaughtering Convention, Brass Band Marathon or whatever else God has up his copious sleeve to shatter my peace. Astoundingly though, nothing happens other than the occasional call of a night bird, and I eventually drift off into a fitful sleep, only to be awakened at about half past five in the morning by the wailing of a soul in torment.

I pull back our hastily tacked-up curtain and come face to face with a huge mouth and a set of needle-sharp teeth, belonging to the howling dervish that has taken up residence on our bedroom windowsill. Hello Smokey.

I groggily stumble out of bed and go round to the front door to let him in, give him some of our cat's food and lurch straight back to bed, only to be awakened about a minute later by more howling.

I can feel Chancery's searing gaze glowering at me in the dark.

"You haven't just done what I think you've just done, have you?" she asks sharply.

"That depends entirely on what you think I've just done," I reply, attempting to stay asleep.

"Tell me you haven't just let a strange tom cat into the house?" Chancery's disbelieving voice drifts into the soft folds of welcome oblivion and sleep is shattered forever.

With a muttered cry of "Oh shit!" I stumble out of bed once again and stagger into the pitch black hall, groping quickly round the unfamiliar room for the light switch.

But my nose is already telling me that all is lost and that it is too late.

Poor Smokey has come home to find that not only are his owners absent but all the furnishings of his house are missing as well, so he has done what any self- respecting tom cat would do in the circumstances: he has re-marked his territory.

By peeing absolutely everywhere.

CHAPTER 3 - WHERE WE START TO FIND OUR ISLAND FEET AND MEET UP WITH A BACKWOODSMAN IN THE FOG

I wake early in the morning of day three, after another restless night's sleep. After years in an unquiet city, with constant noise and glaring streetlamps outside our window, we are intimidated by both the impenetrable dark and the pin-drop quiet, and I toss and turn through the small hours, convinced in my semi-conscious state that the strange repetitive noise that I can hear is the sound of vandals at work the house, and at first light I finally sit up and put the bedside lamp on, determined to deal with the perpetrators.

"What the *fuck* are you doing now?" Chancery's bleary voice demands as I hastily pull a jumper over my head and wince as my bare feet hit the icy cold linoleum.

"Someone's running a bloody spade along our outside wall," I reply, still half asleep and unaware of just how insane this sounds. "I'm going to sort the bastards out."

"God, those delinquent sheep," Chancery mutters from below the duvet, "out there committing acts of vandalism during the hours of darkness. You go see to them, Superboy."

Wakefulness is beginning to impinge upon me by now and the ludicrousness of my proposed course of action comes slowly into focus.

"But what's that noise...?" I falter uncertainly and Chancery snorts, "It's the clock ticking, you idiot. You've just never heard it before. Now either come back to bed or get up, but put the bloody light out."

I flop down again and douse the light, amazed that my new world is so quiet that even a normally filtered-out sound like a clock could have become so amplified, and I realise just how tightly wound I've become over the last few years. I try to go back to sleep, mouthing absurd six-in-the-morning approximations of Louise Hay positive affirmations to myself,

but I eventually realise that I might as well be lying counting off the hours in Big Ben's clock tower, and I finally give in at about half past seven and stumble through to the kitchen to make tea.

Thanks to the excellent marksmanship of our Smokey, it still smells conspicuously of cat pee in here, despite our having spent the entirety of yesterday afternoon scrubbing every available inch of wall space and washing the place down with about a gallon of Zoflora. Muttering about the choice nature of the acrid aroma to our own cat who has now emerged sleepily from her bed, I potter about with teacups and kettle, until I suddenly notice that our spectacular view is missing and that the outside world has completely vanished.

The cat and I pad quickly out to the front porch to investigate this apparent disappearance of all humanity, and I open the door to a silent land of white nothingness, realising that the whole island has been completely engulfed in a thick white sea fog, like crude cotton wool, which has obliterated the entire landscape to the extent that thick tendrils of the stuff are creeping in to softly stroke my face with cold fingers.

"Gosh, Pusskers," I say, shuddering, "I feel like I've just been kissed by a ghost from the bottom of the sea", and suddenly inspired, I ferret into one of the many packing cases that are sitting around the dark house in precarious stacks like sleeping Daleks, and dig out my notebook to quickly scribble down a poem about a drowned girl coming back from the sea to visit her lover, only to be lost when the sun's rays disperse the fog.

It is, of course, a piece of pure unadulterated schmaltz that even Hallmark cards or Orkney's own George MacKay Brown would have binned for being over-sentimental, but it is the first piece of writing I have done in about a year that's not a complaining letter to a mortgage broker, and I am ecstatic at actually getting something down on the page, convinced that the Orkney air is already infecting my creative glands with super-charged positive ions

*

We spend the rest of the day unpacking while the mist continues to swirl silently around the house like a somnambulistic stalker in a Stephen King

novel, and it has a strange effect of making time stand still as it's difficult to tell if it's day or night with all the windows just showing an impenetrable opaque white. However, around two, despite the fact that the light is unchanged, our stomachs start telling us that it's really time to eat, and I volunteer to go out across the blasted heath to the village and pick up some provisions from the local store. Chancery graciously concurs and continues to heft packing cases, and I step gingerly into the fog, shuddering a little as its ghostly cold hands stroke my face again, and hurry quickly down the hill towards the lights of the main settlement.

*

Finstown, like all good Orkney townships, is an old community, sitting cheek by jowl with the sea, and it appears to consist of one long, straight street of grey stone long-houses hugging the main road, with a few tributaries leading off to some newer developments. There's a semi-derelict stone pier that projects into the gently lapping waves and vanishes ominously into the mist, and two shops: Jimmo Baikie's Emporium, a largish grocer's and bakery on two floors, housed in an abandoned Methodist chapel, and Pottinger's, a hand-cranked petrol pump and cramped shoe- box-sized shop that sells everything from Mars Bars to rat poison. There's also a tatty old pub called the Pomona Inn, and bizarrely, a place we later dub Havisham's – a permanently closed restaurant which is Finstown's own Marie Celeste, permanently frozen in a legal wrangle hinterland with its white-linen-covered tables expectantly laid for dinners that are never served.

In my mind's eye I've been seeing a simple lunch of lightly grilled chicken breasts, some vine tomatoes and maybe a dash of fresh basil, if they have it, and, of course, a crusty loaf, and I select Jimmo Baikie's, the larger of the two bazaars, as being the most likely retailer to have what I need. After several years in Manchester, with its plethora of fresh food markets and ethnic grocers of all nationalities, I am well used to always finding what I require in the way of victuals, and nothing prepares me for the startling array of provisions that is about to meet my eye as I push the stiff door of the village store and walk into its dimly lit interior, a brass bell clanging stridently above my head.

It would be unfair to say that there is no fresh food in the shop, as there is

a shelf literally groaning under the weight of strange sponge cakes with fluorescent orange icing and a varied selection of rotund vomit-coloured objects with bits of white stuff sticking out of them –which, a hand-written sign assures me are "Fresh Ogo-Pogo Rolls" – but, except for an ancient browning cauliflower left over from the Viking siege sitting in splendid isolation below the canned vegetable section, there are no fresh fruits or vegetables, and the concept of organic or even natural provisions seems to have been completely lost on a grocer's situated slap bang in the middle of a region of intense agricultural production.

However, despite my townie smugness we still need to eat, and I look quickly around me at shelf after shelf of tinned and packet products, some of which I hadn't realised were still being manufactured, and assemble something to make a half-bearable meal until we can get into the main town of Kirkwall the following day, and, grinning to myself about the tale I'll have to tell when I finally sit down to write my memoirs, I leave the lights of the shop and go back out into the fog once again.

*

A strange dark object like a cattle truck, or a hearse conveying lost souls back to Hades, materialises out of the gloom and almost runs me down, its blaring horn a forlorn sound in the white silence of the world outside, and I strike out across the dark village with not a little trepidation. The mist has thickened considerably now that the afternoon light is starting to fade, and I head quickly back to our house, taking the narrow track almost one step at a time as visibility falls to about three yards in front of me, and I tentatively round the corner by the derelict mill, said to be a Trow's[4] hollow, where the mist is even denser, cross an old hump-backed stone bridge and start the slow upward climb which will eventually lead me home.

The landscape, which is still very new to me, changes drastically in the weirdly greenish fog-light, and there are odd bird noises and strange animal sounds echoing around with no apparent worldly sources. Wrapping my scarf tightly round my face, I quickly mount the steeper part of the hill, near the ruined shell of a derelict burned-out longhouse, and am just about to start the last leg of my journey when I hear a strange

4 - **Trow:** Troll, Brownie, Bad or Evil Fairy etc

scuffling sound from the hillside above me and a ragged figure with wild eyes and long straggling hair suddenly appears out of the mist.

He's a gaunt, wiry creature in his mid-fifties, with long grey hair contained Red Indian style by an old tie made into a headband, and thick sideburns creeping up over sunken cadaverous cheeks. To someone who has read far too much M.R. James and Edgar Allan Poe, he looks like a scarecrow made out of a dead man's frock coat who's crawled up from the graveyard and is out seeking revenge on the desecrators of his ancestors' burial grounds.

All the guide books that we pored over so lovingly in the safety of our fortified flat in Manchester have assured us that here, in the isles, friendly natives delight in stopping to pass the time of day with strangers on the road, and so, trying desperately to find my normal voice rather than the boy-soprano-squeak that seems to have replaced it, I make a pathetic attempt at casual roadside banter.

"Nice day," I peep. "It's foggy... quite mild really..." but the phantom Doctor Syn simply glares at me and then suddenly makes a deep guttural sound before running down the hill towards me with an almost bestial agility.

'Oh my God!' I think to myself as my life flashes quickly before my eyes. 'No wonder there's no fresh produce in the shops, they kill the tourists and hang their bodies from hooks in their caves. Goodbye cruel world!'

He's on the tarmac of the road by now, facing me and blocking my escape route, and he's so close that I can see the whites of his bloodshot eyes.

"Hello there... neighbour," I try. "I'm not a tourist, you know. I've just moved here..." I try again, hoping to placate this emaciated cannibal with my heartfelt allegiance to his native isle. But my efforts fall on stony ground and he just makes a dismissive snorting sound, and then suddenly leaps the ditch at the opposite side of the road and vanishes back into the swirling mist, while I run screaming in the opposite direction, convinced that I have just uncovered the long-lost stomping ground of Sawney Bean[5].

*

28

All our meagre savings have been spent on our epic move to the Far North, and now that we are finally here there's the suddenly pressing matter of eating and the rent to be faced. All the books on downshifting that we have studied prior to our departure have heavily emphasised the need for a financial safety net or other contingency plan to cover this exceptionally fragile transitional period, and, bearing this in mind, we have thought long and hard about our options and come up with the fiendishly cunning survival plan of "something's sure to turn up".

As a freelance illustrator, I have been banking heavily on the assumption that my income will follow me wherever I go, but, if I'm honest, I have to admit to myself that not all of my clients will share this rose-tinted worldview with me, and I know in my heart of hearts that various jobs will certainly fall through over the next few weeks, when clients discover that I can no longer blithely come to their offices to attend their briefing meetings.

Fallow periods like this are, of course, not new to me, and have always been solved in the city with night jobs at call centres or even, if push came to shove, MacDonald's, and therefore the combined necessity to locate the local Jobcentre for a MacPart-time job, plus buy some decent 'real' food, sends us swiftly on safari the next day to Kirkwall, the island's capital city.

"Toon" lies some ten miles away to the east of the island, and it's just a little too far away to contemplate walking, but, though public transport is something of a rarity at this time, all the brochures we have collected from the tourist office at the ferry port inform us that there is a bus, which runs more or less hourly to the capital, and we walk briskly down to the village to suss out the pick-up point. The previous day's mist has cleared and the sun is shining again, although there's a fresh wind that has an abrasive feel to it, which gives a fine ruddy glow to our skins, and we set off optimistically to walk the mile or so to the village wherein lies a road capable of supporting a bus.

---

5 - **Sawney Bean:** 16thCentury Scottish cannibal who lived in a cave in coastal Ayrshire with his wife and over thirty-two, said to be mostly incestuous, children.

"Gosh, this is just so cool," I gush as I take in huge lungfuls of the chilly April air. "I suddenly feel like I'm alive again. I knew there had to be more to life than just walling ourselves up in that flat in Manchester. All these birds and sea and stuff. It's all just so... cool!"

"It's certainly having a profound effect on your vocabulary," Chancery mutters dryly. "Now, could this be the bus stop, d'you think?"

We have reached the nerve centre of the hamlet by now, and are standing facing a slightly foreboding steel structure that has been bowed by the winter gales into a sort of bent-old-man shape, and which creaks threateningly in the stiff spring breeze.

"Well, the road's here, and it looks like a bus shelter..." I ponder aloud. "Hang on a sec and I'll nip into the shop and ask."

"Aye-aye," a miniscule girl perched on a high stool behind a prototype electronic cash register chirrups in greeting as I enter Jimmo Baikie's dimly lit emporium. "Did you like the beef pie you got yesterday?"

I stare dumbly back at her, nonplussed, as I have never clapped eyes on the wench before in my life, and am totally at a loss to understand how she knows what I purchased the previous day. Seeing my confusion, she adopts the special condescending tone that all islanders keep in reserve for dumb Soothies[6] and patiently explains, "Marion, that was here yesterday, said that the new folk in Tumshie John's hoose had been in the shop and bought food. That's how I ken[7] what you had to eat."

"Oh," I say, inadequately, looking round the deserted store. "And is Marion on her tea break just now?"

"Oh no," the girl replies matter-of-factly, "it's just me on here the day, don't you see? Marion phoned me when she got home last night. Now, what can

---

6 - **Soothie:** One from South or "Sooth", or, in other words, anyone who comes from anywhere
other than Orkney.
7 - **ken:** know

I get you?"

Fighting the urge to run screaming out of the door, I quickly purchase a couple of sausage rolls for an on-the-move lunch and enquire about the buses.

"Oh aye, the bus to Toon stops outside, right enough," she tells me. "There's no' really a timetable as such, but they're usually on the hour. Depending on who's driving, of course. If it's Arthur, he's usually quite predictable, but if it's Billy, well, no-one really knows where *he* is. Would you like me to heat your sausage rolls for you?"

*

Forty minutes later a rickety old coach packed to the roof with chattering farmers' wives and back-packin' tourists finally rolls up, and, as the door pulls open via a Heath-Robinson device constructed out of recycled pulley wheels and old clothesline, we are warmly greeted by the aforementioned Billy, Orkney's only full- time bus driver, a pleasant and gregarious sixty-something man with short, Brylcreemed grey hair and a crinkly smile. Billy introduces himself to us, enquires about our health and asks whether or not we are Tumshie John's new tenants, all in the short time it takes him to take our fares and count out our change from the battered margarine tub tucked away below his seat.

"Does everybody here know who we are already?" Chancery asks me in a hissed whisper as a rotund grey-haired old lady, who looks like a hausfrau from an old advert for tinned soup, moves her shopping basket to make room for us on the back seat.

"Aye-aye," Jean McGregor says pleasantly as we take our seats and the back-firing old coach lumbers off. "You'll be the new folk in Tumshie John's hoose. Tell me, how do you like Orkney so far, and which one of you is the writer and which one's the artist?"

Thus our journey continues. Nobody gets tickets, the ancient bus cheerfully stops wherever anyone hails it, and Billy, the driver, loves whistling, humming and outright wailing the Irish Country & Western music he plays loudly on a cassette player hooked up to the vehicle's crackly PA system. Being used to privatised urban public transport

companies in the south, where everyone studiously ignores everyone else and hides behind the opaque screens of their newspapers, we find the music alone deafening enough, but on top of this, all the local people think nothing of questionnairing us, and everyone on the bus talks nineteen to the dozen anyway, often with people at the back holding shouted conversations with acquaintances down the front, and, of course, with Billy the driver chipping in at will, all to the strains of drunken Paddy pub singers caterwauling such classic lyrics as, "Oh come and save our poor little Betty, who's selling her arse at the Dublin jetty", so it's no wonder that after three days of moving, then this, our heads are spinning when we – gratefully – alight at Kirkwall and set out to explore the ancient town.

*

Kirkwall, mentioned in the Orkneyinga Saga as early as 1046, is Britain's most northerly city, and the island's capital and major port, and it forms an untidy ring around the truly magnificent and quite titanic red sandstone Cathedral of St Magnus, which was built by the Norse Earls of Orkney in 1137. Approaching by bus, however, we see the town's arse end first, the outer sprawl of the suburbs being most definitely late twentieth century harled havens due to a building boom in the wake of the sitting of an oil refinery on the neighbouring island of Flotta in the 1970's. A surprisingly large industrial estate dominates most of the coastline to the east as Billy's bus chugs into the city, but we suddenly round a bend and catch sight of the town proper, resplendent in all its medieval glory with the magnificent spire of St Magnus towering over its craggy crow-step skyline. Old Cursiter paintings from the 1940s show the sea lapping up to the very rear of the original buildings that surround the cathedral, but reclamation in the mid twentieth century has pushed the water back again, leaving a strange marooned lagoon like a giant boating lake in its wake, and with typical island pragmatism, the locals have dubbed this sullen expanse of water "The Peedie Sea".

The bus rapidly empties as we crawl into narrow urban streets, and Billy drops us off at a rather bleak and windswept car park behind the Peedie Sea, giving us highly detailed directions on how to find the "Toon" proper, although the cathedral spire is a fabulous beacon in its own right. Heading quickly towards it we walk down a narrow wynd that doesn't quite permit us to walk side by side, and then suddenly fall through a rent in the fabric

of the universe and tumble headfirst into the 1950s.

The three main streets in Kirkwall, leading from the harbour to the cathedral, are paved not in tarmac but heavy stone slabs manually hewn from the island's own quarries over a century ago, and an assortment of odd shops and houses line these thoroughfares in a typically pre-planning-permission era hodgepodge. There are one or two branches of national chains, like Boot's and Woolworth's, which sit cheek by jowl with a huge hardware emporium featuring an enticing display of galvanised metal buckets to tempt the tourist trade, plus some souvenir stores and drapers, one of whom appears to be displaying a window full of big pants and baggy knickers as if this were a positive enticement.

Cars drive insouciantly along the slippery slab roads, narrowly missing ranks of walled-in dwarf-sized pedestrians, and there is a tremendous amount of good-natured horn honking as drivers wind down their windows and hold conversations with friends on foot, oblivious to slowly piling-up traffic behind them. Of a supermarket, however, there is no sign. But we have been reliably informed by our companion on the bus that there are, in fact, two of them on the edge of the industrial estate, and assured that we are not going to have to survive on a diet of Uncle Ben's rice and tinned stew after all, we knuckle down to the serious business of generating some income and thus, go in search of the Jobcentre.

*

The government office in question, when we eventually track it down, turns out to be an ugly anachronistic 1960s prefabricated building, which sits uncomfortably in a narrow seventeenth century lane behind the magnificent red sandstone Cathedral of St Magnus in the heart of the city. There's the usual orange plastic 'Today's Vacancies' board, with a single dog-eared card declaring that the local fish factory urgently requires skilled partan[8] workers; a coffee table with a few dusty, out-of-date government propaganda magazines, and a desk with a hand-written sign saying "Reception".

At first glance, the quiet office appears to be completely deserted, but

---

8 - **partan:** edible crab

slumped very low in his chair, behind the aforementioned Reception desk, sits a glum, boiled-faced man called Robin, who's wearing a bright fluorescent-yellow Ben Sherman shirt, which I assume he must have selected in the dark as it does absolutely nothing for his lobster complexion.

Robin is one of those morose Walter Mitty-type men that you always seem to find behind desks in out-of-the-way government offices, who look as if they're mentally piloting the Star Ship Enterprise, and he glares suspiciously at me when I say that we want to look for a part-time job, plus sign on for any benefits that we might be eligible for.

"Hmmmm...... I've never seen you here before," he muses unpromisingly. "Do you *live* here?"

"Well, er, we've only just arrived actually..." I start, but he stops me dead.

"What? You're just off the boat? And are you going to stay here forever?" he demands, peering at my side as if he expects to see my luggage at my feet.

"Well, hopefully..." I try again.

"No, no," he snaps, "What I mean is, you're not tourists, are you? We get a lot of tourists in here. You'll see them all down Broad Street, taking pictures of the cathedral. You can't get Benefit if you're a tourist, you know."

I assure him that we are definitely not tourists.

"Well, do you have a trade?" he counters and looks at me askance when I say that I'm an illustrator. "You're an illustrator? You mean you draw *pictures* all day? You'll find that there's not much call for *that* around here. Do you not know anything about fish?"

"Well, I drew one once," I say, unintentionally provocative, and he glares at me again, mentally filing me under Useless Southern Bastard, and shakes his head.

"Well, you'll obviously be no use for the fish. What about farm work? Can you drive a tractor?"

"Welllll... no," I say, now convinced that I've completely blown my first ever Orkney 101 exam. "But I've done loads of work in call centres."

"Oh aye," he says with just a hint of dryness, while picking up his pencil in readiness. "And what does that entail?"

"Well, answering phones..." I say.

But this urban skill doesn't appear to impress him in the least, and he drops the pencil again with a skilful cross between a harrumph and a tut. "Oh, I don't ken what to do with you. You'll just need to come in and talk to Inga next week and see if she has any ideas," he finishes, shaking his head.

And then suddenly his countenance brightens as he notices Chancery, who's been skulking behind the empty vacancies board. "Or I could maybe squeeze *you* in right now..."

A frozen smile on her lips, Chancery assures him that an appointment next week will be just fine, and we thank him and exit swiftly, before he has time to demonstrate his Klingon salute.

CHAPTER 4 - WHERE WE UNVEIL OUR MASTER PLAN TO BECOME A TWATT

I come from an old colonialist background, having grown up in the last dying days of non-integration in the British Raj in India, and thus hold some very strong opinions about the correct way to behave as a 'guest' on someone else's turf. So, prior to our move, when all our downshifting manuals unanimously recommend that it is inadvisable to behave like "Ugly Americans" when trying to blend into a small, tight-knit community, we clasp our hands firmly to our chests and swear that we shall commit wholeheartedly to our new land by playing an active role in our newly embraced dwelling place.

We soon discover that this is not a difficult goal to achieve, however, as the Orcadians are an exceedingly friendly race who welcome all their guests with open arms, and we quickly find out that we have, in fact, already earned the title of "Community People" when we put in an appearance at the village hall Beetle Drive on our first Saturday in the parish. This encouraging nomen fills us full of inspiration to become Finstown's Favourite Ferry-Loupers[9] in as short a time as is humanly possible; and we set out to become known in the locale by simply turning up to support every event on the parish social calendar.

Thus we speedily find ourselves imbibing numerous cups of brackish "real" tea at the Ladies' Lifeboat Tapestry Patchwork Display; pitting our wits against teams of plucky ploughboys at the Steam Tractor Society Quiz Night; and cheering on squads of meandering mallards at the annual Poultry Handlers' Duck Race.

However, we soon realise that it is mere child's play to attend only the junior leagues of Orcadian merry-making, and if we really want to be thought of as natives, we need to get out our dancing shoes and patronise one of the many ceilidhs held at the village hall, and so, when we see a poster advertising the "Sensational Wyre Band In Concert" we head down to the local community centre to have our premiere encounter with

---

9 - **Ferry-Loupers:** A derogatory nickname for outsiders who 'leap' onto Orkney via the ferry

Orkney's most-talked-about show business attraction.

*

Rum is flowing like water when we arrive at the hangar-like community hall on the night in question, and there's a lot of tapping of mikes and one-twoing going on as stunted farmer types connect threadbare leads to an ancient PA system while their wives scuttle about the floor in their best Crimplene frocks, but eventually all is in readiness and the lights go down. Remembered images of rock concerts at the Manchester Arena fill our heads as a single flood lamp clunks on, and we crane our necks for our first glimpse of the cool leather-clad idols, but instead of the expected Fender-clutching rock gods the Wyre Band appears to consist of Johnny, a local postman, accompanied by four squat sixty-something guys, three armed with accordions, and the last a Jew's Harp.

There's a couple of seconds of tuning-up noises, and then Johnny the Postie downs a double rum in one gulp and whirls round to the mike growling, "Take your partners for the Eva Three-step," as the band launch quickly into their first number and the floor rapidly fills with scores of tubby "wifies" partnered by mahogany-faced men in braces and high-buttoned slacks. Orkney traditional dance to the uninitiated – I muse to myself, watching the gyrating bodies on the floor –is a sort of unholy blend of African voodoo and a rather huge helping of the Time Warp, and thus, amused by my own referential humour, I turn with a grin to ask Chancery if she wants to "try some folk dancing", but find that she has already been kidnapped by an over-heated farmer in his best navy suit who stands at least four inches shorter than her. I, too, am also quickly baited and trapped in the eager clutches of a fervid wench, already well beyond the boundaries of sobriety, who breathes whisky fumes in my face for the duration of the jig, then sticks her tongue in my ear before she departs into the crowd with a lewd wink.

It's not quite what we've been expecting and we're taken aback at our first night-time encounter with Orcadians, who are a rather staid and emotionally repressed race by day, but, it seems, veritable Jekyll and Hydes when the midnight sun sinks below the ever-present ocean and the locally distilled Highland Park whisky washes away their numerous inhibitions. With some alcohol in their bellies and the worn parquet of the dance floor

dusted with Slipperene – a lethal ankle-busting blend of talc and chalk-dust manufactured to a centuries-old secret recipe that turns any surface into a skating rink in thirty seconds flat – the islanders prove to us that it only takes two lively tunes for their much written-about traditional dance to quickly revert to its decidedly tribal origins.

Chancery is being passed around the farming community like a rag, while a procession of cuddly doll-women, their faces flushed from liquor and exertion, take it in turn to drag me up onto the dance floor. Fuelled with an insane fire as the band crank out song after song in quick succession, they fling me about to the roar of Johnny bellowing, "Strip the Willow!", "Postie's Reel!", "Hooligan's Jig!" with each one eliciting a louder cheer than its predecessor and demanding more and more esoteric and intricate choreography as the whole ceilidh sinks into a maelstrom.

An hour later I'm standing gasping for breath when there's a throaty call of "Are you ready for the Nine Pins?" followed by a raucous cheer of assent, and a wild woman with fifty-proof-breath and huge bosoms grabs my hand with a steely grip yelling, "This Soothie's going to be wur[10] pin!" and I am thrown into a sort of high-speed musical chairs where the men outnumber the woman and have to make a mad dive for a partner when the music stops, which in practice is nothing more than a drunken grope-fest, and I fully expect my Amazon to rip her polypropylene top from her barely-contained bounty and get down and dirty any second.

However, just as things are beginning to really hot up and clothing is about to be rent asunder, virtue is preserved by a resonant cry of "Supper!" and the house lights come up abruptly as the Sports and Social Committee – a fleet of sober women in plastic aprons – hand out tea and heaped plates of dry bere bannocks, cheese, pizza, sandwiches, and enough baked confectionery to feed all the armies of western Europe.

*

Chancery is still imprisoned in the midst of a group of clammy, beetroot-faced men now stripped of their ties, and I am standing in a corner by myself, trying to see if anyone's actually managing to eat all the contents

10 - **wur:** our

of the laden plates of carbohydrate and wondering if there's a handy aspidistra to pour the contents of my large delft cup of navvy's brew into, when a stiffly-erect middle-aged couple come over and introduce themselves to me, just as the music starts up again.

The husband is a bristly, blazered little Englishman sporting a dapper military moustache and razor-like creases in his mail order catalogue trousers, while his good-lady wife is a strapping bean-pole German with long pipe-cleaner legs and big feet, a bit like the result of some kind of unholy coupling between Greta Garbo and Donald Duck.

"Hello, hello," the man says, gripping my hand as if he's recruiting me. "You'll be the artist chappie that's renting Tumshie John's house. Great little character, our John, salt of the earth. Particularly when he's had a few, what?"

"I really wouldn't know," I say diplomatically. "We don't really see that much of him."

"Aha, you wait until Christmastide," the wife interjects. "Then you will see some drinking. No, Hector?"

"Oh yes," the husband says to me, man to man. "My little Hildy is so right. They know how to celebrate the New Year in these parts. You wait and see."

"So you've been here a while then?" I ask, changing the subject, and they both nod vigorously.

"Oh ja, ja," the wife beams. "It is our home now. We are students of the Traditional Dance."

"Oh," I say politely, for want of something better, peering over their heads in the hope that Chancery will see that I have been trapped and come and rescue me. But I see her being led to the floor by one of her new string of beaux and realise that I'm on my own.

"Yes," the little man chimes in, jerking me back into the present, "I'm writing an academic thesis about how Traditional Dance here differs from

the more common Scottish Country Dancing. I'm particularly interested in the Zeitgeist of the Dance in the Isles in general and, of course, the Wyre Band in particular..."

During this lecture, Johnny the Postie has been gutturally caterwauling a slurred rendition of "Goodnight Irene" into the microphone as the assembled multitude grope their way around the floor to a St Bernard's Waltz, and I wonder quite what's so special about these particular musicians, other than their ability to sink copious amounts of alcohol and still remain standing. But my companions insist that the boys from Wyre are, indeed, the pinnacle of the Orkney musical form.

"You see, unlike most bands, these chaps can play for a whole night and never repeat a single dance," the little man insists earnestly. "They know the full repertoire and they keep the whole tradition of The Dance alive almost single-handed. Yes, they're all virtuoso musicians and consummate professionals, to a man."

"Wow," I say, nodding appreciatively, just as Johnny's brother, Edwin, makes a bold flourish on his Jew's Harp, teeters on his equilibrium point for an agonising second, and then crashes off the low stage to the floor below with a loud crump while his fellow instrumentalists carry on playing, completely unperturbed.

*

A frigid May trails lazily into a bright but chilly June. The early summer nights diminish to almost nothing, and as longest day fast approaches, tatty old minibuses full of Druids rattle off the ferry and set up camp on the beaches in preparation for the Summer Solstice celebrations at Orkney's mystical ring of standing stones at Brodgar.

The locals, however, are indifferent to the demands of the old Norse gods and cheerfully leave the New Age Travellers to get on with sacrificing the requisite virgins on the stones, while they, instead, dedicate themselves to their own modern-day summer traditions and rituals.

Great wodges of recycled baler-plastic bunting are suddenly festooning Finstown village's main street and the local shops rapidly all go into fundraising overdrive and cram their counters with books of raffle tickets and mega teddy-bear-naming competitions. This in itself is nothing too unusual as Orcadians are big on raffles and it's essential to keep a supply of mugger money in your pocket at social functions as a refusal to participate is not an option, but we cannot fathom all the flags and sudden over-proliferation of frightening fluorescent-coloured teddies until we discover that the parish's biggest annual festival, the Finstown Gala Weekend, is about to commence and the whole community is gripped in the throes of fervoured anticipation.

Sensing a fabulous opportunity to further our cause to become the island's most Fun Foreigners, we quickly buy our raffle tickets, terrified that we might actually win one of the grotesque furry toys, or, worse, baskets of tinned herring tails and oatcakes, and, on an icy windswept Friday evening in June, join the assembled villagers in celebrating their Viking heritage on a narrow strip of stony beach at the Bay of Firth, to witness the official opening of the Gala, and our first Finstown Raft Race.

We have been unsure what to expect, but the raft race seems to be a fairly low key affair, and shivering in a bitter wind that's blowing straight in off the sea, there are six teams of apprehensive-looking oarsmen standing beside a motley fleet of home-made rafts and dinghies. There is a single team of earnest sporty types in team colours and matching life-jackets, three squads of fat beery punters in baggy rugby jerseys and shorts, some kids with a blow-up dinghy, and in the far distance, a team of old ladies who appear to be downing several flagons of cider prior to splash-down, but who on closer inspection turn out to be some of the village lads in drag[11].

Other than this impromptu imbibing session, however, nothing much else appears to be happening, and we stand shivering with typical townie impatience in the exceedingly nippy wind that's coming in off the sea.

"Aren't these guys supposed to be dressed in hats with horns and wrapped in still-bloody sheep fleeces?" I say to Chancery in what I think is a discreet

---

11 - Dressing up in general, and drag in particular, is big in Orkney, in a masculine sort of way, of course, and many a football team has toured the "Toon's" watering holes dressed in their aunties' frocks.

aside, but a cynical and distinctly Central Scottish voice from behind me audibly replies, "Hell no, that's Shetland where they dae that. Don't let them hear you mixing the two up or they'll hang you aff the nearest standing stone for the crows tae eat."

We turn abruptly to see a fat scruffy guy with wild grey-streaked hair, clad in jeans and an ancient jumper that appears to be sporting samples from every meal he's ever eaten in the last year.

"Hallo, I'm Shuggie," he says, proffering a grubby paw. "I take it you pair are new here?"

We nod cautiously and he continues, "And you want them tae embrace you as one of their ain? It's never gonna happen. Oh, they're friendly enough, and they'll tolerate you quite cheerfully if you play by the rules, but you'll never be one of them. The first rule for surviving here is tae keep your own eejit half-baked opinions to yoursel'. They've got long memories and they're still fighting vendettas over slights tae their grandfaithers' grandfaithers. And don't ever mix them up with Shetlanders, or folk from the Western Isles either. And don't, whatever you dae, call them Scottish. Nobody's broken it tae them yet that that's who they are. They'll never forgive you for that yin!"

"So you're not from here then?" I ask, stating the bleeding obvious, and he shakes his shaggy head amusedly.

"Hell, no!" he exclaims. "Came up fae Clydebank a year an' a half ago in search of the good life. Still hav'nae found it, or a fucking job either. Seems I'm no' a Twatt and that's apparently really important doon at the fish works."

"Come again?" I say, perplexed, and he looks at me like I'm some helpless imbecile child trying to master the concept of thermodynamics on re-entry.

"Orcadian surnames," he says with weary patience. "They don't mind you living here but they won't employ you over one of their ain. And they can tell if you're one of their ain or no' just by your name on a form. So if you're called Twatt – no, don't laugh, it's an ancient parish here and a really valued old Orkney surname – or Isbister, or Flett, or Clouston, or Firth,

then you're at the top of the food chain when they're picking folk, but if you're just called Smith you go right doon the bottom. What *is* your surname, by the way?"

"Scratchmann," I say and he laughs mirthlessly.

"Bloody hell, you'd better just pack your bags and skedaddle now," he says shaking his shaggy head. "There's no way you're going tae be able to show a reference tae your family in the Orkneyinga Saga any day this week."

"They actually *ask* you stuff like that?" I say, having myself been hearing an ominously deafening silence over the last couple of months from the local employers regarding some part-time work, and my new friend chuckles bitterly.

"Hell, yeah!" he replies. "They've got parish registers going back tae the Vikings, and if your granny – or at least your auntie's auntie – isnae one of them you're totally fucked."

I look at him incredulously and he nods sagely.

"I kid you not," he says in the weary tone of one who has already explained this many, many times to dewy-fresh newbies, and my head suddenly fills up with all the niggling anxieties that have plagued me over the last few months. I'm about to ask him to elaborate when a starter's pistol suddenly goes off and interrupts our discussion.

The raft teams quickly throw down their beer bottles and stumble through the icy water to their crafts as the scrap yard armada finally sets sail. There's a lot of splashing and clambering, with people falling into the water, and when they eventually cast off, most of the 'boats' just go round in circles while one sinks completely. However, the kids in the blow-up rubber dinghy, who are probably the only sober competitors there, manage to dart out to the front and head for the finishing post on the other side of the bay amidst cries of "Cheats!" and "Peedie Gobshites!", while a lurking orange lifeboat picks up the already blue survivors from their sunken crafts.

We wait around expectantly for the survivors to be set alight and pushed

out to sea on their marooned vessels, but it seems that the party's already over.

"They're all off tae the pub now," Shuggie, our new buddy, explains as people begin to pile into cars or walk up across the fields to the village. "It's an island tradition tae get as rat-arsed as you can before nine o'clock on Gala Friday, and stay that way for the whole weekend."

"Should we go too?" we ask, but Shuggie merely shakes his shaggy head.

"I don't recommend it," he says, deadpan. "They'll no' respect you in the morning.

*

Saturday is the Gala's big day and starts about lunchtime with "Activities" and a burger barbecue in a lumpy field opposite the village hall that's about half an inch deep in very moist goose shit. "Activities", we soon discover, however, consist primarily of drinking in a rickety beer tent, but there's also a haphazard assortment of Tombola, Hoopla, and Find-the-Needle-in-the-Hay-Bale type stuff to keep children occupied while their parents get themselves totally sozzled at the al fresco bar.

Chancery whispers to me, sotto voce, that it's all a bit like being at the Craggy Island Annual Fete in an episode of Father Ted, but I remind her to keep her opinions to herself, and, smiling like Westminster's most seasoned legislators, we're doing our patriotic bit and eating quarter-carcass mad-cow burgers from the barbecue stall when Lynn, a petite forty-something village lady in a beige cardigan and taupe print frock, sidles up.

"Aye-aye," she says, her ingenuous blue eyes wide. "We were wondering, do you pair play Rounders?"

Now, anyone who has seen me on a dance floor knows that co-ordination is *not* one of my gifts, and neither of us gives off an air of being remotely interested in sports, so they're either being more than exceptionally friendly or are desperate for people for their play-offs, but before we know what's happened we hear ourselves agreeing to be in one of the teams for

the following day's death-before-glory Rounders Tournament.

"Oh good, good," Lynn says, the bargain sealed and our souls safely in the depths of her fawn leather bag. "It's not my team you're in, it's Doreen's, but she's a peedie bit shy and didn't like to ask you herself."

She waves and quickly makes a secret victory sign to the aforementioned Doreen, a strapping lass in her twenties with wide child-bearing hips and breasts the size of Yorkshire – who, by the way, doesn't look in the least bit shy – and she lumbers over to make formal introductions. The niceties being quickly dispensed with, we get our instructions for the following day and they move on, stalking off through the crowd on their mission to find more hapless saps who don't know their modus operandi of old and have an excuse ready to hand.

*

My Dad, like many men of his generation from the bleak grey sandstone metropolis of Dundee, spent several decades working in an Indian jute mill and brought my sister and myself up with a strict ethos about not, under any circumstances, giving money to beggars in Calcutta street bazaars, as it would put an invisible mark on us and cause every vagrant in the place to sense a soft touch and home-in on us for the remainder of the day.

I have always regarded this as part of his normal paranoia, but today it seems that we have barely surrendered our virtue to the Rounders mafia when a callused hand snakes round my shoulder and a honey-dew voice whispers Satan-like in my ear,

"I hear you're in the Rounders team. Do you want to be in the Tug of War too?"

I turn to see a steel-wool-haired woman called Linda, who I have often seen riding an ancient bicycle up and down our road, and who has always appeared to be fairly normal up to now, but today seems to have been possessed by the spirit of Competitiveness Past. Her eyes shine with a frightening fundamentalist hue as she fills us in on the bitter conflict between the north and south ends of the parish and tells us that we must enlist in this combat, via her Tug of War teams, and obtain the dubious

benefit of possessing a cast-plastic trophy, for one year, on behalf of our end of the locality.

Since refusal to participate in this inter-tribal blood feud is obviously not an option we quickly feed our half-eaten BSE burgers to the seagulls and dash over to the impromptu gladiatorial coliseum, where I am led into the centre of a group of men with determined red faces and arms like steel chords, all of whom are all about half my height but at least twice my girth.

"This is Max," Linda says to her lead combatant, a scrubbed bullet-headed fisherman who appears to be chewing the discarded beer cans of his team-mates. "He's a lightweight, so put him in the middle somewhere and use him for balance," and, with nary a 'May the Force be with you', she gives her personal Jedi salute and vanishes, leaving me alone in the seething wash of testosterone.

My certain humiliation is made complete by the arrival of Matilda, a very large woman from the Parish Council who has something of the air of Don Corleone about her, despite, or maybe because of, her huge bosom and an ill-fitting wig. She has arrived with her militia-issue clipboard and calls things to order while my fellow teamsters are all slapping great wodges of dirt onto their hands, which they seem to be making into some kind of clay with their spit. I'm guessing that something is about to happen when a heavy rope that appears to have been salvaged from the anchor chain of the Titanic is suddenly slapped into my mitts and I'm inserted by main force into the middle of the Finstown Mean Machine.

The heavy-set and somewhat gaseous old guy in front of me, with whom I am now intimate in an uncomfortable way, grips the rope tightly and settles his buttocks back into my belly, saying, "Get your feet dug well into the dirt and lean back on the rope, bhouy[12]." He pauses just long enough... "And if I fart, dinnae let go."

*

Six o'clock eventually comes around and we all assemble at a bit of lumpy grass – laughingly referred to in the programme as the tennis court –

---

12 - **bhouy:** boy

outside the local pub for the fancy dress parade which marks the start of the grand Gala Day Procession.

There are about twenty people in costume milling around the grass judging-area, and about three or four floats are parked at the side of the road. Other costumed characters are standing by the pub door, downing bottles of Skullsplitter[13] and a few more are amongst the crowd, chatting to their friends. This being 1999, there are large and small Millennium Bugs sporting tinfoil hats and matching metallic wellie boots everywhere, and the whole thing feels a little like standing by the catering trailer of an old Ed Wood movie set.

Eventually though, and only a mere twenty minutes behind schedule, Matilda, the intimidating local councillor with the squint wig and imposing clipboard, calls things to order, and stray entrants are chased to the parade or their floats. There's a minor fracas when two pencil-thin German tourists in matching neon ski suits and wrap-around shades are shooed off to join the procession and it turns out that they're not actually *in* fancy dress, but otherwise it all goes without a hitch and the parade sets slowly off along the main street to the village hall, and the most drunken ceilidh of the year.

*

Several hours of wild dancing later, we slowly walk the couple of miles from the village to our house through the perfect stillness of three-in-the-morning Orcadian sunlight. A still summer dawn just before Longest Day has to be one of the most beautiful times of the year to view an Orkney landscape, and as we climb the steep incline of the slumbering Snaba Hill, the sun is already bright and we can see a whole panorama stretched out ahead of us; the majestic Bay of Firth sapphire-blue and like a sheet of glass, the fields lush and green, the new corn moving like slowly-brooding water in the gentle morning breeze.

Although we are determined to make a go of our new life we have had more than a few moments of indecision during the three scant months we have been on the island, but here, in the almost deafening quiet, with the

---

13 - **Skullsplitter:** locally brewed strong ale

only audible sounds being the shrill cry of gulls and the mellow quee-quee of oyster catchers, we stand drinking in the vista before us, feeling smug and self-satisfied as any lingering doubts about the suitability of our new environment melt away with the fragile dawn mist.

Despite the isolation, the high cost of foodstuffs and the lack of work opportunities, we have, very obviously, come to the right place.

*

Sunday morning finds us in a far less smug frame of mind, particularly as we remember that we have actually volunteered to play bloody Rounders, and we drag ourselves down to the appointed field at the village with something less than enthusiasm.

There are an awful lot of similarly hung-over people milling about on the same goose-shit-covered grass as the previous day, but we eventually manage to track down the wholesome Doreen and meet our team, which appears to consist of a gaggle of giggling teenage girls and a smug middle-aged balding alpha male who spends all his time flirting with the pubescent Lolitas.

Anyway, as previously stated, I am totally crap at all sporting activities and anything that involves co-ordination and teamwork in general, and I'm standing here in this very shitty field trying but failing to blend into the grassy knoll while being forced to listen to my only adult male team-mate and some fifteen-year-old exchanging seriously cringe-making naive double entendres about all-over body massage, when the comely Doreen steers her breasts over in our general direction.

"Okay, this lot are all crap," she says to Chancery and myself in a not-too-discreet stage whisper. "I'm relying on you two to win this for us."

"Us?" I say, thinking that one or other of us must definitely have had one rum too many at the dance the previous night. "Are you sure you mean us? Isn't there some aggressive three-year-old you can recruit to thrash the enemy?" But Doreen is unimpressed by what she perceives to be my urbane modesty and brusquely hands me an ancient cricket bat.

"They're going to try and fast bowl us," she whispers. "Whack the hell out of every ball that comes your way and run like the wind. We only need to get about fifteen rounders to win this."

Too afraid to tell her that I wouldn't know what a 'rounder' was if one jumped up and bit me, I squelch gingerly up to the impromptu batsman's plate and wield my cricket bat in what I hope is an intimidating manner, trying to meet the steely gaze of an eagle-eyed fence-erector on the opposite team with a suitably manly nonchalance.

However, it's all a piece of pointless bravado as the members of the opposition actually have some experience of playing this game, not to mention sporting ability, and my opposite number hands out a punishing humiliation as tennis ball after tennis ball flies past my reeling head before I eventually manage to deflect one of them with a resounding thwack!

Amazed that I've actually hit something, I go skidding off through the foetid goose guano like all the demons in Hell are after me, but I've only squelched about twenty steps when I hear somebody yell "Out", and I retire gratefully to the furthest fielding corner I can find.

Chancery is sent up next, but while she has much better hand to eye co-ordination than I do, her natural defence instincts make her an even worse batsman as she repeatedly ducks every time a ball is flung in her direction, and after witnessing our team's complete humiliation, we both slink quickly off back home to lick our wounds when Doreen's Dreadnaughts retire all-out with no score and are ignominiously expelled from the tournament.

*

Thinking it's all over we are sitting quietly reading at about four o'clock that afternoon when there's an emphatic pounding at our front door and I immediately dive behind the sofa thinking that it's Doreen come to beat the crap out of me for screwing up her Rounders game. But the caller turns out to be a bloke called Charlie, a coarse-featured smallholder from a tiny farm further along our road. Charlie is a tall, denim-clad, balding man with big ears, who bears a striking resemblance to a Mr Potato Head toy. We've seen him around a few times and said hello, but have never actually

met him, and have no clue as to why he should be trying to knock down our door.

To our surprise, however, it turns out that Mr Potato Head is the president of the Gala Weekend Sports & Social Committee and, impressed by our willingness to join in with all events, he's come over to invite us to the after-show party at his house, for which we're told to show up at his farm any time after six.

"Oh my God!" I say to Chancery, flattening myself on the back of our crude plank door as it shuts behind him. "We're in. We're on the team!"

"Yes, and after our amazing success on the playing fields of Finstown too," Chancery muses with just a tiny hint of foreboding.

*

We show up at Charlie's house later that evening, clutching the best bottle of wine our limited budget and the village store can run to, but find all in darkness.

However, there's a definite scent of barbecue coming from the side of the building and we thread our way through the farmyard past a falling-down poly-tunnel to discover practically everyone from the village crammed into a hastily swept out lambing shed. Charlie appears out of nowhere and makes introductions, and before we know where we are we are fed and watered and led into a long dark room that's absolutely crammed full of people who all seem to want to welcome us to the fold. Which, I suppose, is par for the course in a sheep shed.

*

It's a great party and our first brush with the famous Orcadian Magic Refilling Glass experience, whereupon your island host will ensure that all his guests have enough to eat and drink at all times, achieving this by hovering by your right side all evening, making sure that your glass is always kept full to the brim, while his wife, or worse, mother-in-law, will flank your left side and pile sides of beef and whole cheeses onto your plate every time you take a mouthful.

Thus we are beyond butt-toasted by midnight, when the party is starting to break up, and the evening has long since become a blur, although we have a hazy recollection of many strangers, who have only nodded to us before, coming over to 'talk', which always seems to involve pouring more spirit into our glasses, and which achieves the dubious result of getting ourselves signed up for five different committees and a lifetime's voluntary activities.

Our new green cards and our corresponding induction onto the A-list also seems to afford us entry to previously restricted subjects of conversation, and it appears that on a small island where everybody knows everyone else the two major pastimes are gossip and adultery. The trick, it seems, is to know everything about everybody and spread it absolutely everywhere whilst trying to keep your own name and reputation squeaky clean. Unfortunately, this is not an easy balancing act to perform, as you only have to be seen with someone who is not your designated partner to wake up to find the whole island buzzing with the news of your threesome or lesbian affair, and we hear some exceedingly gory details about the sexual faux pas of other villagers, some of whom are only feet away gossiping about our confidants with equal aplomb.

*

We are, of course, not the only downshifters in Orkney and the slow and steady drain of young people who go off to university each year and never return is matched by a balanced parallel influx of retired art teachers and would-be potters, all armed with their downshifters' dreams and wholesale job-lots of Patchouli. We have, of course, passed a couple of these old-school hippy-types like ships in the foggy Orkney night, and have heard the whispered tales of the hardcore Soothie settlers who live circumscribed off-the-grid lives on the outermost outer isles, surrendering material comforts in exchange for a foolproof milking of the state benefit system. But until now our personal version of the Orkney Experience has been limited to hobnobbing solely with the indigenous population.

However, on a mild night in late July when the sky is a Turner watercolour of blood- reds and mood-indigoes, we are standing in the shelter of our open front door listening to the symphony of summer birdsong when I

become aware of an odd refrain that sounds like digging coming from the hollow at the bottom of our hill.

About half an hour later, at around midnight, just as the long summer light is finally beginning to fade, I'm almost certain that I can now hear the distinctive sound of an old push-pull lawnmower.

"Listen..." I say in a portentous tone worthy of an old Bela Lugosi melodrama. "Do you hear that sound?"

"God damn those voodo drums," Chancery immediately deadpans. "Once again the natives prepare the dead so that they may walk this earth –and clean up the mess after Stromness Shopping Week."

"Oh, ha ha," I reply. "But seriously, listen. Does that sound like..." my voice drops an octave or two, "a lawn-mower to you?"

"I can't hear anything for bloody twittering birds that don't have the sense to sleep when it's dark," Chancery says in her barely-humouring-me voice. "But if it makes you happy we'll go and find the white zombie who's been sent to cut grass at midnight. Damn islanders. Recycle everything. Even their dead."

I make a grumpy 'very bloody hilarious' sound and we both tiptoe out into the purple twilight to investigate. As we get closer to the bottom of the steep slope, it's obvious even to Doubting Thomasina that somebody most definitely *is* cutting grass with what sounds like an old-fashioned hand-mower, and that the bizarrre sound appears to be coming from the low, ramshackle much-extended house whose vegetable patch abuts the grass at the bottom of our garden slope.

"Jeeze, it's comin' frum the ole Radley place," Chancery whispers in an abrupt change of sarcastic disrespect. "Maybe it's ole Boo out a-lookin' fur souls with sharp ole scissors..."

"Shhhhh!" I hiss. "I'm trying to listen."

But the mowing sound has ceased and we can't see anyone, so believing ourselves invisible, we skulk closer and closer when suddenly a razor-

sharp figure rears up out of a hollow right in front of us, alarmingly silhouetted with enormous pointy garden shears, like a sinister paper cut-out against the sunset sky.

"Hello!" it cries, like some kind of demented jovial grim reaper who thinks he's Santa. We leap back at least three feet and push each other out the way in a scramble to get back up the slope to safety.

But the voice saves us further embarrassment by reassuring, "I'm Hordun, your neighbour. You must be the new folk in Tumshie John's house. Nice to meet you."

*

Despite the lateness of the hour, and adding to the bizarreness of mowing the lawn at midnight, Hordun insists on taking us inside his house to meet his wife, Marigold, a raven-haired earth-mother with glassy green eyes, who appears to currently be in some other universe, but who robotically shakes hands with us and doles out runic hand-thrown mugs of something murky and herbal while Hordun leads us into their large folksy living room. At close quarters, and under the light of an electric lamp, he's not nearly as scary as he first appeared, and turns out to be a likeable, sallow old hippy in his mid-fifties, with long, lank hair and a droopy Zapata moustache.

"I worked as a postman and did lots of odd jobs so that I could build this house myself," he tells us in a strong Geordie accent. "We started out here thirty years ago with just the two rooms, but when we wanted a family I had to add more space, so we've just extended it as we could afford it. It took a lot of letter-delivering to pay for this place, I can tell you."

He pats the battered old sofa he's reclining on affectionately to emphasise his point, oblivious to the cloud of dust that rises like a mushroom cloud, and surveys his kingdom with pride. Despite its somewhat ramshackle appearance from the outside, Hordun's palace is indeed a cosy and comfortable haven, with attractive felt hangings on the rough-plastered walls, a low smoke-stained ceiling, and a rough-hewn stone fireplace taking up most of the far wall.

"And are these your children?" I ask, indicating a dead-eyed boy who sits playing a guitar in a corner by the fireplace, while a curvaceous olive-skinned young Latin-American girl gazes at him adoringly.

"Oh, not both of them," Hordun laughs. "Most of ours are grown up and living abroad by now, but this is our youngest, and Maria here's on a student exchange from Costa Rica, so we're putting her up."

The boy just keeps on playing his tuneless melody regardless of his father's introduction, but the girl makes a friendly hand gesture of acknowledgement and I realise with my first unexpected pang of nostalgia for the life that we left that she's the first person I've met here who isn't a pure White Caucasian.

"Actually, Maria's having a Fiesta Night to raise funds for street theatre for Brazilian crack orphans next week," Hordun says, smiling at her. "We're going to do some Salsa dancing and eat tapas. All very un-Orkney. Would you like to come along?"

It's as if the kindly old hippy has entered my mind and seen the last four months of going to constant country gatherings spread out like a hall of mirrors, and we accept his invitation with an alacrity which is nothing short of embarrassing.

"They take a bit of getting used to, the Orcadians," Hordun says, smiling again. "When we first came here we would have happily taken tea with Mussolini just for a break from making small talk about silage grass. But don't worry, you'll gradually come to love them, and all their odd little ways."

*

A week later we don our sombreros at the appointed Fiesta hour and trot down the slope to Hordun and Marigold's house to enter a strange hidden country within the even stranger world that we have slowly been coming to know. The large and comfortable room is packed, not with the customary hobbit-like creatures that we have come to expect, but exotic tall Amazons, gypsy beetle-browed swarthy men from another world, clad unashamedly in cheesecloth and coarse weaves, and dark-eyed women

with strident BBC accents dressed in bright coloured kaftans and muumuus, the air thick with the scents of musk and patchouli as sandalled feet shuffle to Latin rhythms and long grey hair is flung around with gay abandon.

There is nary a synthetic fabric or a bere bannock in sight, and the youthful Maria, who has spent all day cooking a tapas buffet which tantalises my nostrils with hints of alien aromas, now insists that everyone learns to tango properly. It becomes a bit like being caught up in the parallel universe of a Posy Simmonds cartoon when I am paired up with a tall gangly brunette with long flowing locks and big glasses who bears an uncanny resemblance to Wendy Webber, and we stride up and down Hordun's hessian carpeted floor together in a poor-man's parody of a Brazilian salsa.

It's like discovering a secret door to the world of hot burnt-orange Buenos Aires café-house culture in the middle of Orkney's cool Nordic-blue colour palette, and I'm having so much fun doing something that doesn't involve accordion music and tray-bakes that I take to the task at hand with great gusto, oblivious to my complete lack of choreographic ability, and in the course of an elaborate gaucho turn, inadvertently snag a large lock of my partner's free flowing tresses.

"Sorry!" I gasp, sweeping her into my arms in what I think is a suitably Valentino hold and letting her head drop backwards towards the floor.

But Wendy makes an odd little squirming movement before coming back upright again, whispering in my ear as she spins back up onto her feet, "That's alright. I love having my hair pulled. Particularly while I'm tied up."

CHAPTER 5 - WHERE WE JOIN THE GRAND MARCH AND ENJOY THE LONG LIGHT OF AN ORKNEY SUMMER

The placing of an inauspicious poster in the post office window announcing the "Firth Parish Annual Parish Picnic and Grand March" in early August fills us full of disproportionate excitement and glee. Not because the idea of a picnic, per se, is particularly thrilling in its own right, but because it offers us the opportunity to be whisked off to some as yet unseen part of the island. Engage any Orcadian tourist board official on the subject of motor transport in the isles and they will happily quote you mind-boggling statistics about how Orkney has more cars per head than any other region in Britain, but what they will omit to tell you is that public transport in the isles is almost nonexistent as a result[14].

Having now almost completed our first half year in the isles, the novelty of isolation is wearing off and we are beginning to be painfully aware of this very noticeable lack of transportation and of the narrowness of our personal universe, with the village and the bus trip to Kirkwall being all that we have, as yet, experienced of our new island home, and now, in the height of the mild summer weather and the long daylight hours, we are literally champing at the bit to explore the rest of Orkney's historic terrain.

All the guide books have, of course, told us that the traditional Orkney picnic is now a thing of the past, so we are overjoyed to discover that the custom still holds good in Firth parish, and we spend endless evenings poring over the Ordinance Survey map, looking at all the places that we have yet to visit and visualising what a group outing to one will entail.

According to all the local history books, the annual parish picnic was the big event of the summer months in the immediate post-war era, when any available carthorses or tough little David Brown or Massey-Ferguson

14 - My publisher, fearing swift and punitive litigation from the Orkney Tourist Board, asks me to remind you that we are talking about 1999 here, and that a much improved bus service now runs in mainland Orkney throughout the summer months.

tractors were traditionally pressed into service so that a whole parish could pile into trailers and head off for food and games at some scenic beauty spot like the Brough of Birsay, a tidal promontory boasting its own Neolithic village, and long the happy haunt of Orcadians on a fun day out.

Thus we eagerly hurry down to the village store on Thursday – "paper day" – to pick up this week's Orcadian and learn the details of the big event that is going to surpass a personal invitation to the royal garden party. However, as we stand in the middle of the lane with the open newspaper in our hands, our disappointment is crushing when we read that we will not, in fact, be going to the mystical ring of standing stones at Brodgar, the rugged promontory at the aforementioned Brough of Brisay, or even the popular white sands of Scapa beach at Kirkwall, but that the location for Firth's one-day wonder-of-the-world extravaganza is to be Big Ed's Field, a lumpy, cow-pat-strewn piece of grass about a mile from our house.

Also, the much-anticipated Grand March will entail no tractors, trailers or horse-drawn vehicles, but instead all participants are being asked to assemble at the village hall car park and then march the mile or so to the picnic site in formation, with an all-banners-blazing pipe band leading the way, which is a decidedly un-Orcadian method of doing things and, we privately think, all far too Braveheart for words. But, that this is not the way to make friends and influence people in our new Jerusalem, we keep our bitter disappointment and our townie opinions to ourselves and duly show up at the car park in question at the appointed time.

It's one of the most beautiful days of the summer, with genuine sunshine and only a moderate sea wind, and we expect the parking area to be mobbed with fun-loving Finstownites. But we discover to our surprise that there's not exactly a huge turn-out for the grand procession that is to rival the Lord Mayor's Show, and even most of the organisers are notably absent when we arrive at the commencement point with sickening urban punctuality. In fact, there are so few people in the car park that we think we've got the day wrong, but we eventually discover a small posse of about a dozen "peedie dumpy" farmers' wives cowering in the shadow of the community centre porch with some sullen-looking children who look as if they've been bullied into coming under pain of having their Play Stations confiscated.

"Hello," I say to a heavily fleeced woman who I vaguely recognise from one of the neighbouring farms. "Are we in the right place for the Picnic Parade?"

"Oh aye," she replies with a certain tremor of trepidation in her voice. "But there's only a peedie crowd of us, is there no'? Folk'll no' like to be oot so brazen-like in the street."

I smile reassuringly and mutter something noncomittal about how more people will turn up soon, and settle down for the customary wait for something to happen.

However, I am surreptitiously glad that the promised "pipe band" are also blissfully conspicuous by their absence, and I am about to heave a heartfelt sigh of relief when an unassuming low-slung blue saloon drives up and Kenny the Pipe Mannie, an oddly over-groomed silver fox in his late sixties, piles out into the sunshine, ostentatiously dressed in full bandsman's uniform.

However, of the stormtrooper Matilda and her army clipboard there is no sign, and we all hang around making self-conscious small talk for about twenty minutes until it's clear that, even by Orkney time, which is a bit like Mexican time, no-one else is planning to show, and as it's as close to blistering hot as Orkney ever gets and poor Kenny is sweating in his pipe band uniform, it's decided by popular plebiscite to start the grand parade.

Kenny quickly cranks up his pipes to a scalded cat pitch and launches, not into some heart-wrenching Orcadian ballad, but a death-defying medley of Hampden Park Scot-pop choruses, including "There Wuz A Sodjur" and other tartan sick-makers. Infected by the strange but persistent discomfort palpable around us, we reluctantly follow his lead as he suddenly strides manfully off towards Big Ed's Field.

But when we all-too-soon reach the village we are obliged to march down the middle of the road, with the entire fifteen of us by now cringing into our shirt collars, scarlet with embarrassment. Orcadians have, of course, written the book on observing the "Tall Poppy Syndrome", and the lack of bodies is making the assembled few very uncomfortable indeed as they feel that they are in imminent danger of Making a Public Statement, which

is not something that anyone wants to have to their credit here on Selkie Isle.

Normally, of course, it would be possible to walk naked through Finstown on a typically sleepy afternoon and not be noticed, but of course it's high summer and the parade time has synched perfectly with the Scrabster Ferry tourist influx and the road is crawling with liner-like Winnebagos stuffed full of Twitchers and earnest camera-snapping Canadians in search of their ancestral roots[15]. Plus, of course, one of the local sheep farmers is moving his flock and has halted the normal progress of the traffic, so we are obliged to squeeze past thirty stalled vehicles and their gawping drivers.

An alarming sound of digital clicks and whirrs accompanies our painful progress as our biblically shamed assembly shuffles its way alongside the idling traffic, and I visualise the strange images of bowed-head prisoners on their walk of penance that will soon be pasted into numerous albums on distant continents as typical of the 'colourful' ethnographical customs of the isles.

"Hey, Buddy!" a fat Canadian calls out to me from his driving seat, winding down the window of his mobile home with an electronic ease, "what's the parade in aid of?"

"Human sacrifice!" Chancery yells back. "We're looking for volunteers. You interested?" But the whine of of his window closing and the accompanying clunk of his automated locking system engaging is her only reply.

*

It takes us an excruciating three-quarters of an hour to make the twenty-minute walk to Big Ed's field where the resident cattle – or "kai" as they're locally known – have been removed earlier that morning and a rickety marquee has been erected to house the tea urn. I have been hoping to sidle in unnoticed and write my part in the by now mortifying procession off to history, but our arrival is heralded by a small cherry-cheeked child dressed

15 - Orkney was a popular recruiting ground for the Hudson Bay Company in the nineteenth century.

in Bermuda shorts, a chunky Icelandic-knit sweater and wellie boots, who rushes back into the field yelling, "They're home!" and we are greeted with a resounding cheer and the glare of the Orcadian's photographer's flash gun. We are thrown to discover that there is a veritable mob of merry picnickers already milling about behind the cover of the dry-stone wall, with scores of cars parked in the ditches and in the neighbouring grassland, and bitter realisation dawns that the true cognoscenti have just skipped the humiliating Grand March and come directly to the picnic site.

However, we have learned something in our few months in the Arctic Circle, and when the ubiquitous Rounders posse comes around looking for people to shanghai I have an injured back excuse at the ready; although you would have thought that our performance at the Gala Weekend tournament would have precluded us from *ever* being asked to be in anything sporty ever again. Nonetheless, the press gangs procure sufficient bodies for two teams and the game eventually gets under way, with today's competition quickly turning into a gladiatorial fight to the death between two clans of Finstown's alpha males, and blood is spilled before the abattoir-men of the Orkney Meat team finally reign victorious, being spurred on to success by the arrival of their manager, a young(ish) go-getter called Edgar, who pulls up in his sleek black sports car.

At the Gala Day debacle we had used our ignominious defeat as the perfect opportunity to slink away unnoticed, but today Matilda, who seems to run absolutely everything in this township, is rationing the tea urn and refuses to issue a single drop of beverage before the tournament is over, and we are all forced to endure the prize-giving before anyone gets anything to eat or drink. We have, however, blissfully missed the "primary bairns" sports, and there have thankfully been no entrants for sword-dancing, so the distribution of prizes is deliciously quick. But I am intrigued when the victorious Rounders Team are presented not with a cup or shield but a discreet brown envelope that looks like something dispensed to the parish poor.

"What do you think's in there?" I whisper to Chancery. But she just grins.

"Matilda's car keys," she replies with a smutty smirk, and I wish I'd never asked.

But I am unable to assuage my burning curiosity, and later, when we are hefting the now familiar delft tea mugs and whole-pig hot dogs, I sidle over to the orange-tanned Edgar who is busily offering autographs to adoring school girls, and enquire about his prize in the nearest I can manage to a jocular blokey tone.

"Hello Ed," I say in my best I'm-really-a-sport's-jock-like-you-under-this-aesthetic-exterior voice. "What's in the little brown envelope then?"

Edgar's face whips round to me as a hush falls. Even the birds go silent and the sheep on the hillside hold their breath. The crowd of fangirls quickly escapes to the sidelines as Edgar's glare becomes distinctly flinty, his countenance saying I would probably have committed less of a social faux pas if I had asked for his inside leg measurement or the date of his mother's last period.

"That's *personal*," he manages between whitened lips, and he turns and stalks away.

*

The annual agricultural shows mark the zenith of any Orkney summer, when agrarian workers from all over the islands head to town to show off their prize livestock, and tractor-makers cross the Pentland in their droves to display their latest implements via 'hospitality tents' designed to lure drunken farmers into placing lavish orders for new John Deer combines.

Orkney's myriad local charities also come out in force and there are literally hundreds of fund-raiser stalls: from Hoopla to second-hand books, more home-baked Ogo-Pogo Rolls and raffles than you can handle, some excruciatingly bad street performers who foot the ferry bill to come up from Sooth in search of fame and glory, and fairground rides of every description. Almost the whole population turns out to meet their friends, win prizes and get drunk, which is followed, of course, by the local paper running pages and pages of earthy scowling farmers' pictures, showing them clutching unhappy roosters, which are headlined, "Fred Flett, gold medallist for the largest cock" with no sense of irony whatsoever.

Needless to say, we are seduced into going along and eating tray-bakes

with the rest of the populace, but this year it seems to mark the end of what has passed for summer: only eight or nine scant weeks of frequently cold and windy sunshine. The harvest is brought in quickly to minimise losses from strong searing winds, and by the end of August the tourist chalets in the village are already half-shuttered for the winter. The treeless landscape creates the illusion of there being no Autumn, and, as the September winds start getting nippy there's already a hint of frost in the early morning air. Winter, it seems, is already here.

A stray black and white cat called Pifco has taken up temporary residence under one of Hordun's numerous tumbledown sheds, and one morning, after about two week's absence, arrives on our doorstep complete with a convoy of seven tiny kittens. Chancery immediately wants to feed all the hungry little bundles of fur but the last few months have seen my worst earning figures in the last twenty years and I'm in a state of high anxiety, which makes me immediately start chanelling my father as if possessed, and I refuse to spend any money on food for them, only agreeing to give them some household scraps.

Chancery is, of course, rightfully incensed at my over-zealous parsimony and takes to making a constant stream of pointed remarks at mealtimes: "Is it okay if I put some milk in my tea? I could drink it black if it's running us up too much money."; "Shall I recycle this teabag?" or even, "I wonder if we could drink our tea straight out the teapot? Imagine how much money we could save if we didn't have to spend money on detergent to wash the cups." In fact, she is frosty around me for most of the day, every day, but I am my father's son and am by now firmly convinced that bankruptcy and debtor's prison will be just around the corner if I indulge in the odd tin of Kitekat for the feline refugees, and so stand firm in my resolve not to take responsibility for the strays.

However, Pifco, the mother cat, spurns my meagre aid package, or lack of it, as she has been happily fending for herself for years without my intervention, and cheerfully decimates the young of some of the local hares in order to feed her motley brood. She slinks off into the furze behind our house each morning, only to return with some hapless leveret in her mouth, which the kittens quickly rip to pieces, and despite the fact that we are desperate to attain our Orkney citizenship, we revert completely to Southern squeamishness in the face of all this rural nature- in-the-raw and

are totally grossed-out to discover dismembered limbs and, occasionally, eviscerated entrails all over our front step each morning.

The final affront to our namby-pamby ways, however, comes when we arrive home one afternoon at the same time as Pifco returns from one of her hunting trips and we find the kittens happily ripping the ears off a still-living baby bunny. Although we chase all the cuddly flesh-eaters away there's still the matter of the bleeding leveret that's lying gasping for breath on our grass.

"It's too far gone," Chancery says tearfully, after inspecting the body. "You're going to have to kill it."

"*I'm going* to have to kill it?" I say, aghast, trying not to look into the pleading eyes of the half-skinned bundle. "I'm practically a vegetarian. Why do *I* have to kill it?"

"Because you're the one who's too mean to buy a tin of cat food," Chancery immediately retorts, and then puts the final nail in my coffin by adding as she slams the door, "Kill it quickly, it's in pain."

*

Needless to say, I now have no hesitation whatsoever about buying cat food and we purchase six-packs of whatever's cheapest in the village shop almost daily, but it doesn't go far over seven fast-growing kittens and their mother. The youngsters, who started out as feral, quickly domesticate and come running over to our door for food whenever they see us or hear us and it doesn't take long for us to develop a strong bond with them all.

The whole brood are all full of insatiable curiosity and happy to play with us for hours on end, and there is a huge temptation to adopt them all. Particularly one ragamuffin named Tribble – so called because she is nothing more than a tennis-ball-sized bundle of fluffy fur, but has a voice that can wake the dead –and a rambunctious young tom called Pink Nose, thus named because, yep, he has a pink nose. He quickly forms a tight bond with me and regularly comes over to sleep on my lap when he's not busy kicking the shit out of his siblings.

Therefore, with possible adoption in mind, we tentatively try bringing them all into the house, which they instantly take to. But Pusskers, our poor old cat, hates them all on sight and their presence stresses her dreadfully, so we have to quickly relegate the entire brood back to the great outdoors again.

Banned from their newly discovered inner sanctum, however, the kittens simply take to registering their protest by congregating like flocks of furry owls on our kitchen windowsill, their eyes round and pleading like soulful Hallmark 'ickle kitties'. Tribble, in particular, perfects the art of heartbroken wailing whenever she sees me washing-up or at the stove, and it becomes obvious that we really need to concentrate on finding them all proper homes before the winter comes.

We're almost into a steely October, with bitter sleet-laced winds, and summer's sunny days and long evenings have already become but a hazy memory, so when one of the ladies from a croft house further along our lane offers to put us in touch with Sigurd, the island's ultra-macho, I'm-the-animal-law-in-these-here-parts, gaucho-moustached charity worker, we reluctantly agree, and his little navy-blue van pulls up at our house a few days later.

"Hello," bellows the mustachioed Sigurd in a booming voice as he bustles into our narrow hallway, stroking his handlebar facial hair like something out of a Sergio Leone movie. "So it's a home for your cats you're wanting, is it? I've had to pull a string or two for you, I can tell you. Wur sanctuary at Harray's absolutely full to bursting point with peedie cats just now, but I've managed to get you a place in the Sanctuary at Caithness."

"Caithness?" I say, thrown. "But that's across the water. How are we going to get seven kittens all the way to Caithness?"

"Ah," Sigurd says smugly, doing the thing with the moustache again, "you're forgetting that you're dealing with a professional here. I'll get them on the boat, nae bother. You just round all the peedie scamps up and keep them in the hoose overnight, and leave the rest to me. I'll come and get them the morn's morning.[16]"

---

16 - **the morn's morning:** first thing tomorrow morning

*

The first part of Animal Clint's cunning master plan is easy enough to fulfil, as the offer of food and a warm place to sleep has the kittens into our kitchen faster than a mob of paedophiles being granted free access to a children's home. But things don't go quite so smoothly the next morning when the animal kingdom's answer to The Man With No Name arrives bearing a large livestock transport cage and no real plan for how he will persuade seven wilful kittens to embark, Noah's-ark-style, inside it.

Pink Nose takes one look at the large figure in his big black puffer jacket and leather gauntlets and flees under the nearest chest-of-drawers, Tribble claws at his leg, and the rest of the brood quickly join in the new chasing game and disperse themselves throughout the house.

"Are you needing a hand there, Sigurd?" Chancery asks sweetly as kittens fly in all directions, but 'the professional' is adamant that he has the situation well under control and so we happily stand back and leave him to it, trying our hardest not to laugh as every time he manages to corner two kittens and open the cage door to drop them inside the previous two promptly jump out.

Eventually, when it's getting dangerously close to sailing time, and Tribble has attached herself to El Moustachio's leg and is hanging on for dear life, Chancery steps in and we finally, and sadly, manage to round all the little villains up and pack them off to their new homes on the mainland.

*

By the time the black November rolls in, the cold and sleety weather of the previous month has deteriorated completely into a dark and miserable arctic winter.

Mornings are late in dawning, the scant grey daylight is usually completely gone by half past two in the afternoon and the howling gales become bitter and constant. Ferries are cancelled, planes are unable to land, effectively halting the delivery of mail and national newspapers, and fresh fruit and vegetables become a rarity on the supermarket shelves.

It becomes physically difficult to go out at all, the ferocious wind being like a giant's hand pushing you backwards when you step outside the door, and when we finally make it to the supermarket in Kirkwall one particularly bleak grey Thursday, we get caught in a freak hail-storm on our return and have to walk the mile or so uphill from the bus stop to our house under the torrential onslaught of frozen needles hammering down on our skulls. So swift is this cosmic ice-dump that not only do our laden carrier bags inflate with lumps of ice like peas going down the hoppers into their bags at Birds Eye, but our shoes also fill up with the icy gravel, the hail fall so dense it is literally firing into the microscopic gaps between the heels of our socks and shoes like sixty mile per hour pea-shooters.

Tumshie John's house, which had seemed so ideal in the spring, makes a poor winter residence, with its draughty plank door and no real fireplace to keep the large living room warm. The rest of the house has only electric night storage heating, which is hard-wired to turn itself off during the nine to five working day, and as we're actually in the house between those very same hours, we are forced to go out and buy a couple of second-hand electric heaters, thus pushing our already uneconomical bills through the roof.

In the spirit of all good transplanted townies, we complain incessantly about the bad food and the bad weather, and we have to keep reminding ourselves of what our life was like previously on a housing estate in Manchester. But one morning in late November, a brilliant ray of sunshine arrives in our darkness with the delivery of an unexpected letter bearing a local postmark, and containing a brightly coloured invitation card to a silver wedding party in the village hall.

It's just what we need to raise our spirits, and though there's a heavy blizzard raging on the night in question, we gleefully don our party clothes, pack our dancing shoes into a rucksack and pull on our wellie boots and wax cotton coats to plough through ten inches of snow to join the merry-making.

The hosts are sparing no expense and have invited practically the whole parish, and despite the blizzard, the hall is buzzing when we get there. There are thick clusters of flushed farmers everywhere, including Tumshie

John, our gnome-like landlord, all smelling faintly of camphor and suitably kitted-out for the occasion in their "good" funeral suits, and still more broods of homely women in 1980s' synthetic frocks seated round the walls and foyer, with everyone gossiping about everyone else while the local favourite after whisky – rum – flows like water.

Eventually, however, everyone finds their place-cards, and we find ourselves seated at the end of a long trestle table next to two identically-dressed girls who are attired in black Diane-Arbus-like puff-sleeved velvet dresses with little white lace collars like the Grady Twins in The Shining.

"Aye-aye, whit like?[17]" says the first, as surly adolescent catering staff fling plates of cold meat covered in mushy vegetables and congealed gravy at us. "You're the folk from Sooth in Tumshie John's hoose, are you no'? I'm Rhona from Buttaquoy."

"And I'm Shona," chimes in the second. "We're from doon the road. We've seen you aboot."

We have been here for eight months now and the mildly stalkerish tendencies of the natives still disconcert us slightly, but the twins look relatively harmless and so we sit down and permit friendly overtures to be exchanged. Both sisters are typical young island women in their mid-twenties: short, brown-haired and wholesomely pretty. But although they look and dress like peas in a pod, their personalities couldn't be more different. Shona, the "peedie lass" of the pair by three minutes, is a quiet, introverted local primary school teacher, and obsessively fixated with how she appears in the public eye. A lonely vegetarian in a land of hardcore beef farming, she is grazing contentedly on the sole carrot that has been untouched by gravy on her plate, and appears to normally exist exclusively on a diet of cheese toasties and extruded polystyrene snack products.

Rhona, however, unlike her carrot-nibbling twin, thrives on a completely carnivorous diet of pure red-blooded gossip and rumour. A walking compendium of foolishly shared confidences, she, like many other Orcadians, has an encyclopaedic knowledge of the entire island's

17 - **Whit like?:** How are you doing?

population, and she quickly treats us to the life histories of everyone at our long Oliver-Twist-style table, peppering her thumbnail biographies with sotto voce little titbits like, "That's Katrina Isbister. She's never had an orgasm during sex with her husband, even though she bought one of those stimulator things at Ingrid Norquoy's Ann Summers' party," or "That's Sigurd Petrie. He used to be married to Ola over there but she caught him at it in the byre with her auntie's cousin that went Sooth to become a lesbian, so now he's reduced to buying it down at Kirkwall harbour."[18]

However, both Thompson Twins appear to be well pleased at having drawn Finstown's Favourite Ferry Loupers in the table-seating-plan lottery, and we chat away quite amicably, staying on with them after the boards have been cleared away and the floor Slipperened for dancing. Abruptly, mid-speculation on the possible sexual orientation of the hosts' émigré son, Rhona asks us if we ever frequent Matchmakers, the island's sole disco in Kirkwall.

"Disco?" I say incredulously. "You guys have a disco?" And the twins nod in unison.

"Of course!" Rhona replies.

"We're not all country yokels here, you know," Shona adds with a slight hint of reproach in her voice.

"Or nuns," her twin continues, her tone distinctly suggestive. "Do you pair want to come along and shake it aboot on Saturday night?"

*

It is sleeting heavily with a wind so cold it takes the top layer of skin off your face on the Saturday night that the twins call to collect us in Rhona's ancient mustard-yellow Volkswagen Beetle. Tonight, as if to match the vehicle, the sisters have favoured a vintage look and are clad in identical knee-length boots and short plaid pinafore dresses with matching polo-neck sweaters, which make them look like a doo-wop backing group, and

---

18 - Needless to say, I made these stories, and the people named in them, up; Rhona's real accounts are completely unprintable.

they bicker unceasingly between themselves for the entirety of the journey to "Toon" about whether or not their skirts are too short and how this will affect their ability to snare men.

We, meanwhile, are squashed into the back seat of the car, looking forward to what we think will be a relaxed and fun night consisting of getting a couple of drinks and then going to the nightclub, unaware that we have just entered into the Twilight Zone and have been transported from Orkney to Twin Manhunting Land, a complex and multifarious world with an intricate sociological infrastructure built upon layers of complicated social mores and conventions, all of them more convoluted than anything that can be found in the combined novels of Elizabeth Gaskell and Jane Austen.

Rhona parks the car in her "secret spot", a pitch-black canyon between two tall, weather-beaten stone buildings near the town's original thirteenth century harbour, and we all bundle out quickly through the cutting wind and freezing fog towards the glowing yellow lights of an ancient seafront pub. We've been to the local pub a couple of times and played at watching to see if Village Worthy One moved his foot before Village Worthy Two, so I'm expecting a cosy quiet place with a cheery peat fire crackling welcomingly in the grate and dusty bottles of Skullsplitter behind the bar, but when we open the door, loud rock music literally punches me in the solar plexus and we crawl into a tiny room that is so wall-to-wall with bodies that it makes rush hour on the Tokyo tube look deserted.

There are drunken limbs dangerously brandishing glasses and lit cigarettes everywhere and I'm slowly backed into a tight inglenook that appears to already be occupied by some very drunk girls who are putting bright-red lipstick prints around the rims of empty vodka-shot glasses, and who don't appear to notice that some strange Ferry Louper has been shoe-horned onto their laps. Chancery, meanwhile, finds herself pinned to the old panelled-wood wall with Rhona. It's impossible to make out what anyone is saying, a state of affairs which doesn't appear to deter Rhona, who seems to be treating Chancery to an uninterrupted monologue, which I'm later told consists of biographies of all the people who'll be joining us this evening,including full catalogues of all their sexual proclivities.

I, in my big city innocence, had thought that tonight's posse was to comprise only of ourselves and the twins, but there are apparently three more people still to come, plus, of course, "The Bhouys[19]" who, apparently, won't be part of our party but will join it later. Confused? Try attempting to make sense of it with six hundred decibels of music in your left ear. Anyway, three turnip-shaped farm girls, who are to play tonight's Pips to the twins' Gladys Knight, eventually appear in the doorway and there is an awful lot of pantomime beckoning and waving as they fight their way through the sea of bodies and into my inglenook, the previous incumbents having now deserted it for pastures new, leaving only their bizarre lipstick-print artworks behind them.

"Right, we need a drinks kitty," Rhona yells over the blare of the music. "Is twenty quid a head enough?"

I immediately blurt out, "Twenty quid! Jesus Christ, how much are you planning to drink?" in a loud Victor Meldrew voice. But fortunately for my reputation as a sophisticated socialite, no-one hears me, and one of the Pips yells, "Twenty? No, no, that's no' enough!" while another interjects, "Drivers pay ten?" and a long and arduous discussion on a par with a local government sub-committee ensues, eventually settling on the sum of twenty-five pounds for non-drivers and fifteen for everyone else. Greatly relieved that I actually have fifty quid in my wallet, I'm as quickly dashed when I'm told with a withering stare that I can't have a mixer because we're "starting with doubles", a threatening manifesto that fills me with dread.

*

There are six pubs in Kirkwall which have the twins' seal of approval, and it's apparently vitally important that we be seen in all of them. Thus I have barely poured my illicitly-purchased Coke into my to-the-brim double rum when Shona puts her mouth against my ear and yells, "Scoop!" and when I look at her quizzically, puts on her let's-tolerate-the-idiot-foreigner voice and says, "Drink up, we've got places to go," and we are all dragged off to the next venue of the night, an equally miniscule establishment called The Auld Motor Hoose that seems to be populated entirely by kids who don't look old enough to be in long trousers, let alone drinking in a licensed premises.

---

19 - **The Bhouys:** the boys

We are barely in the door of this particular hell-hole when a pasty-faced loon drapes himself around Chancery, attempts to plaster a kiss on her face and tells her that he loves "mature women". But before I can get over to her rescue, I'm set upon by a group of shaven-headed boys in immaculately pressed Ben Sherman shirts who all want to know if I'm "somebody".

"What do you mean, am I somebody?" I bellow over the discordant blare of Big Muff, a raucous three-piece head-banger band squeezed onto a tiny podium in the corner. "Everybody's somebody."

"Aye, but we ken you're not anybody, you're somebody," their leader replies. "I ken I kent you from afore."

"Obviously my fame has gone before me," I mutter dryly, trying to get myself out of their sphincter-like circle. "But I don't think I'm nearly famous enough for you to have heard of me."

"But we have!" they all cry. "We've seen you on the telly."

"I don't think so..."

"Yeah, you were getting your arse kicked by Pakkies!" they chorus gleefully.

"What?" I say, totally baffled now.

"You're that Salmon Rushdie," the runt of the group pipes up. "Can we have your autograph?"

"Scoop!" I yell to my party, who gladly oblige. "Let's move on to the next place before someone mistakes me for some other old trout."

*

A little after midnight the twins eventually decide that they now have a full dossier on who's "oot" tonight and we all finally head for Matchmakers. The nightclub, to our surprise, turns out to be a fairly classy if small-scale purpose-built disco, not, as we've been expecting, a ratty old

pub with coloured lights propped up on beer crates, and we are suitably impressed by the smoke guns and mirror balls and the half-decent sound system. Chancery and I immediately start to head down to the crowded dance floor with its iridescent streaming bubble machine, but Rhona suddenly pulls us back sharply in the opposite direction.

"No, no! You can't just go on the floor like that," she admonishes into my left ear, her breath hot and her speech slightly slurred. "Not when you've just come in."

"We need to have a peedie walk first," Shona instructs into my other ear, appearing out of nowhere and gripping my arm, while her sister puts a similar half-nelson on Chancery, and we are quickly led to a narrow, crowded walkway that runs along the front of the bar for a distinctly unsteady perambulation that assumably announces our arrival in the assembly rooms of Orkney's equivalent of Bath.

The three Pips have already gone ahead and are exchanging rather slavery kisses with some drunk boys at a table, but they hastily disengage when they see us and flutter ahead of us along the crowded Birdcage Walk, making sure everyone knows we're here while scouting the room for objects of desire.

It's a Saturday night and the bar is an impenetrable sea of drunken bodies, but the head Pip suddenly lets out a piercing shriek, or at least a fishwife's yell, and starts pointing into the crowd of imbibers in a way that is supposed to be coded and discreet but is really the equivalent of semaphore flags under a flare-light. Rhona goes on point and Shona's hand grips my arm like a tourniquet – I can feel the bruise forming even as she speaks – gasping, "It's The Bhouys..." into my ear, like one about to swoon.

*

"The Bhouys" are a sort of island Rosencrantz and Guildenstern called Kecks and Specs, a pair of almost identical caricature suicidal farmhands with no social skills, dressed predictably in faded Levis and neat checked shirts. Being, of course, a typical grouchy middle-aged male I find it hard to comprehend why the arrival of these glassy-eyed misfits should be

causing quite so much excitement in the assembled harem, but even the pragmatic Rhona has already flipped into serious flirt mode and the Pips are buzzing round the two drunken cowboys like crazed flies around a cowpat.

However, the kill has already been bloodied in advance, and, with paradoxically explicit innuendo being flung between them like discarded underwear at a Tom Jones concert, Shona the vegetarian twin develops a distinctly predatory gleam in her eyes, and with the wisdom acquired from generation after generation of shrewd buying at the local cattle mart, struts forward to declare her newly-found carnivorous interest in the shorter of the two specimens.

Chancery and I, meanwhile, decide it really is time to suss out the dance floor and melt gently back into the crowd to make good our escape.

*

The DJ plays a smoochie Walker Brothers classic at about two in the morning and the lights slowly come up, indicating that it's all over for the night, but the twins have other ideas, and, for them, the most important part of the evening is just about to begin.

Eternally grateful that I've brought my –however inadequate –overcoat and scarf, which is fighting a losing battle against the cutting gale-force wind that's coming straight in off an angry sea, we are led through some of Kirkwall's ancient back wynds to the most important social venue of the night, a battered old caravan converted into a mobile fast-food outlet in a litter-strewn car park just off the harbour.

Outwardly, the Burger Van is just a place to eat, but to the Saturday night cognoscenti it is the place where bargains are sealed and dreams come true. Many a marriage has started its life at this fragrant altar to fried manna, and if gossip is to be believed, many an Orcadian has been fathered in the dark back lanes behind its spitting deep fat fryers.

In a faithful recreation of the cattle ring at the local auction mart, the twins and their Pips strut their stuff while armed with bags of strange criss-cross chips that look for all the world like shrunken baby waffles, and although

a willowy lesbian called Peedie Olga tries to tempt Chancery to sample some of her Grootie's meat and potato patties[20] it seems that somehow "The Bhouys" have managed to vanish into the inky night and there are just no other takers.

Eventually, just as frostbite is about to claim all of my fingers and toes, the twins admit defeat and decide to call it a night, and we all pile into Rhona's Volkswagen and are finally, thankfully,allowed to go home.

20 - **Grootie's Patties:** A strange concoction not generally listed on official Taste of Orkney propaganda, consisting of beef and mashed potato shaped into a ball and then usually deep-fried.

CHAPTER 6 - WHERE I BECOME THE LOCAL POSTMAN PAT

The long dark winter continues on its unrelenting way, and a heavy frost falls in December as the whole island freezes over, creating spectacular red and green aurora borealis in the night skies. The cutting winds are still ferocious and unrelenting, but it doesn't stop us wrapping ourselves up in coats and scarves and standing outside the house at night, marvelling as the sky turns from purple to deep indigo, and sometimes even from glowing ruby to emerald green, as "The Merry Dancers", as the locals call them, flicker across the majestic heavens like God's own personal lava lamp.

However, our current financial situation is much less pyrotechnic, and after only three-quarters of a year as downshifters, bankruptcy is looming and I am seriously considering having to give up our island idyll and return to the city and more work possibilites when the phone rings one icy morning and the unexpected caller is Anne, the local postmistress, bearing financial good tidings.

"Aye-aye, Max," she says, "whit like the day? It's rare and frasty[21] weather we're having, is it no'?"

"Hello Anne," I say back, already well used to island preamble. "What can I do for you today?"

"Aye weel, now that you ask..." she says, obviously glad to be shot of social niceties, "would you be free to earn a peedie bit of money for Christmas?"

"Always glad for some money, Anne," I say immediately. Then realising I may be committing myself to the crab works, or worse, I add, "What would I have to do for it – and how 'peedie' an amount are we talking?"

"Weel..." she says, taking a deep breath, "Sinkie, that's your postie, as you ken, weel, he needs to take two weeks holiday before the end of the year. And Charlie, doon the bottom of your road, you ken, weel, he usually fills

---

21 - **frasty:** frosty

in. But there was a peedie incident between him and a wife doon in Rendall and, weel, he doesnae want to do it again. So we were wondering if maybe you'd like to help us oot and cover Sinkie's round for a couple of weeks?"

Now, while this monologue is going on I'm mentally protesting, 'What, get up at five every morning for a fortnight, in the pitch black and freezing cold, and then be out in the howling gales all day? Not a chance...' when I hear the people-pleasing part of myself exclaiming in a hale and hearty manner, "No problem at all, Anne. I'd be glad to help you out. And the money will be very welcome. When do I start?"

*

It should, perhaps, be explained at this point that rural Orkney is somewhat different from most other places in Britain, in that the entire "country" part of the island is split up into parishes. Most of these, like Toab or the unfortunately named Twatt, consist of only a few far-flung cottages which do not have a nucleus to them, thereby making it exceedingly difficult to know when you've left one village or entered another. Particularly as most of them don't have signs or even boundary stones.

Therefore, when Anne informs me that my round is to cover only the twin parishes of Firth and Rendall, I have absolutely no idea of exactly what size of an area I'll have to cover each day, and studying the Ordinance Survey map in advance proves to be of little help to me.

Firth parish, where we live, is unusual in that it has the village of Finstown with a couple of numbered streets at its epicentre. But its evil twin, Rendall, is truly rural, with no catalogued settlement of any description, and consists solely of sporadic, far-flung crofts clinging perilously to its rocky coastline, and it is with some trepidation that I drag myself out of bed in the frozen dark on the first morning of my training period, and walk down to the sleeping village.

Sinclair, the postman I'm covering for, is a calm, silver-haired, twinkly-eyed old bloke who seems to have been Finstown's local postie for as long as anyone can remember, and is an encyclopaedic font of knowledge on absolutely everyone in the two parishes that he services. Our first task

together is to spend about two hours sifting through the large polypropylene sacks of incoming mail, crammed into what's laughingly referred to as the sorting office, which is, in actuality, an unheated narrow hut behind the miniscule post office.

I assume – naively – that sorting will consist of slotting all the letters into the wooden pigeon-holes on the wall that match their addresses, but I should have known that Orkney post would never run so logically, and it seems that every letter I try to categorise appears to be in the wrong place.

"But it definitely *says* Glebe Cottage on this one, Sinkie," I say as Sinclair corrects me with an imperceptible shake of the head, and when I am foolish enough to remonstrate further, he explains patiently, "Aye, but Sigurd's oot on the farm all day so his mail goes to his mother's hoose at Renaquoy, don't you see. Except on a Tuesday, of course, when she's at the Mart and it goes to his sister's at Doon-a-Biggin," until I finally admit defeat and get a notebook to write it all down. By ten that morning I have a novel-sized pad under my arm as we pile all the sorted mail into the van and drive out on the round.

With a typical outsider's arrogance, I think that I already know my local terrain fairly well, but as we drive out through a hidden gate in an ominous-looking hedgerow, and up and down little-known tracks and lanes miles from the main road, I soon realise that I have absolutely no clue about where I am or what I'm doing and that I have only a few days left to learn anything helpful at all.

However, we pull up at the first house without major mishap and Sinclair hands me a bundle of mail to deliver, an amused smirk on his face as he says, "Let's see how you get on with that."

Insulted, I clamber out of the van muttering, "I'm fucking university educated. I think I can fucking manage to push a fucking envelope through a fucking letter box." And am about to attempt to do just that when I realise what all real Orkney postmen know in the womb.

Island houses have no letter boxes.

A letter box in Orkney, Sinkie informs me as I come shamefacedly back to

the van, is not a convenience but merely something to rattle all night long, and let in a ferocious draught when there's a gale blowing. As nobody ever locks their doors anyway, their installation is considered completely impractical and unnecessary. In fact, in a coastal community plagued by icy sea winds all year long, polar draughts are such a problem that the resourceful Orkney islanders invented their own 'gadget', the hooded Orkney Chair, a heavy wooden contraption that looks a bit like an antique dentists' chair with a wickerwork coffin nailed to the back of it. The wicker hood effectively stops freezing draughts, and cups the heat from the fire around the sitter at the same time, and nearly every home used them extensively right up until the late 1960s and the eventual arrival of central heating.

"Now," Sinkie tells me, "you'd better get your notebook out again, because there's a way to go into folk's houses. With Sooth folk like yourself you just open the door and put the mail in on the mat, but in an auld farm where there's a wife in the hoose you cannae do that – we have to go inside and take the post to the kitchen table and pass the time o' day. I'll take you round and introduce you so that you'll not be a stranger to them. But they'll all offer you tea and a bannock. We've not got the time to stop, but be very careful how you refuse so that you don't offend anybody."

"Is any of this going to be straightforward?" I ask, a mite sarcastically.

No," Sinclair replies in all seriousness, "it's not."

*

We continue for another hour, Sinclair making the necessary introductions when we need to enter farmsteads and meet the lady of the house, and I'm just beginning to get a little more comfortable when we pull up at a run-down farmhouse with a tumbledown gate and a front door that looks as if it was last painted during the attack on Scapa Flow – the *Viking* attack. But when I try to get out, Sinkie motions to me to be still as he looks furtively all around him.

There's only one letter, a circular from a feed company, and I am about to ask why we're not just delivering it when he whispers, "This is a very important hoose to remember. You *never* just walk up here and open the

door."

"Alright," I reply cautiously. "What happens here then?"

He laughs quietly. "Just watch," he says in an exaggerated undertone. "Okay, the coast's clear..."

We get carefully out of the van and Sinclair fumbles behind the gate post and produces a large stick like a club left behind by one of those Scapa Flow Vikings, which he brandishes in front of him like a madman.

Having already made a complete idiot of myself more than once this morning, I say nothing, but assumably now armed against possible attack by rival delivery firms, we proceed quietly up the overgrown path to the front entrance like rustic commandoes, where Sinclair quickly pushes the stick hard against the bottom of the door before deftly opening it and throwing the mail inside. However, he isn't quite quick enough and there's a scratching slithering skid of claws from inside the rank-smelling darkness of the hallway and a malodorous dog hurls itself bodily against the door, clamping its teeth onto the lower half of the stick like something out of a cartoon.

"*That* is why we don't ever just open this door," my mentor tells me sternly.

*

In my more romantic moments, I saw myself as Rendall's harbinger of good tidings when I decided to save the parish and be its local postman, but in practice most of the mail we deliver consists of bills and advertising circulars, and when we're out in the van again the next day my head is spinning, trying to remember where all the hidden track entrances are, and which old ladies it's okay to collect mail from and which it isn't.

In fact, I'm so preoccupied with the order of the route that I don't notice the creeping greenish-grey clouds that are looming ominously over the restless sea, and suddenly, without warning, the icy-cold wind that's been blowing in from the North Pole all morning turns into a fierce swirling blizzard, bringing complete white-out in the space of five minutes.

Sinkie is possessed with the indigenous Orcadian's stoic acceptance of his native climate and is perfectly calm about this, but I am in total panic as I watch all the landmarks I've carefully memorised being completely obliterated, and I sit stiffly in the van, trying to look disinterested, while my insides turn to water as I contemplate the blank, featureless landscape before me.

My track record for day one in the job has hardly been brilliant, and even with Sinclair at my side I have taken more than four hours longer than the allotted time to complete the round; fallen into muddy ditches on several occasions, and as the fin touché, run right past the actual post office van and jumped into a post office red Renault driven by a shocked village woman, of whom I demand, "What are you waiting for, Sinkie? Drive."

It is no wonder then, that I'm eyeing the eight foot drifts ahead of me with a neurotic trepidation, and I'm seriously wondering if the van is even going to make it across the ordinary snow-covered roads without mishap or misadventure. Sinclair, on the other hand, came out of the womb in his postman's uniform, behind the wheel of a Morris Station Wagon, and the blizzard conditions don't faze him in the least, as the sturdy little van chugs confidently along snow-covered single-track and up and down bumpy farm ruts, under his beyond-advanced control.

However, even the Mighty Sinkie, lord of all the Norse gods, is no match for the fury of a fully-fledged Orkney snowstorm, and although we manage to proceed without mishap for most of the day, the van suddenly skids and careers blindly into a ten-foot-high snowdrift a little after two o'clock, slap bang in the middle of a deserted country road, just as it's getting dark.

From inside the van it's like looking out of an aeroplane window as you fly through an impenetrable bank of cloud, and the vehicle is quickly smothered front and back in the densely packed snow, the wheels spinning impotently when Sinkie tries to reverse out of it.

Darkness is falling by the minute now as I quickly get out and try to push. But it's to no avail, and there's a bitter wind that's abrading layers of skin off my face faster than any Bel Air plastic surgeon ever could, and eventually Sinclair motions me and all my penguin pals to get back inside

the vehicle.

It's now completely dark; there are no lights or houses for as far as the eye can see, not another vehicle on the road, and the snow is still belting down with a vengeance, already starting to submerge our marooned vehicle.

"What do we do now?" I ask, trying desperately to maintain my demeanour of cutting-edge cool in the face of all this rustic disruption to the natural order of things.

Sinkie just smiles.

*

To my complete astonishment, Sinclair's master plan is to do nothing, and incredibly, after sitting in the van for just five minutes, powerful headlights appear out of the darkness like the arrival of the mothership in Close Encounters, and we hear the throb of a heavy engine as an ancient snow-covered David Brown tractor chugs into our line of vision.

Quickly switching our movie metaphors from science fiction to classic horror, a muffled figure in a parka like something out of the terrorised ice station in The Thing, yells, "Are ye stuck?" from his open-to-the-elements driver's seat, and Sinclair gestures assent.

The parka waves a gloved hand in an all-scientists-battling-the-elements-together salute and shouts, "I'll get Rognvald,[22]" as he vanishes back into the blizzard, while Sinclair sits back satisfied in his seat and flashes me a that-showed-you look.

"Help's coming," he says, as I try to fathom exactly how he, they or anybody knew what was going on, but sure enough, five minutes later we hear a second deep-throated engine and this time a large yellow JCB digger appears out of the swirling snow, and after a couple of deep scrape and dumps, the road's clear again and we're back en route to deliver our bagfuls of electricity bills and Reader's Digest circulars, waving our thanks to the faceless driver who is, I assume, the mythical and mysterious Psychic

---

22 - **Rognvald:** old Orkney name, pronounced Ronald

Rognvald of The Snowy Plough.

*

The whole point of delivering mail at all becomes meaningless to me as we spend the next day risking life and limb negotiating snowy roads and scrambling up and down fourteen foot snowdrifts to deliver the junk mail that we know is going to end up straight on people's fires. Nevertheless, I'm just getting confident that I can actually make a stab at this by myself when a severe overnight frost turns all the furrowed snow to iron, the narrow roads turn into lethal skating rinks and the deeply rutted farm tracks become obstacle courses to be negotiated with great care.

Sinclair, of course, rises to the challenge and glides along the icy tracks with a tantalising flash of red livery and a Torville and Dean-style ease, but even under his expert hand it's too much for the van when we descend a particularly rutted track where the frozen snow between the ridges is like an iron girder lying on its side, and there's suddenly a horrible metallic shriek from the undercarriage as the exhaust parts company with the rest of the vehicle.

Sinkie merely shrugs, and I'd like to say that I, too, remained polished and unruffled and didn't really scream, "What the *fuck* was that?!" as I jumped out of my skin and blew yet another audition for Incomer Who Blends Seamlessly With Natives.

However, my mentor thankfully doesn't insist that we continue the round by pack mule and matter-of-factly says, "We'd best go to Kirkwall" as the darkness begins to fall.

It is ten minutes to two in the afternoon.

*

The van sounds like a motor boat with diarrhoea, but Sinclair coaxes it skilfully through Rendall's twisty lanes and back onto the main road which has, thankfully, been recently gritted, and we limp to the Royal Mail depot in Kirkwall. They give us their only remaining vehicle – an old wreck of a van with a flickering orange light on the roof – to finish our round, and we

head back out to Rendall in the dark.

We have a lot of mail left to deliver, and there's a particularly large bundle for a big farm where all the tracks are beautifully clear, as the farmer owns his own snow plough – an impulse purchase at a farm sale in Shetland, Sinclair informs me. Said farmer is standing in the bitter cold, smoking a rolly-up at his byre door, when we finally limp and cough into his yard at a very late just-after-five that evening.

"Fuck's sake, Sinkie. Where the fuck have you fucking been? And what the fuck's that fucking heap of fucking shit you're fucking driving?" the fat little farmer grumps as I fumble for his mail, and Sinclair decides that introductions are necessary.

"This is Wishart," he says with a twinkle. "He likes to fuck."

*

Sinclair finally goes on holiday and I start to get into the rhythm of being an island postie. In fact, once I get used to the intricacies and eccentricities of the round, I start to relax and enjoy myself, and driving the van, of course, suddenly opens up parts of the island that have previously been denied to me. The inaccessible and off-the-guide-book parish of Rendall is a different face of Orkney, and is far more rugged and untamed than the gentle agrarian Firth where we live, and there is a certain thrill involved in driving out to its distant houses along rough tracks that are so close to the sea that, at high tide, indignant waves splash up across the road and soak the windscreen of the van. Miles from the tourist trail, crow-stepped eighteenth century farm buildings are commonplace, and there's even a medieval dovecote sharing a muddy field with a handful of hardy grazing cattle, but my favourite 'hidden' destination of all is the lonely Isle of Gairsay.

Gairsay is a tiny barely-inhabited island that sits just off the coast at Rendall's southernmost promontory, a bleak piece of rock in a stormy sea with a scanty toupee of arable soil providing a meagre living for its inhabitants. Well-mentioned in Orkney ballads and songs, and the setting for many a plaintive dirge about selkie-men emerging from the waves and preying on unsuspecting maidens, the tiny islet originally housed thirteen

families, but poverty and hard living conditions have long since driven them away, and today the isle is inhabited by a solitary hermit who occasionally rows over to the mainland in his open boat to pick up supplies and collect his mail from the tiny shed where I leave it each day.

The time quickly passes, and in the manner typical of smug incomers, I'm about to claim my Blue Peter Badge for a job well done when, on my last day, I discover a letter in the unsorted mail for an address that I've never delivered to before. On enquiry I am informed by a suspiciously amused Anne that it's an old croft that's been empty for years after the original occupant slit his wrists and bled himself dry in a sheep trough.

Some keen sod has, of course, now decided to move in and has been sent a letter from Reader's Digest to mark the auspicious occasion, and it's up to me to see that 'I Fought a Grizzly Bear for the FBI While Wearing an Iron Lung' arrives clean and pristine on his blood-spattered doormat.[23]

It's been a stormy, unsettled day and by the end of my round the strong wind has worked itself into a full-blown gale, and of course the House of Death is in the middle of nowhere, so it's pitch dark by the time I reach its alleged location. I ask for directions at some of the neighbouring longhouses, but this far from civilisation any house that's not a working farm can only be occupied by twitchy-faced incomers from the Home Counties who all keep goats on their front lawns, and none of them have ever heard of it. Eventually, however, I find an old farmer mucking out his byre who gives me directions, totally unaware that he should really say something portentous like, "Beware the dog o' doom, bhouy" to make this story more colourful, and I drive blind down a narrow, overgrown track, finally coming upon the dark looming shape of the squat ugly house.

Orkney's landscape doesn't boast any genuine trees because of the constant high winds, but this building is surrounded by the usual scrubby hedges and a couple of mournfully stunted elms which stretch their malformed branches across my path.

And, of course, there's not another house or light in sight.

---

23 - What? I'm an artist. I'm allowed a little poetic licence now and again.

It's darker than a tar baby's arse when I douse the van's headlamps, but thankfully Sinkie keeps a torch in the glove compartment and I circle the deserted cottage like the world's most northerly Fox Mulder, but it's boarded up tight, with no sign of life. The mean wind that's been picking up all afternoon is now screaming like a chorus of mad Mrs Rochesters, while the battery in Sinclair's torch is starting to fade and I can't see hide nor hair of an unlocked door or any other orifice in which to divest my missive.

I know that the Post Office Creed I've been forced to learn by heart states that all mail must be delivered somewhere, somehow, but I'm holding an advertising circular for an empty property, and this is one temporary postie who's giving up the ghost, and I quickly bundle myself back into the van and put the headlights on.

I start up the engine to leave, but the space at the side of the house is narrow and muddy and there's only the crumbling wall of the Byre of Sorrows on one side and a very deep and unfriendly-looking ditch on the other, so I have to try and turn the van around in six-inch-increments while unable to see my hand before my face.

The wind is getting louder and louder and my fertile imagination is already furnishing phantom crofters in every glimpse of undergrowth caught in my headlamps, when suddenly there's a horrible grinding sound and the whole vehicle abruptly tips backwards as the van drops down into the darkness of the ravine-like ditch at the side of the road.

*

I'm sitting with the front wheels in the air and the back half of the van in the ditch of a haunted house in the middle of nowhere, with a hell of a storm brewing up, and wondering what the fuck to do now. After discounting all the ridiculous ideas that fly into my head – like breaking into the house only to find a dead phone with a cut line and, of course, a guy in a hockey mask – I try the obvious and put the van into gear and try to drive myself out. I've divested myself of all the mail order muumuus, free feed catalogues and million pound prize draws, so there's nothing in the back to weigh me down and, miraculously, the rear-wheel-drive actually manages to find a grip in the rocky soil and claw me back up onto

the track. I can't believe that I've actually rescued myself without having to run for help for once, and I tank back to the welcoming lights of Finstown like a latter-day Tam O'Shanter fleeing his furious Cutty-sark.

CHAPTER 7 – WHERE WE SPEND OUR FIRST FESTIVE SEASON IN THE ISLES

The village hall is hosting a Millennium Hogmanay Party to say goodbye to the twentieth century, and we go along to meet up with our new friends, Rhona and Shona, who are tonight attired in matching little black numbers to which Rhona has added a cheap silver-gilt "2000" brooch which Shona, her more-inhibited twin, notably, has not, and I somehow guess that they have argued about the suitability of this bauble for the entirety of the journey to the community centre.

The party has no formal bar or catering and everyone has been told to bring 'plenty' of food and drink, a red flag to a bull for Orcadians, and when we arrive the buffet counter already resembles something out of the Beano, with literally hundreds of plates of sandwiches and mini sausage rolls piled at least eighteen inches high up and down its length, and there is enough alcohol on the tables to keep the entirety of America drunk for ten years if prohibition is ever reintroduced.

It seems that the entire parish and their sheep dogs have turned out, and the big hangar-like hall has already divided itself into dyed-in-the-wool farmers' tables groaning under the weight of tuna and sweetcorn sandwiches and home-brewed strong ales; patchouli-scented hippy tables with coarse hessian cloths covered with wine bottles and bowls of Japanese seaweed crackers; and trendy young Orcadian tables where sulky teens imbibe suspiciously innocuous, and almost certainly, spiked, family-size bottles of Coke and communicate with each other across the table by text.

The twins have already charted the inhabitants of all the various corners before we arrive, and, after we have been on the obligatory 'turn about the room' with them, they eventually cast their vote for the best place to sit. Rejecting the teen tables because the boys are too young, and the hippy happenings because the men are too old, they finally settle at a drunken farm-boys' cluster-fuck where a particularly odious specimen called Spunky[24] has indicated –by ignoring them completely – that he might be "up for it"; a bait which the sisters take by competing ferociously with each other for the dubious benefit of a night discovering how he earned his name.

Meanwhile hordes more people continue to flock into the room and the hall slowly fills, and then fills some more. By the time twelve o'clock is on the horizon it's Sardinesville, with standing room only and dancing totally out of the question.

There has been a lot of talk about a live BBC link to welcome in the New Century. Having gone to too many such events in Manchester, I've been visualising a video link with a booming Big Ben being projected onto a huge screen outside. But the isles version of this grandiose concept is simply an ancient transistor tuned to Radio Orkney, which has had a crackly old mike taped to the front of it, which in turn is fed into the exterior public address system so that fireworks can be launched into the night sky as the sadly shrunken magnificence of Big Ben is just about discernible chiming tinnily from a studio in downtown Kirkwall.

Thus, as midnight approaches, everyone crowds into the car park to witness this pyrotechnic wonder, and as twelve o'clock strikes and the soft tones of Radio Orkney give way to Brian Perkins, we hear the familiar sound of the Westminster chimes taking us into the new century. There is muffled stage whisper of "Light it now, Brian!" and a splutter of sparks emanates from the dark field adjacent to the car park as a single brave little rocket shoots about ten feet into the air and fizzles out into the starry night sky.

A lady beside me tells me that it's supposed to spell out "two thousand" but it just looks like a burst of coloured sparkle to me. However, further contemplation of the Zen meaning of this is interrupted by uproarious cheering and I'm suddenly engulfed in an orgy of handshaking, back-patting and moist embracing as a barrage of drunk women, most of whom I have never met before, plant happy new year kisses all over my face.

*

Having both been reared in Central Scotland, Chancery and I are both

---

24 - Getting to know the men that the twins lust after is a bit like being thrown into the world of a Tennessee Williams drama, and strange nicknames like Spooty, Dimmer and Cheesey abound.

familiar with the Scottish New Year and know the drill for first-footing on Hogmanay, so on Millennium night, after the Hall party folds at a surprisingly early one a.m., we simply follow the crowd and visit several open houses in the village as we make our way steadily homewards, overdosing on rum, shortbread and esoteric flavoured Pringles as we go.

Rhona and Shona have deserted the village in pursuit of Spunky and his mates, who have absconded to the "superior" street celebrations in "Toon", but we have declined their invitation to accompany them as our close encounter with frostbite on the last occasion is still fresh in our minds, and four in the morning sees us safely home and in bed.

*

We sleep late on New Year's Day and are pottering around with breakfast just after noon, blissfully unaware that any other social obligations are scheduled, when there's a loud knocking at the front door and Rhona and Shona bluster into the hallway in large overcoats and matching woollen hats, scarves and ear-muffs, looking like a double helping of Nanook of the North crossed with Eskimo Nell.

"Hello, are you two going ice fishing?" I ask in as jocular a tone as I can muster for that hour of the day, and a bellyful of last night's rum and cake.

However my jape falls upon deaf ears as the two fur muffins stare at me and Shona blurts, "Oh my God, you're not dressed yet. Come on, they're throwing up in half an hour!"

"And do we really want to watch someone throwing up?" I ask, now genuinely perplexed.

"Oh... my...God. Do you pair not read the pepper?" Shona demands, and I begin to wonder just how much she had to drink last night.

"Read the pepper...?" Oh Christ, what weird new custom was this? "Is this a tarot thing... like reading entrails...?" I ask with more hope than enthusiasm, praying that the mad women will leave soon.

Chancery immediately clarifies, "The paper, you prat", and I realise that

there has obviously been some local news item that I have missed.

"It's the New Year's Day Ba'," Rhona explains, and Chancery adds pointedly, "In *all* the guide books..." as the penny finally drops.

*

The Ba' is an ancient Orcadian game played in the streets of Kirkwall between the Uppies and the Doonies. It involves a heavy leather ball, or ba', which is "thrown up" in the centre of the town, and which the teams then fight over to try and get it to the designated goal area on the other side of town, preferably before night falls. It is a sort of unholy blend of Rugby, American Football and a street riot, and involves two teams of several hundred men[25] who jostle together for several hours, moving neither forwards nor backwards, in a giant rugger scrum that is even more boring than cricket. However, huge amounts of spectators brave the icy January gales to watch this legendary 'action', and the local council boards up all the shop windows and doors with old railway sleepers while smothering the entire town in non-liability statements for injuries and fatalities sustained during the drama of the 'game'.

It's a cold but bright day when we arrive and find a "safe" parking space well away from any possible trauma, and hordes of stocky young girls yell ribald greetings to the twins as we make our way with the crowd to the traditional throwing up point at the doors of St Magnus' Cathedral for the official start of the game. The broad street is already packed to bursting point as more and more folk show up, and the combatants, a motley ménage of shaven-headed men of all ages, most clad in rugby jerseys and already red-faced with the cold, bob up and down, full of nervous energy as they wait for the contest to begin.

The whole place is literally stewing with excess testosterone, much to the delight of the many, many clusters of women who are already hoarse from raucous cheering and bawdy cat-calling, and other than the freezing weather, it's a bit like

---

25 - Originally there was a Women's Ba' as well, but it was discontinued due to the large amount of uncontrolled aggression and near fatalities. (Honest!)

back in time to the days of gladiatorial combat in Ancient Rome.

We have found a spot on the grass in front of the Cathedral, but the crushing crowd soon separates us, and although I can still see the rest of my party, I find myself in close proximity to a woman from Finstown with whom I have only a nodding acquaintance. Being New Years Day, there are no pubs open, but most of the viewing public have supplied their own refreshments and the, I'd thought, demure lady pauses momentarily from screaming obscenities at the opposite team to offer me a drink from her shiny silver hip flask, which she seems to have inadvertently filled with surgical alcohol or home-stilled Icelandic vodka.

"So, how do you get picked for a team, then?" I ask, more out of a desire to stem her flow of 'encouragement' than any genuine curiosity.

"Picked?" she says, looking at me as if I've just insulted the Shaolin temple. "You don't get *picked for* the ba', bhouy. You're born either an Uppie or a Doonie and you stay that way till the day you die. There's no choice involved."

"Oh," I say. "So what about me? I wasn't born here – what side would I play on?"

"You? Play?" she says, suppressing, I fancy, somewhat raucous laughter. "I guess you'd have to be an Uppie, since you came in on the Stromness boat. But I don't see you being called on to play any day soon. You're useless, you Doonies. We're going tae skelp your hairy gobshite arses!!!"

This last shriek is accompanied by a uniform roar from the assembled crowd as an unknown, and largely unseen, male in a provost's chain flings the tan and black ball into the air from the church doorway and all the shaven-headed combatants make a dive for its anticipated landing spot. Limbs flail in all directions and within ten minutes huge clouds of steam begin to rise from the tight crush of humanity that is inching its way down to the harbour in what seems to be a meaningful progression to every person in the street except me.

I have already become separated from my new acquaintance but I can still hear her hurling abuse at the opposing team, and I fight my way through

the tight press of bodies until I eventually reach Chancery and the twins who have fought tooth and claw for a coveted niche on the cathedral steps.

"Is that it then?" I ask with not much hope in my voice. But the twins just look at me witheringly.

"It's only just started," Shona admonishes me. "It hasn't had time to get exciting yet."

"And anyway," Rhona adds, "Spunky's playing. We want to see if he manages to handle the ba'!"

I somehow feel that it's going to be a long afternoon.

*

We assume that the festivities must now be finally concluded for the year and are sitting in our living room with mugs of tea at seven o'clock that evening, listening to Radio Four, when there's a loud hammering at our - locked – front door. Chancery goes to answer it and is surprised when Tumshie John, our under-sized landlord, and his young live-in farmhand blunder drunkenly into the hall and shake her hand so vigorously it loosens her watch. This is obviously not a formal visit as they're not wearing their "good" suits, but although they're both still in their obligatory farm clothes they've swapped their wellies for hob-nailed boots and are wearing freshly pressed overalls, along with combed brilliantined hair, so that they look oddly like a pair of garishly-painted lawn ornaments.

We invite them inside, thankful that we bought a hospitality bottle of Highland Park after all, and in the course of the ensuing conversation learn that an Orkney New Year will carry on for three or four days until you have visited absolutely all your relatives and neighbours. Tumshie John tells us that as our landlord he will be shamed by proxy if we don't accompany him to pay our respects to the rest of the parish, so we change out of our jeans and all bundle into his old van to commence what turns out to be a truly epic journey.

*

John is not drunk, per se, although he's already well over the legal limit to drive, but although it's a cold wintry night there's a full clear moon and no frost, and he never drives much faster than ten miles an hour anyway, so we figure that we'll all be fairly safe. The hillside is dotted with longhouses and bungalows all glowing with oil lamps and twinkling fairylights and we call at house after house where I attempt to only sip at each of the quadruple-doubles I am given, but rum, shortbread and black bun is still coming out of my ears by the time we finally reach the village.

Tumshie John, on the other hand, is downing the free liquor like it's going out of fashion and his already wobbly driving is getting more and more erratic as the little green van sways drunkenly down the twisty single-track road. I'm just about ready to call it quits at around two in the morning when our motley crew finally arrives at the home of a burly retired policeman called Len, who looks like the kind of scowly-faced copper who always played Bad Cop in witness interrogation scenarios. Judging by his festive greeting of, "Oh, it's you, you little shit", the glowering ex-PC doesn't appear to be any too pleased to see the intoxicated John, but it's New Year's Day and he is a good Orcadian, so of course he invites us all in to his home.

The visit doesn't go at all well, however, as the host's wife apparently has some unhappy history with Tumshie John, who is now exceedingly drunk. Living up to whatever it is he has done in the past – and by her face it was something terrible – John behaves obnoxiously and insults her repeatedly, taking no advice from any of us to, "Behave yourself, John."

The atmosphere is getting more and more uncomfortable and when it reaches the host's face by way of a thunderous brow and ferociously scowling mouth, I'm starting to think that it's time to go, when the silent farmhand, who has not said a word the entire evening, miraculously reads my mind and quickly makes our excuses and heads for the door. Tumshie John, in the meantime, has improvised a little song of his own and is singing it under his breath, and although I can't exactly make out the words it's my belief that they are not exactly complimentary to our by now fuming lady of the house.

Chancery quickly hustles Tumshie John to the door before things get any worse and Len follows us out, I assume to make sure that we all leave his

property and don't simply drop John on his lawn, but instead he takes me to one side and says that there's no way John can be allowed behind the wheel and instructs me to drive him home.

"He won't like that," I say cautiously, indicating the bouncing dishevelled ball who is determinedly pushing off Chancery's assistance while telling her how much he's never liked her. "How are we going to get him into the van?"

"Leave that to me," Len says with the closest thing to a smile that's been on his humourless face since we first darkened his door. "Come here, you!"

Len is a good six foot three to Tumshie John's four foot nothing and he wrenches the rear door of the van open with one hand and grasps the squirming little dwarf by the scruff of the neck and physically flings him into the back of the vehicle like a sack of turnips going into a cargo hold. I quickly get into the driver's seat and try to start up, but although John's keys are dangling obligingly in the ignition I can't get the engine started.

After a moment's confusion the farmhand confesses that John must have turned the security code on, knowing full well that someone somewhere would try to stop him driving the van during the course of his night's revels.

Len lets out a roar of frustration and aims a kick at Tumshie John's supine body.

"What's the code, you little shit?" But Bilbo Baggins only chuckles to himself and goes on singing his peculiar little ditty, which is now fairly audible and by no means complimentary.

"Oh Len's got a pen where his dick should be... it's awful when he needs to pee... the doctors raised an awful stink... when they saw oor Lenny peeing ink," croons the gnome. For which he receives a hefty kick from Len's, thankfully, slippered foot. But he is totally unrepentant.

"He's a prick withoot a dick... is that no' sick?" he caterwauls in reply, heedless of the kicks and blows. "He needs a peedie stick tae be his prick." Len kicks him again, shaking him in a brain-loosening way that would

probably do serious injury if he had been sober.

"What's the code, you raggedy-arsed wee gobshite?" he demands as he lifts John up off the floor by his dungaree straps and drops him down again with an almighty crump.

"Two, six, seven, ten, Len cannae get it up again!" Tumshie John giggles.

Len bangs him off the side of the van and pulls him out by the feet then shoves him in again as if he is trying to rattle it out of him. But it's obvious that John can't or won't tell, so the livid policeman has to content himself with merely confiscating his keys and dispatching John's mortified farmhand to take his inebriated boss home on foot.

We mumble something totally ineffectual and grasp this opportunity for escape with both hands, making for home before Len slaps the bracelets on us.

*

The New Year celebrations go on and on, and we're well sick of fruitcake and shortie by the fifth of January, so it's a relief to know that the last festivity of the season is to be Hordun and Marigold's Annual Music Night and that this will be a strictly grappa and tapas affair.

It's snowing heavily on the evening in question but it's only a short walk down the steep slope from our house, so we wander down at our leisure, threading carefully through the parked Renaults and Volkswagens to arrive fashionably late. We find Marigold alone in the kitchen, mixing strange things in a bowl and lost in a world of her own –an occurrence that is to become a regular feature of our Zen-like encounters with her –but the evening's entertainment is obviously already in full swing in the living room.

A goatee-bearded Glaswegian, dressed in skinny black jeans and black tee-shirt is reworking some old 1960s' comic song about a double decker bus, much to the delight of an appreciative fifty-something English audience who all seem to think that they're watching Billy Connolly.

Next on the bill is a stoned performance poet with a strange Doctor Seuss-style hat, although nobody's sure if his fragmented verse is abstract or he's just too out of his head to know that he's reading stanzas from alternating poems.

Miscellaneous guitarists and fiddlers follow, then there's a welcome interval at half past ten to allow time for food and group singing in foreign languages before the concert programme recommences. Ten minutes of blissful non-music have gone by and we're standing, plates in hand, amidst the numerous stacks of guitar and fiddle cases in Hordun's hallway, talking to some arran-clad Norwegian geography teachers about Orkney's geological strata, of all things, when the whole room, one by one, becomes aware of what sounds like raised voices and what can only be described as drum-related violence coming from a nearby broom closet.

"Oh my. Now this is just not good. I'm sure this is out of tune," mutters a neurotic high-pitched voice like Alistair Sim playing a decrepit headmistress in some flickering Ealing comedy.

"For goodness sake, it's a bodhrán,[26]" an irritated male voice replies. "How could it be out of tune?"

"Well, it's all very well for you, right enough, James Foubister," the agitated one replies with a snap, "but it's *your* bare arse that's going to be oot there flapping in the wind when we go on and it's no' right."

"Nobody's arse is going to be oot there flapping anywhere, you know that, but folk are waiting to hear us play... tonight, so will you come on?"

"Oh my, well I never. Well, you ken *I'm* ready," the lady rector of St Trinian's insists right back. "But I really don't think that we should do Lonely Scapa Flowat all tonight. It's just going to be a muckle shambles, so it is."

"Can we just play?" the deeper male voice almost pleads in exasperation, and the cupboard door is abruptly thrown open. But instead of the two

26 - **Bodhrán:** Celtic musical instrument, a cross between a drum and a tambourine.

cantankerous pensioners that the altercation has led us to expect, the occupants turn out to be a pair of tweed-clad genteel boys in their late twenties. They stand there blinking uncertainly in the sudden glare of the electric light, when suddenly one of them spots us and descends on us like a widow-woman greeting her lost husband home from the sea.

"Oh my, this is affa[27]fine," he squeaks in his hyperactive way. "Is it no' yourselves, and whit like the night? I've seen you pair walking on the old Scapa road. What a grand thing to meet you here, an a'."

I'm about to yell 'Help, help! Stalker Alert!' when I realise that our paths actually *have* crossed and that we have, indeed, met this somewhat camp couple before, bowing and scraping around a village ceilidh, dancing attendance on all the blue-rinsed old 'wifes' that usually line the walls, and had assumed them to be an eccentric visiting couple from somewhere even stranger than Orkney – like Shetland, perhaps – but we now learn that they are in fact local lads called James and Jasper, and that they are alleged to be both sane and straight.

"You'll have to excuse him," James, the taller of the two interjects. "He had to buy a gallon of petrol to get here tonight and he's still in shock."

"Whit a thing to say!" Jasper, the more effete one immediately splutters back. "His idea of splashing oot is staying home and putting an extra lamp on."

"Jasper, these folk are not wanting to hear all this banter. Come on and get ready, we're on in a peedie minute!"

"Oh my, yes, I'm coming." Jasper says, not moving an inch. "Now... well... do you pair live doon here?"

"Yeah, just next door," I say without thinking. Chancery clears her throat loudly and I try desperately to think of another house 'just next door' to cover up my faux pas. But it's already too late.

"Oh my, away. You're no' the two folk from Sooth that are in peedie

---

27 - **Affa:** awfully

Tumshie John's hoose, are ye'? Is it true that you're both antique dealers?"

Wondering where the hell he has picked up this piece of ancient history, I scratch my head and start to say, "Well, we *used* to deal in collectibles about twenty years ago..." when the two of them go on point and literally pounce on us.

"Oh collectibles! We're great men for the collections," James says, clapping his hands. "We've both got huge ones."

"Oh aye," Jasper adds. "We're men with huge ones, right enough."

James immediately snaps, "Jasper!", going decidedly pink, but further innuendo is, thankfully, avoided by Hordun calling the two gay caballeros into the main room, and they go through their set numbers, still bickering, and conclude their act with a selection of exceedingly bawdy "auld Orkney" stories from a coyly filthy Jasper while James sits, mortified, with his head in his hands at the rear of Hordun's impromptu stage.

However, we are saved from further revelations of Celtic crudity as the clock strikes midnight and aged Afghan coats are draped over devoré velvet shoulders, and paunchy potters and grizzled ethnographers alike start heading for their ancient Renaults. But not before Marigold's sojourn with her spirit guide is apparently over and she returns to our galaxy, appearing in the living room resplendent in a bejewelled emerald-green floor-length kaftan, and bearing large cards with the correct words to Auld Lang Syneinscribed on them so that she can lead the community singing that signifies that the evening, and the party season, are – blissfully – finally over.

CHAPTER 8 - WHERE, CAUGHT UP IN THE EUPHORIA OF BEING PARTY-GOING NATIVES, I LET MY VANITY GET THE BETTER OF ME AND ALLOW MYSELF TO BECOME INFATUATED WITH A COUNTRY WENCH

The long and gale-racked winter finally passes and the puffins return to the outer isles as May tentatively approaches. Stir-crazy after nearly four months of virtual imprisonment in the house and now desperate to see more of the island, we buy a dubious pair of second-hand bikes and head out onto the open road.

Cycling takes me quite a bit of getting used to, however, as I haven't been on a bike since I was a teenager and I can't sit down for the first week, hobbling around complaining like somebody's decrepit old grandfather. However, we're soon fighting the strong spring winds and pedalling the ten miles to Kirkwall and back without too much effort and, emboldened, we even begin to tour the locality and manage to get out to see some of Orkney's numerous tourist attractions – aka heaps of Neolithic stones.

Rhona and Shona, the twins, continue to take us out manhunting on weekends, and as the fragile May slides into a raw and chilly June, they arrive on our doorstep one evening with their eyes aglow and the metaphorical blueprints of a master plan tucked neatly under their arms. Gala Day is fast approaching and a couple of Stromness lads called Digger and Spader are rumoured to be judging this year's fancy dress parade, and the twins are determined to enter the competition and win their hearts, or at least their bodies, and have nominated us to be their accomplices.

"Now hang on," I say. "Why do we have to be in the parade if it's you two that are after the judges?"

Rhona casts her eyes heavenward as if to say, 'Have you learned nothing at all on the nights we've been out together?' and Shona explains patiently, "Because we've never been in the parade before, folk'll think it's funny if we just suddenly turn up on our own. But if we go with you it'll be alright."

"I'm still not getting this..." I begin, but Shona jumps in as though addressing the thickest dunce of her most retarded kindergarten class.

"Listen, you two are incomers. You don't have a history, so you can do what you want. And because we're your friends, if you go in for something then we can go along too, because we'd be going with you, we wouldn't just be there as us. We'd be you. Do you not see?"

"What costumes did you have in mind?" I ask, defeated.

*

Rhona and Shona decide, predictably, on St Trinians schoolgirl costumes and set about constructing the shortest gymslips known to man. We, however, having no judges to pull, decide that if we're going to do this we might as well treat it as a creative exercise and, rejecting the conventional gorilla suits and furry creature costumes for hire in the Kirkwall joke shop, come up with our own take on the old Universal Frankenstein movies.

Chancery fancies a 'Black Widow' costume and I cannibalise some old dresses from her drama school days to create a disturbingly sinister figure complete with torn weeds and a long train of ripped and decayed old lace and an ominous head-dress and veil which completely covers her face. For myself, we go to the Salvation Army shop in Kirkwall to buy a ghoulish old suit which doesn't fit properly, much to the consternation of the lady behind the counter who clucks around me in despair when I say that I intend to purchase it.

The worn-out old suit has obviously been cut for a typical Orkney short-arse, and as I'm well over six foot, the sleeves just make it past my elbows. This is great, as it makes me look just like Boris Karloff, and I further accentuate this by painting stitches on my exposed wrists.

*

Thus attired we go out to Shona's house in the village to collect the twins, impervious to the number of small children who run away screaming as we glide past, but her doorbell refuses to work and, when the gymslip-

clad bobbysoxers finally answer our emphatic knock, we see that the hall behind them is in complete darkness and that their scowling countenances are even blacker.

"Oh it's you," Shona says, disappointment writ plainly upon her face. "I was expecting Iain Denistoun the electrician."

"Because bloody Billy Flett's gone and blown all her fuses," Rhona interjects. "Wiring a lamp that I could have done in two seconds."

"And I've told you before that we'll never get a man if we go changing oil filters and fixing fuses ourselves," Shona replies tartly. "But that's no' the worst news."

"No, not by a long shot."

"Why, what else has happened?" Chancery asks cautiously.

"Oh just the worst thing..." Shona sighs.

"...the very worst," Rhona echoes. "They're saying now that Digger and Spader are no' judging the parade."

"It was all just a vicious rumour put aboot by that Ingrid Clouston from the craft club," Shona says, shaking her head in despair. "And now the word is it's those two weird fogies frae Toon that are doing the actual judging."

"And what kind of points are those two going to give these two?" Rhona demands, jiggling her little breasts in her hands, much to her sister's horror. "Best lime jellies?"

*

Apparently the identity of the judges is kept secret until the very last minute in the interests of Island Security, so we all trot off to the parade in fevered anticipation to join the merry flotilla of Vikings and radio-active leprechauns already on the village green. The twins are biting their nails down to the quick while they wait to see if the rumours are indeed true, and even Chancery and I get into the spirit of things and start conjecturing,

but our impromptu guessing-game is brought to an abrupt halt when I hear barely-repressed exclamations of disappointment from the twins and see that the predicted "weird fogies" are, in fact, here, and that they are none other than the legendary James and Jasper, who, still bickering between themselves, are being led up to the judging table along with a pair of curvaceous thirty-something ladies called Roberta and Henrietta.

The boys faff around and repeatedly rearrange their chairs like crabby old cats trying to get comfortable in their baskets, but eventually they pronounce themselves ready and we're all obliged to do a self-conscious lap around the green area.

There's a lot of animated chit-chat between the four judges and it soon becomes apparent that the girls have cast their votes, but the two fey lads are still arguing between themselves, calling for the assembly of characters to perambulate around the judging area for a second time.

However, it seems that little Jasper still can't reach a decision, and after much squabbling between the two boys the four judges come over for a closer look.

"Oh my, well, it's yourselves," Jasper gushes. "You're being The Monsters, are you no'?"

We decide to stay in character and just stare coldly at him, but it's over the top of his head as he's too busy arguing with James to notice.

"It's not The Monsters, it's The Munsters, you eejit," James snaps.

"Oh my, now, The Munsters... are you sure? Now, I thought it was The Monsters... with thon fellow with the bolt in his neck, and the Grandpa. Do you mind the Grandpa, James?"

"Oh for God's sake, Jasper, no-one wants to hear about the Grandpa just now."

"Oh my, no, now I'm sure it was The Monsters. Henrietta, did you not watch that when you were peedie? Was it not The Monsters? There was the Grandpa, and the bonnie lass, and the auld witchy one..."

"Jasper, will you shut up and judge the contest? Folk are wanting to get on, they don't want to listen to you yarning."

"Oh my, yes, and there's so many bonny costumes as well. But are you *sure* it wasn't The Monsters...?"

*

The judges finally hand over their entry sheets to an official from the Sports and Social Committee and the parade gets underway, with everyone marching down the road jingling charity cans. My skeletal makeup and Chancery's blank-faced veil prove to be slightly unnerving to our fellow villagers and we easily extort money out of them for the entirety of the parade. Everyone piles in to the village hall for the results, and we sit through twenty minutes of awards for Best Child's Handwriting and Best Jam Tart before we finally get to the accolades for best fancy dress costumes.

A little girl in front of us goes up to accept the award for Best Costume Under Ten Years, and I'm about to make the quip, 'Is it the costume or the child that has to be under ten?' when I see that the infant in question is clutching one of the mystery brown envelopes that had been handed out at the village picnic last summer.

"It's one of those brown envelopes," I whisper, craning my neck for a better view. "What the hell do they put in them?"

"Well if it's Jasper's car keys, you're 'It'," Chancery smirks, and I elbow her in the ribs. She's about to retaliate when Rhona hisses, "Shhhhhh!" and we realise that they've finally reached the prize for Best Adult Costume.

Matilda, Finstown's ubiquitous parish councillor, peers short-sightedly at the clipboard in front of her. "The prize for the best adult costume goes to..." she says, screwing her eyes up and taking her glasses off, "...is that the munchers or the mumblers? Och, whatever, it's Max and Chancery. Well done, the pair of you. Come away up and get your prize."

"We're getting an envelope! We're getting an envelope!" I exclaim jubilantly as we bound up to the stage to collect our prize, and we run quickly back down the steps ripping it open, desperate to see what's inside. I've been expecting an indiscreet picture of last year's Carnival Queen, or at least the freedom of the island, but instead the envelope simply contains two neatly folded one pound notes.

"That's it?" I say, crushed. "After all this MI5 stuff, it's just money? I thought it was the secret recipe for Orkney Fudge, at the very least."

"Oh well,"Chancery consoles, "at least our financial worries are finally over."

*

Tonight's annual Gala Night Dance is the usual sozzled affair and the village hall is packed to the rafters with lecherous farmers in hot pursuit of comely wenches that are certainly not their wives, and all the island's professional gossip-mongers sit like knitting women around the guillotine, memorising every gory detail so that it can be stored up and rationed out when the long winter nights finally return.

As if hiding their eyes from their parents' drunken indiscretions or perhaps simply just keeping away from the official bar and whatever vestiges of the licensing laws that remain, the village youngsters are holding their own private party outside, taking advantage of the mild evening to throng in the car park with their mobile phones and the ubiquitous family-sized bottles of 'Coke'. Inside, an intoxicated Wyre Band hammers out tune after tune and puny ploughboys are flung around the dance floor to the rhythm of frenetic fiddles and squealing squeeze-boxes.

We enter the warm hallway from the car park with the twins and their entourage and have our hands stamped for admission. Inside, however, our party is immediately split by the crush of the huge crowd, and I'm barely in the heaving squash of bodies when Roberta, one of the judges from this evening's Fancy Dress Parade, pounces on me like a black widow spider, and under the pretext of "teaching me some Orkney dances", proceeds to commandeer me for the entire evening.

It's the parish's annual night of adultery as, dulled by the long and arduous nights of the protracted wintery spring, the village lets its hair down and throws all the rule books out of the window as they prepare to welcome in the summer. I'm flattered to have been so purposefully singled out for one of these Spring Fever Flirtations by a woman some ten years my junior, and the evening rapidly degenerates into a scene straight out of Bertolucci.

I am, of course, far too overwhelmed with the concept of being someone's first choice for one of these bucolic fertilty festivals to realise that this sudden surge of fervid feminine attention has nothing whatsoever to do with my irresistible charm or boyish good looks and owes much more to Roberta's current circumstances than to my masculinity.

The lady in question is an indomitable Orcadian farm girl in her late thirties with pleasing curves and thick chestnut hair, who has been swept off her feet as a teenager by a passing squaddie and has left the isles to marry him and bear his children. But now, some sixteen years later, after a stormy divorce and a recent affair with a philandering turnip-faced farmer, she is back on her home territory and aggressively on the prowl for a man – any man.

However, one of the downsides of growing up in the isles is that you've met all of your possible partners during childhood, and when Orkney women find themselves post-divorce they often discover that the only available men are Geordie Flett, who lives with his mother on some distant farm without running water, or strange little Erland Isbister who used to poo his pants in primary school and looks like he probably still does.

Thus, outsiders become highly desirable commodities and everyone from dodgy travelling salesmen to 'married' old gits like myself are suddenly painted with the gilded brush of mystery and become prime targets. If I had had any sense on the night of the Gala Dance mating rituals, I would have realised that Roberta had a determined gleam in her eye that should have sent me running screaming in the opposite direction.

*

Summer, before the harvest, when the cattle are put out to pasture in Orkney's verdant buttercup fields, is one of the most active times on the

island social calendar. Freed from the chore of daily mucking-out for six weeks, jubilant farm wives sit down to plan their numerous August activities, and the Gala Weekend Dance is barely over when the twins sweep us off, protesting, to the next event of note in their busy summer schedule.

We try pleading physical exhaustion and then poverty, but neither suit is successful, and the sisters raise their eyebrows at the mere thought that we might want to miss the "Last Night" of Stromness Shopping Week which, in Orkney, is like someone who works for Vogue saying that they "don't really feel like" going to Paris Fashion Week, so, defeated, we don our party clothes yet again and accompany them to the ancient port town.

Stromness was originally developed during the herring boom of the late nineteenth century and has changed little since then. The main street starts at the harbour and weaves its narrow serpentine way along the coast, protected from the fierce sea winds by Brinkie's Brae on one side and the town's weathered stone buildings on the other. An old school and some big houses sit on the crest of the Brae, but most of the original town nestles below in a series of wynds and narrow cul-de-sacs, and the high street itself is paved, like Kirkwall, with heavy stone slabs rather than conventional tarmac. Some crooked houses interspersed with eccentric shops contain its population, and it's normally a placid, sleepy town, even on a Saturday night.

Tonight, however, the 'town centre' is alive with bodies, and the street and harbour areas are covered with hundreds of human ants scrabbling all over every available surface. There are costumed people everywhere, talking, dancing and drinking lethal two-hundred-percent-proof homemade cocktails from plastic lemonade bottles, and an old woman even appears to be peeing into the harbour, but as she's doing it standing up it's probably just a boy in drag, but there's no way I'm going to go over and find out.

A recent newspaper story about Orkney women having bigger bums than the rest of Britain has inspired a tableau-trailer called Fat-Bottomed Girls, where the participants have photocopied their bare derrieres and used the results as wallpaper for their float. And now coteries of eager boys are plying them with moonshine in exchange for privileged information about which image matches which girl.

In the midst of all this Rio-like frivolity, the twins, dressed tonight in rather conservative denim dresses and matching flatties, are hacking through the crowd trying to find Rhona's current beau, a ferrety little joiner called Doofer who is playing hard-to-get, but is believed to be amongst the two thousand people who are milling about the street.

Other than ourselves and the sisters there are six other people in our group tonight, all armed with lethal bottles of moonshine – "Iron Bru and vodka!" a blonde dwarf says encouragingly to me as she thrusts a blood-red concoction into my hands – and I have no idea who any of them are and am far too afraid to ask Rhona for fear of what she might tell me.

The crowd is overwhelming in the harbour area, but as we move further up the narrow street it's like being funnelled into the killing tunnels at an abattoir, and it becomes more and more difficult to move as throngs of people crush into the constricted stone canyon. However Rhona is not to be dissuaded and, her hand clasped around my wrist like a tourniquet, we press on through the assembled multitude in search of her elusive paramour and, in the process, lose most of our party in the tightly packed crowd, including Chancery and Shona, and I discover, too late, that we're now just a party of me and Rhona.

"We've lost everyone, Rhona," I manage to croak as a tributary of girls dressed as Kewpie Dolls flows into the main current and press bottles of homemade alcopop to my lips as they pass by. "Shouldn't we go back?"

"Aye, in just a peedie minute," Rhona replies, her rigor-mortis-like grip on my wrist unwavering. "I think I can see Dooffer up ahead. Look, over there."

I can just make out the top of Chancery's head vanishing into the crowd as Rhona pulls me into the fray, but, astoundingly, we actually do stumble over the aforementioned Dooffer, a shifty-eyed little hamster who looks like he should be rubber-stamping documents in a basement office somewhere in Soviet-Middle-Europe.

Leaving Rhona to make the necessary overtures, I'm about to depart and go in search of Chancery when I'm suddenly collared by one of the

hamster's party draping an ample arm around my waist, and I look up to behold Roberta from the Fancy Dress parade gazing into my eyes.

"Hi there, Sexy Legs," she breathes into my ear, having obviously never laid eyes on the knock-kneed limbs in question. "Want to hold me in your arms again?"

"What? Now?" I falter, but it appears that the predator's plan is far more plotted as there's to be a homecoming ceilidh on the neighbouring island of Rousay the following week and Roberta is adamant that I – and Chancery, she tacks on as a hasty postscript – should come along.

It's an open invitation to pledge my troth, but, blaming my rashness on the plastic bottles of dosser's alcopop that everyone's carrying around, rather than Roberta's generous bosoms, I recklessly promise that we'll be there, without even bothering to consult my beloved, and, satisfied, Roberta vanishes back into the seething crowd, taking Rhona's pet marsupial with her.

*

We all meet up the next week for what is to be our maiden voyage to one of the outer islands, in a windswept rural car park at a place called Tingwall, where a tiny ferry boat embarks for the "commuter" isles of Rousay, Egilsay and Wyre.

The Orkneys consists of one very large island called Pomona or the Orkney Mainland, where we live, which is surrounded by lots of smaller isles. Some of these are only a short hop away and are considered commutable, whilst others like Westray and Sanday involve much longer ferry trips and tend to be more isolated, self-sufficient places. However, all the islands are fiercely independent and tend to have their own personalities and characteristics.

The regular Rousay ferry has long-since packed up for the day, but there's a special "dance boat" been laid on for the occasion and there's already a veritable mob of people gathered at Tingwall waiting for it to berth at the minuscule dock. The car park is full to bursting point with vehicles of all shapes and sizes from a sleek silver Mercedes to ratty old vans and pick-

ups, but the boat only has enough room for four cars and I wonder aloud if the dance is being held near the ferry point on the other side.

"Oh no, it's a peedie way to the dance," a very wizened old lady leaning on a gnarled stick says. "It'd be finished by the time you got there if you walked!"

"So how are we all getting over then?" I ask naively. "Is there a bus or something laid on?"

My companion laughs. "You're no' from here, are you, bhouy?" she says. "Dinnae worry. The Rousay folk'll make sure you get to the party."

*

The little ferry finally bumps onto the line of old tyres that clings to the old stone harbour wall like a row of black rubber limpets, and, as the front of the boat lowers down like a World War II landing craft to form an impromptu gangway, we move uncertainly onto the shore, looking about us like a herd of fresh immigrants on turn-of-the-century Ellis Island. The Rousay landscape is like Pomona, green and lush with a few grey stone buildings and not much else, but in the nearby car park, a veritable fleet of ancient vehicles sits awaiting our arrival.

"What's wrong, bhouy?" the old lady who had spoken to us earlier cries as she deftly pushes in front of me and elbows her way to the front of the queue. "Never seen an Isles Car before?"

"Quick, get a good one!" someone else says, taking my arm, and I turn to find Roberta and her friend and fellow judge from the fancy dress parade, Henrietta, who quickly hustle us past what appears to be an old Ford Anglia and into a battered old Volvo that sits against the grass verge with its engine idling.

"Aye-aye," beams a good-natured old bloke dressed in his best suit and wellie boots. "It's a bonny night, is it no'?"

"Aye, it is that," Roberta replies. "Are we seeing to the kai first or going straight to the dance?"

"Oh, dinnae worry aboot the kai, lass," he says. "I saw to the beasts afore I came doon, so we can all just get straight to the party!"

"Oh good, good," Roberta replies, settling down as the old car pulls out into the stream of rusty old vehicles that's now filling the narrow lane that leads to the school and community hall. "And will you be up for a Palais Glide with me later on?"

"Oh I will that, bonny lass. You can count on it," he says, and I wonder how long these two have known each other to have developed such an easy familiarity.

"Aren't you going to introduce us to your friend?" I ask and Roberta laughs.

"Oh, we've only just met," she says to me, and then, addressing our host, continues,

"I'm Roberta and this is Max, Chancery and Henrietta. We're over from Kirkwall."

"Oh aye, lass, I ken who you are. You're auld Archie Rosey's peedie lass, and your two friends here are the Soothies that bide in Tumshie John's hoose at Firth, are they no'?"

I'm about to marvel in astonishment at the kind old man's ability to read people's entire histories at a glance when he suddenly says, "Hold on a peedie second now!" and swerves the car suddenly into the heavily overgrown verge at the side of the road.

I've barely had time to utter "What the fuck?" when our host turns and beams engagingly at me, saying, "Aye, she's a good runner, right enough, but the brakes went a couple of years ago. Good thing the verge does just as well."

*

"You've never been in an isles runner before, have you?" Roberta asks me

with a grin as we make our way up to the tiny school hall in the long crocodile that's formed at the little pay desk and impromptu raffle ticket booth.

"I'm frightened to ask, but just what *is* an isles runner?" I enquire and Roberta laughs.

"There are no police here on Rousay, so the local people just run old cars that work but wouldn't pass an MOT test on the mainland," she explains. "Lots of folk keep their proper cars at the ferry dock at Tingwall and use them for going to Kirkwall or if they want to go Sooth. It's too costly to take them to and fro every day on the ro-ro ferry."

"And do any of these rust buckets have brakes?" I ask sarcastically.

"Not many," Roberta replies in all seriousness.

*

The dance is due to start at eight and the little hall is already throbbing with farmers' wives in their best dresses rushing around with trays of dead animals wrapped in pastry when our task force of "Pomona Toonies" arrives, but Isles Time is even more elastic than standard Orkney Mean Time and it's nearly nine before the band finally strikes up. The impromptu bar in the school tuck shop has been doing a brisk trade since the back of seven, however, and a lot of the people here are ex-Rousay residents and have been visiting friends and relatives all day and have already been imbibing freely before they arrive, thus ensuring that a suitably partyish atmosphere for the evening is guaranteed.

We have been hoping to make use of the long summer light to go and see some of the island before the Bal Masque commences, but Roberta informs us that this is not feasible and we are instead issued a VIP pass to join her peer group.

There are about fifteen people in this tiny clique and they have already commandeered their very own corner of the compact gymnasium where they are meticulously exchanging their footwear for highly polished dance shoes. Other than Roberta and her Rubenesque friend, Henrietta, most of

the folk here are strangers to us, but they are all, Roberta tells us, tucking her hand firmly into the crook of my arm, Orkney's Traditional Dance Elite – a gang of party-going banditos, we are later told, who are less flatteringly referred to as "those bloody traditional dancers" and whose modus operandi is the seeking out and invading of dances up and down the length and breadth of the isles.

However we are welcomed into the gang with open arms and Roberta takes us round, making introductions, but it soon becomes apparent that everyone in the group is divorced or single.

"This is the fucking Arctic Circle Matchmaking Club," Chancery hisses in my ear. "What the fuck have you landed us into now?"

"No it's not," I say, exuding a confidence that I really don't feel as I peruse the northern latitudes' answer to Dateline. "It's just a... coincidence that none of them have got partners."

"Coincidence my arse," Chancery snorts. "There's a bachelor over there already cruising the place for fillies to keep his farm books and bear his children."

"Rubbish!" I exclaim as I follow her line of vision to a guy with a Brillo-pad-like shock of ginger hair who is staring at Roberta with an unblinking gaze. "He's probably just trying to work out if he's related to her. It's a homecoming dance after all."

Chancery makes a noise like a constipated horse with colic, but further debate on the subject is abruptly halted by the arrival of the head honcho of the dance group, a rotund midget with a shiny, billiard-ball head known as Rodeo Raymond or the Babe Magnet. The eagle-eyed Raymondo, having spotted new blood in his corral, has sped over to claim his droit de seigneur, and he chassés confidently off with Chancery over the lethal skating rink of Slipperene before I can blink an eyelid.

However, I'm not left alone for long as it seems that I'm designated to be on tonight's menu for the ladies of the group. I'm kidnapped by Roberta and dance a couple of reels with her before I'm passed onto her best friend, Henrietta, who had been co-judge at the Fancy Dress Parade, and we take

to the floor just as the band unexpectedly announce a St Bernard's Waltz.

The St Bernard's is a slow, intimate sort of dance that usually turns into a grope-fest when it's performed late on a boozy night, and people are a bit self-conscious with it this early in the programme with the bright evening sunlight still slanting through the windows, but Henrietta takes it in her stride and steers me through the assembled throngs of couples and children with a deft mastery of the form. I've never really spoken to her before, but find that I'm very relaxed in her company and that she is both smart and funny and possessed with the most beautiful sea-green eyes that I have ever seen.

We sit and talk animatedly together after the dance is done and then go back to the heaving dance floor together time and time again, and Chancery's face is distinctly unamused come eleven o'clock, but I choose not to notice, just as I'm also not noticing that my new friend is just post-divorce, and, like her friend Roberta, actively looking for a replacement man, but I choose to ignore that too and blithely exchange telephone numbers with the promise to be in touch in the very near future.

CHAPTER 9 – WHERE, AFTER TWO SUMMERS ON THE ISLAND, WE GO BACK TO MY ANCESTRAL HOME FOR A COUPLE OF DAYS

Shona has temporarily hooked up with a strapping navvy called Digger while Rhona, having failed to snare his best mate Spader, is left on the shelf, thus creating a temporary rift between the sisters, and, disgusted, the spurned twin decides to head "Sooth" to visit friends and asks us if we'd like a lift as far as Inverness. It's the first opportunity that we've had to leave the island since we came, and although we really can't afford it, we elect to go along and see what we've been missing in civilisation, and we quickly work out a cunning plan to obtain free board and lodgings for our 'holiday' by going to visit my father in his gloomy semi-detached bungalow in Dundee.

We catch the old St Ola from Stromness with Rhona and her ten-year-old son, Sean, and have a smooth easy crossing. It's a clear but windy day and in the long summer light Rhona's Volkswagen soon eats up the miles and we even find time to stop at the Chinese take-away in the tiny red-sandstone village of Brora. Not far out of Inverness, however, Rhona tilts her head to one side like a spaniel dog that's heard a fridge door open and expresses grave concern about an alleged imperceptible noise that she's picking up from the engine. Conversation stops and everyone dutifully listens to no avail, and the car's running without a problem, but Rhona's now certain that some terrible catastrophe is about to befall us.

I'm squashed into the cramped back seat of the old Beetle with bags of luggage and Sean and his Gameboy and have been enduring some very strange music and sound effects for the last hundred miles. So, as revenge, I volunteer Chancery, who's successfully tendered for the front seat under the ticket of car sickness, with the unenviable task of rigging up the hands-free attachment on Rhona's mobile phone to let her summon assistance, and a myriad of wires are hastily attached to facilitate this.

I, naive metropolitan man that I am, assume that the troubled twin wants to ring the AA or the RAC, but it turns out that in times of crisis Rhona *always* goes to the fourth emergency service –her sister, Shona.

Sean is still busy on his Gameboy, unperturbed by the imminent vehicular disaster, and its odd metallic bleeps form a strange descant to the sound of a ringing tone from Rhona's phone which is now on speaker.

However, after only three rings there's a hissing noise and we all suddenly hear Shona's tremulous voice, sounding extremely breathless, as if she's been running or is reciting the ransom demands of a horde of bushy-bearded terrorists.

"Hello. You're speaking to Shona. Whit like? [Long Hiss] I'm no' here. [Another long hiss] You'd best leave a peedie message. Bye!"

"Shit!" Rhona mutters. "No, don't listen to that bit. [Loud bleeping from rear of vehicle as Sean's virtual self kills several hundred ninjas] Sean, will you turn that fucking thing off! Shit! Don't listen to that bit either. Hi, it's me. Rhona. Are you there? We're ootside Inverness and the car's making a funny noise. Can you get Digger to call me back and listen to the noise and tell me what it is."

Rhona wipes the sweat from her brow and breathes out deeply.

"So we're all sorted now?" I say, trying my hardest to remove every last trace of amusement from my tone.

"Oh aye," Rhona breathes, relieved. "Digger'll ken what's wrong."

*

It should now be a simple matter of boarding a train at Inverness to get down to my dad's home in Dundee, but British Rail ensures that we arrive five hours behind schedule, our train being held up to make way for a late-running luxury express service, and the railway company eventually has to taxi us from Perth; but Dad is waiting up and all appears to be normal when we finally arrive at the place of my ancestors.

My mother had passed away just prior to our maiden voyage to the isles, and this trip to the old homestead is the first time I have seen my now-widowed dad in the flesh since the funeral, so I am somewhat

apprehensive about what I am about to find.

However, I needn't have worried, as Dad is a fiercely practical man who frequently weeds his herbaceous border with a flame thrower and has just concreted-over his front lawn in order to rid himself of daisies, and he appears to have tackled the task of dealing with the loss of my mother with the same lack of subtlety. His normally barren sideboard is now groaning under the weight of three dozen newly framed photographs of Mum, but other than that he has dealt with the raw feeling of loss by eradicating all traces of my mother in a vain attempt to assuage his grief and anger, and all my mother's numerous personal knick-knacks have been carefully rounded up and transported to the municipal tip with military precision.

My father is a portly man with a thick neck, jar head and large sticky-out ears who looks like a Kulak who's just stepped off a collective in the Ukraine, and during his years in the Far East was always being hailed by Russians who greeted him warmly in the mother tongue and then experienced extreme perplexity when they discovered that he was not a long-lost Red Army comrade. In his old age, however, he has taken this kinship with Soviet-Central-Europe to ridiculous extremes and has been driving the same blue and elastoplast-coloured Lada with a dodgy heater for the last twenty years, duly kitted out for the occasion in a suitably Stalinist fur "car coat" and fleece and leather hat.

Thus attired, on a warm day in August, he wakes us at the crack of dawn the next morning and takes us out in the said ancient Lada to visit the garden of remembrance where my Mum's ashes have been interred, brooking no argument about the time of day or his eccentric choice of apparel.

He's silent on the drive to the little country graveyard, a strange low-rise sort of place that has fairly modern antecedents and consists solely of small headstones marking little urns of ash; but, as we thread our way carefully through the miniature city of the dead I notice that my Dad is scrutinising all the graves and periodically stops and takes a tape measure from his pocket and measures a headstone; and I realise that he needs to know that nobody here has a bigger or grander memorial than my mother.

We have brought a modest bunch of flowers and, thankfully, no-one has

left any giant floral tributes today, but instead of spending a few reflective moments at Mum's final resting place my Dad, measuring tape now tucked back into his pocket, looks angrily heavenwards and makes a fist and then, indicating the gaudy granite pergola he has had erected, almost shouts, "And that's all that's left of your Mother!" before blustering off between the adjoining tombstones loudly blowing his nose.

*

We have intended to spend the remainder of the day quietly at my Dad's house but unfortunately the family has other plans. Other than a brief pit stop for my mother's funeral, the last official visit we have paid to the old homestead was eleven years ago for my niece's wedding, and her resultant children are now desperate to meet their long-lost aunt and uncle, and my sister, June, phones to say that a gathering of the coven has duly been scheduled at her house for four o'clock that afternoon to facilitate the reunion.

My Dad's face briefly appears from behind his newspaper as I lay down the receiver to mutter that we should not attempt to attend this introduction to the family's youngest division empty-handed, and, being granted the keys to the collective's Lada, we embark on an impromptu trip to the town centre to buy some presents for the sprogs in question.

This manoeuvre, however, takes a little longer than anticipated as our Orkney lifestyle has us firmly in its rustic grip, and we wander bug-eyed through the tunnels of unadulterated consumerism in the trendy new malls which seem to have mushroomed up since we were last here, gaping open-mouthed at all the coloured lights like caricature bucolic tourists. It is ten minutes to four before we eventually return to the car park clutching what we hope will impress ten-year-old children, but it's only a fifteen minute drive to June's house from here, and although Chancery frets that we'll be late for the ritual breaking of bread in my tribe's main hut, I'm confident that we'll be there in good time.

Fate, however, is playing another of its little jokes, and, as I try to navigate the stately old Lada back to the boonies through the already choked-up traffic, I find that a new one-way system is in force and before I know where I am we're being streamed out towards Teuchterville[28] in the midst of the afternoon commuter exodus. Swearing vociferously, I negotiate my way through the honking lanes of the fleeing four o'clock lemmings and eventually spot a route off the main thoroughfare but, infuriatingly, it just takes me round in a circle and we find ourselves back on the rat-run lane once more. This is exceptionally frustrating as I still know the geography of the town well enough and can see umpteen streets ahead which will all take us to June's hut, but all have sprouted ugly red 'No Entry' signs like mutant lollypops since I was last here, and it is almost half past five before we eventually roll up in my sister's drive.

Of course, it's a full house at *Chateau de Ma Soeur* by now and the noise hits us like a wall when we go in. One of the more endearing habits of my family is their tendency to all talk at once, so the volume level naturally rises steadily as they all try to shout over each other to be heard, and, of course, they've all been here for about two hours by now so the decibel level is reaching industrial earphones level.

My Dad is milking his role of Patriarch and has commandeered the remote and quarantined himself in a corner with the television where he is watching his favourite Australian soap opera, and everyone else in the room is talking simultaneously and yelling to be heard over the TV soundtrack and each other. Bill, my brother-in-law, recently the happy recipient of a surgical hip-replacement, prods me in the chest with his walking stick and demands to know where we've been as he's been kept waiting for his tea, and when I hang my head in shame and admit to getting lost in my own home town, complete pandemonium breaks out.

In a soaring chorus not dissimilar to a closing crescendo of a Wagnerian opera, cries of derision and disbelief are yelled out, accompanied by a swelling refrain from the sopranos of "You got lost? Why did you not just come up Cleppington Road?"; and this in turn countermanded by a deep bass retort of "No, no, just straight up the Kingsway's the best route by far."

No-one, of course, can actually agree the ideal route and a fight immediately breaks out over what really *is* the fastest way here from the

---

28 - **Teuchter (pronounced chook-ter) :** peasant, yokel, or in modern Scots, one who lives outside the commuter belt.

centre of town, and the din just gets louder and louder until my Dad is eventually forced to break from his sacred Aussie hour to silence all dissent and name the definitive journey plan.

Silence reigns blessedly for all of a fraction of a nano-second after the Head of the Clan has spoken, and then the cacophony merely swells up again as half a dozen different conversational threads are promptly renewed, and, despite the fact that this morning's visit to my mother's grave is still fresh and raw in my mind, the idea of just dying and being cremated is, at this moment, incredibly appealing.

*

Bidding farewell to my Dad we set off on Thursday morning on the long trek back up the length of Scotland to its most north-easterly tip, glad to be going "home" again, and there is something reassuring about the slowly thinning traffic on the roads the further north the coach takes us, and when we finally get to the windswept ferry port of Scrabster at a little after five on a bright August evening the quiet streets are almost deserted. A friendly farmer collecting a package from the bus station recognises us as neighbours of his Orcadian cousin and offers us a lift to the boat terminal, and, filled full of a rosy glow of contentment, we arrive in Orkney a little after seven that evening and bow down and kiss the sacred island turf.

The cost of a few days away from home have eaten into our scant cash supply like a bleach bottle pictogram, and as we walk down the gang plank at Stromness harbour we have scarcely ten pounds left in our pockets. The last bus has, of course, long since departed and, rather than attempt to walk the ten miles home, we bag the sole taxi that's hanging about at the pier head looking for stragglers and head for Finstown, telling the driver to stop when her meter hits the ten quid mark some two miles before we reach our house.

However, with a typical islander's knowledge, the driver knows full-well where we live and demands to know why we would want to be dropped-off in a field full of frisky newly let-out "kai" instead, and, when she hears our story, merely shuts off the meter and drives us the rest of the way home for free. Quite overcome by these random acts of unprovoked kindness, we sit in our living room thirty minutes later, the cat purring in my lap and

sea birds trilling and swooping against the beautiful orange and red sunset sky and vow to stay in this wonderful, tranquil place for ever.

CHAPTER 10 - WHERE WE DON OUR GREASEPAINT AND APPEAR IN THE VILLAGE PANTOMIME

Our second all too brief summer on the island is coming to an end and September has already rolled in with its chilly winds and freezing sea fogs when we see a snippet in The Orcadian about a Finstown woman called Lorna who's putting a pantomime together for Christmas and is looking for village people to participate.

Chancery wonders aloud if this is something that we should get involved with, and, as if the universe has read our thoughts, the phone promptly rings and it's an English guy called Danny the Computer Mannie.

Danny is a programmer from Macclesfield in Cheshire who has committed some corporate sin down south and been summarily exiled to the isles to be his company's most northerly maintenance guy, and, despondent, he spends his days pacing the corridors of a rundown farmhouse like some cyber Sleeping Beauty surrounded by malodorous old sheep, waiting for someone's mainframe to crash and free him from his inactivity; and, thus, is perfect prey for club secretaries everywhere.

The panto press-gang have, therefore, quickly followed his paper trail and tracked him to his bunker, and Danny has taken very little seducing to be signed up. Of course, as a fellow Soothie, he has now been delegated the task of recruiting us, and he asks just a little too casually if we'd be interested in joining the show as our performance in the Gala Day Fancy Dress Parade has been duly noted by the Orkney Bureau of Observation and Surveillance.

"Lorna and Alistair are organising it all," he lies unconvincingly, adopting a well-worn Orkney method of persuasion, "but they were too shy to phone and ask you themselves..."

*

The community centre looks like a scene from a between-the-wars Punch cartoon that would be captioned "The Squire's Daughter Puts On A Show for the Village Folk". Everyone is drinking tea and eating strange-coloured melted-marshmallow cakes, totally oblivious to the hordes of children climbing up the stage curtains or the multitude of sulky teenagers who sit in a silent group in the darkest corner, texting each other while they chew on thick wads of fluorescent-coloured bubble gum.

Lorna, the show's organiser and Finstown's nearest equivalent to Linda Snell, is a diminutive blonde with long flowing tresses and a penchant for Pod shoes and striped socks, and she sits at a long trestle table stuffing large squares of chocolate dipped marzipan cake into her mouth. A tall, thin, sixtyish guy in a beret sits to one side of her, holding forth on some lofty ideal, and a beefy, beetle-browed guy has her other flank.

"Who's the bloke that's boring Lorna to death?" I ask a grim-faced lady sitting next to me.

"That's Ernie," she says in the reverential tone of someone telling an idiot that this is the Pope or Ayatollah. "He's the best director in Orkney and he doesn't normally do shows ootside Toon. We're extremely lucky to have him."

"Wow," I say for want of something better. "And who's the fat guy?"

"Oh, that's Alistair," she says with a tight-lipped smile. "Some people think he's funny."

"Wow," I say again, lost for words for a second time, as the aforementioned Alistair begins chucking M&Ms into the air and catching them in his mouth, crunching loudly and interrupting the flow of Ernie's lecture.

The grumpy director glares at Alistair, who is unrepentant and crunches back defiantly, and a major lovie fight looks imminent but is thwarted at the last moment by Lorna finishing her cake and standing up to call the meeting to order.

"Aye-aye. Whit like? Glad you could all come to wur show. We're no' serious actors here," she says, laughing. "We're just wanting to have a night oot and a good laugh."

Ernie the director has been going various shades of puce during this short introduction and he quickly stands up to assert his authority, and, purposefully straightening his notes, he begins to address his cast.

"Now I expect everyone here to give their very best and be punctual," he says, glaring at Alistair who crunches impudently on another M&M. "And everyone in the cast must treat their fellow actors with respect. You there, down the front, be quiet when I'm talking. You'll get your chance to speak when I give you a part. Now, we'll read through the parts and I'll take notes, then I'll give you all my decision once we've finished auditioning."

Lorna and Alistair exchange puzzled glances and Alistair mouths 'Auditions?' while Danny the Computer Mannie, who is seated behind me, leans forward and whispers in my ear, "What's he on about? They've already decided on the parts."

"Wow," I say, noncommittally.

*

We had thought that an Orkney pantomime would be something suitably Nordic like the Tale of Sigurd the Singing Selkie or Rognvald the Rambunctious Rabbit, but it turns out just to be boring old Hansel and Gretel and Ernie quickly runs through all the gangly Lolitas in search of his principal boy before getting the squat girls to read for Gretel. He makes numerous notes on his clipboard, and utters little comments under his breath which Alistair silently mimics, and then turns to the adult members of his cast.

"Now then, the Wicked Witch. You and you," he says with some relish, pointing to Chancery and a wild-haired old woman. "Read that part for me."

The truly scary woman with grey hair reads the Witch speech first, a clunky rhyming monologue with exceptionally bad meter, waving her arms about to emphasise her evilness, but Cecil B. DeMille is underwhelmed.

"No, no, that's no' a witch," he says, shaking his head in exasperation and

pointing to Chancery. "You. You try it."

Chancery reads the part slowly, ignoring the bad meter and giving the dull lines an underlying sinister feel, and Ernie's scowly face lights up.

"Not bad, not bad at all," he mutters. "Yes, we'll have you. You're evil, you are. Now then, the men's parts. Alistair, you're playing the gorilla, and you there, Sooth Bhouy, would you read the dame for me?"

There's a pin-drop silence in the big room as Alistair and Lorna exchange frantic glances and I see Alistair mouth 'The gorilla?' as I stand up and realise that I have just been thrown into the mother of king-sized political quagmires. Chancery urgently whispers "You'd better hope you blow this," as I walk up to the director's table, and I can feel Alistair's beady stare boring into my back as I pick up the script and find the marked place.

The speech is hardly brilliant and it's a simple matter of just reading it flatly to screw up the audition, which I do, but Ernie's wise to this one and is not buying my roll-over belly-up act.

"No, no, NO!" he yells at me. "Give it some wellie. You can do better than that."

Now at this point I should have just read the part badly again and allowed myself to slink back to some minor part in the chorus and let Alistair take his rightful role as the leading lady, but some long-buried spirit of competitiveness rises up and I find myself launching into the role like Jack Milroy wowing the Gods at the Glasgow Pavilion, and the character just seems to flow out of me. Some kids in the front row start to snicker three or four lines in and then grown-up-people begin laughing as the monologue picks up momentum, and I can tell by Ernie's glowing fizzog that I've just landed the leading role.

"Oh good, good. Good potential, bhouy," the old Thespian beams, scribbling on his clipboard. "Aye, you'll be great in a dress, so you will, once I've finished with you!"

The general air of merriment quickly evaporates like cold water being poured on hot stones, and there's a general hissing which I tell myself is

just a shuffling of feet.

Alistair chucks one of his sweeties into the air and lets it fall to the ground, grinding it deliberately into the floor with his boot, and Lorna looks uncomfortably at her clumpy Pod shoes.

"Are you nuts or what?" Chancery whispers frantically into my ear. "Decline the role. Quickly!"; which is good advice that I would normally have taken, but just then someone at the back of the hall mutters, "Fucking ferry loupers coming in and stealing all the starring roles," and, annoyed, I simply smile at Ernie, accept the challenge and leave quickly before we both get mugged.

*

We're on our way to the village hall on our bikes at the appointed hour for the second rehearsal when a sleek four-wheel-drive suddenly screeches to a halt in front of us, barring our way, and I'm thinking, "Oh God, this is it, farmers in Fedoras are going to take us for a ride and drop us off the pier at Burwick" when a very irate woman jumps out to confront us.

At first we think that this is nothing to do with last night's panto rehearsal and that we're about to be mugged for our bicycle clips, but once we see past her throbbing temples we recognise our assailant as the lady who had been sitting beside us when I'd asked who Ernie the director was.

"Thank God I've met you," she gasps breathlessly. "Have you heard what's happened?"

'No?' we mouth silently, shaking our heads, as she almost screams. "They've gone and sacked Ernie!"

I stifle the urge to shout back "Oh my God, they've sacked Ernie!" in my best South Park voice but content myself with simply asking her what's happened.

"What's happened? They're smearing him, the dirty so-and-sos, that's what's happened. They're saying that he was screaming at all the peedie bairns[29] and that he had whisky breath," she yells, waving a stubby finger in my general direction to emphasise her point. "Did you smell whisky on his breath?"

"No-ooo," I squeak, shaking my head and flinching like a girl, and she goes on, stampeding a curious herd of young heifers who have stuck their heads over the dry-stone dyke to see what all the fuss is about. "They want that Alistair to have the leading role and Ernie won't back down, he's far too much of a professional to compromise his values, so they're smearing his good name all over the village. He won't be able to lift his head here again."

"Gosh," I say, having completely worn out 'Wow' the previous night. "What's going to happen?"

"Yes, will it all be cancelled?" Chancery chips in, a little too eagerly to my mind.

"Cancelled? It'll be more than cancelled," the irate woman spits. "It'll be a complete bloody disaster, that's what it'll be. They can't put on a show without Ernie. It'll be a sure-fire flop and I'm certainly not going to be in it."

*

One of the troubles of being reliant on a push bike for transport is that it's impossible to follow through with a story when all the other participants are in motor vehicles, and although we've had supporting roles in the impromptu street theatre production, our new friend arrives at the village hall some fifteen minutes ahead of us for the evening's main dénouement; where upon she signs-up most of the adult cast for her all-star mutiny and there is a major no-expenses-spared melodrama and resignation-fest.

Typically, all the fun is over by the time we eventually get there and the adult numbers are looking severely depleted, but Lorna is still hell-bent on putting on her show and has stepped into Ernie's still warm shoes and taken on the role of director herself, quickly assigning the tubby Alistair to the disputed leading role of the Dame and buying my compliance with the

---

29 - **peedie bairns:** small children

offer of the comic lead while relegating poor Danny the Computer Mannie to sweat it out as the aforementioned hairy gorilla.

*

Nine excruciating weeks of half-arsed rehearsals later the first night eventually rolls round and the hall is bursting at the seams when the curtain goes up on a spot-lit Chancery in her witch's hat delivering her evil prologue. There's an ominous silence from the auditorium as she cackles gleefully about how she's going to kebab Hansel and Gretel and eat them with chilli sauce, and I'm cowering neurotically in the wings expecting her to be stoned or at least booed off the stage at any moment, convinced that the capacity audience is a flotilla of hard-core Ernie supporters who've all come out to stage an impromptu lynching. But Chancery makes it off stage in one piece as a chorus of stage-struck nine-year-olds are shooed on to look at their feet and murder a popular song from the hit parade.

"Are they hostile?" I whisper nervously into Chancery's ear beneath the floppy brim of her tall chimney-pot hat. "Did you spot any firearms?"

"Will you just relax?" Chancery whispers back. "If they'll sit through an hour and a half of the Stromness Ladies' Choir they'll sit through anything."

"But this show's crap," I start to plead, when Lorna shushes me from her prompter's chair, and the song grinds to its excruciating conclusion and the kids stampede off the stage like liberated lab rats.

"You're on, Alistair," Lorna barks to her portly dame, who is still fiddling around with his enormous false bosom, and, hastily affixing his bubble gum to the back of a wobbly stage flat, Finstown's answer to Robbie Coltrane waddles confidently onto the stage.

I can hear him delivering his first line as if he's reading it, and, peering onto the stage through the wings I realise that this is because he actually is reading it, and that our leading lady has saved himself the bother of learning his words by planting scripts all over the set.

"That's it," I mutter woefully, slapping my hand to my forehead. "We're

done for. They're going to murder us all."

As if in answer I hear a low rumble spreading from the back of the hall, swelling up and getting louder and louder. "This is it. They're killing him." I groan, pulling my hands over my eyes. "It's the death of Falstaff, I can't bear to look, is he bleeding?"

"No, you prat," Chancery says exasperatedly. "They're laughing. It's a pantomime, remember? And you're on."

With a muttered exclamation of "Fuck!" that, hopefully, doesn't go much further than the wings, I do the first of my many ungainly tumbles and blunder onto the stage where I have to trip and fall and land at Alistair's feet, and the roar of laughter from the audience is almost deafening as the two of us end up in an undignified heap on the floor.

There's a bright yellow glow of reflected footlight shining on the front few rows, and, from our tangle of limbs I can actually see line upon line of happy faces, actually laughing.

"I can't believe it," I whisper sotto voce to Alistair. "They really like it!"

"Welcome to Orkney," he says with a grin.

CHAPTER 11 - WHERE WE MEET A TROPHY WIFE AND HEAR ABOUT THE INFAMOUS SHAVED PUSSY INCIDENT

One of the leading lights of the Traditional Dance fraternity is a silver-haired, gold-medallion-wearing local builder called Ewan, who made his packet in the mid-seventies and built himself a luxury "lurve pad" from the proceeds. Twenty-five years on, and one quickie divorce later, a considerably thicker-round-the-middle Ewan, who still sports his original Beatle-fringe and tight white Levi's, has allegedly been Sharon-shopping on the mainland and has set up house with a petite, chestnut-haired trophy girlfriend almost thirty years his junior.

Come Christmas, some twelve weeks later, the transplanted lass doesn't appear to have withered and died on Orkney's frozen soil, and, overjoyed with his purchase, our aging Lothario invites everyone to a huge New Year party in his ostentatious retro mansion to be introduced to his latest acquisition.

We, meanwhile, after two miserable years of near abject poverty living off sporadic illustration fees and the wages from odd pieces of casual work, place some old costume jewellery for sale on the then fledgling eBay and are astounded by the price it reaches. Having successfully dealt in collectibles some twenty years ago, and aware that Orkney jumble sales are rich with beautiful old domestic fabrics and vintage kitchenalia, we tentatively start buying and then reselling the choicer pieces to wealthy Japanese and American collectors, and money, astoundingly, starts to pour in.

Thus we arrive at Ewan's purple and ochre salon resplendent in our newly mail-ordered designer outfits, but we have hardly removed our coats to show off our finery when the host's new acquisition, and purpose of the party, is swiftly eclipsed by the triumphant entrance of a jubilant Roberta, the judge from the Fancy Dress Parade, on the arm of a scary-haired farmer called Silent Philip, and a ripple of gossip speeds through the large room.

"You'll never guess what's happened," Henrietta, the other judge from the

Fancy Dress Parade, and now very much my new best friend, breathes into my ear as I sink into the depths of Ewan's white leather sofa beside her.

"The Planning Department have finally condemned Ewan's decor?" I quip and she punches me playfully.

"No, you idiot," she laughs, taking my hand in hers. "Roberta's getting married."

I had danced with Roberta for over an hour at a ceilidh just days before Christmas and at that time she didn't have so much as a one-night-stand, let alone a boyfriend, on the horizon, and I am intrigued as to where she has managed to procure a spouse at such short notice.

"Please tell me that you haven't been letting her go on the internet unattended again," I groan, but Henrietta shakes her head.

"It's worse than that," she says, indicating with her head. "She's marrying him."

I follow the line of her gaze to the large G-plan table where a jubilant Roberta sits gazing adoringly at her new beau – who's currently ploughing his way through a huge plateful of clapshot[30] and mince – and I am momentarily hypnotized by his electrifying mop of ginger hair which looks like a cross between the youthful Malcolm McLaren and a radioactive Brillo pad.

"You *are* kidding?" I say.

"I wish I was," Henrietta replies.

The entire place is, of course, buzzing with the news by now, and more and more people join us on the sofa, Henrietta being considered the best source of insider information as she's Roberta's best friend. Everyone wants to know when the proposal was made, although I, personally, am far more interested in the 'how' as no-one has ever heard the erstwhile groom actually speak.

---

30 - **clapshot:** a popular local dish of mashed potatoes and turnips

However, it's a tale often told. Silent Philip, like many an Orkney farmer before him, has remained happily single for most of his adult life, but now, with fifty staring him in the face and his parents recently deceased, he has ventured out into the world to find himself a suitable filly to help deliver the spring lambs and propel a can of Mr Sheen around his bachelor abode, and he has been dedicatedly wife-hunting in the dance arena over the last few months, haunting the bleachers of ceilidhs like the Ghost of Hamlet's Father.

He has, however, quickly singled out the capable Roberta as being Danceland's most able woman to perform Wifely Duties for him, and has invited her to dinner in one of Kirkwall's more expensive hotels where he has broached the subject over dessert – it's anybody's guess how many words she managed to get out of him during the starter and entrée – accompanied by a folder-full of property deeds to prove his husbandly worth. And Roberta has promptly accepted the deal and seals her part of the bargain in her bedroom when she finally manages to get rid of all her children for a night.

*

Winter rolls on with its painfully short days and long windy nights and life on the island goes into virtual hibernation with only sporadic sparks of gossip to keep it warm. A lady who runs a bar in Kirkwall somewhat bizarrely accuses Rodeo Raymond of shaving the left flank of her tabby cat, and pursues the matter doggedly to the Sheriff Court, oblivious to the fact that it is gossiped about over the length and breadth of the island as the "shaved pussy incident" and prompts every drunk in Kirkwall to lurch up to her counter and slur their own personal take on the pun.

I, meanwhile, appear to also be setting tongues wagging over my "good friendship" with Roberta's friend, Henrietta, as it seems I have blatantly ignored the first cardinal rule of successful Orkney living – "Keep a low profile at all times". I become aware of little groups of whispering women in dark corners when I am in Henrietta's company, and strange accounts of fictitious secret assignations begin to circulate amongst complete strangers who have never even heard of the traditional dancing fraternity.

As if this isn't bad enough, another of the fringe benefits of my 'bond' with Henrietta is a sudden surge of attention from the zaftig's mother, Backpack Bertha; a strappingly-built, sixty-year-old divorcee with a weather-beaten face and motherly demeanour. Bertha promptly adopts us, and deciding that we need to be taken under her capacious wing, hauls Chancery and myself off on her numerous organised rambles. Refusal is not an option, and we spend many wind-blown days being dragged over the spectacular rocky Cornwall-like coastal paths of Yesnaby, or over to the neighbouring isle of Hoy where, like school children on a nature ramble, we are shown the dramatic beaches at Rackwick and the tiny hidden loch deep in a ferny gully which is the sole habitat of Orcadian dragon flies.

There isn't much sunshine yet, but we know that summer has officially come around again when Rhona and Shona insist that we help them design a float for this year's Gala Day parade; and, once a theme has eventually been decided upon, we busy ourselves with paint and costumes for the next couple of weeks, designing outlandish Sunday hats and recreating the interior of the local church in the back of a battered old cattle trailer that Rhona has cajoled out of one of the neighbouring farmers.

The real village kirk is currently being renovated and the congregation have been relocated to a tiny community centre in the next village, but our tableau depicts them all at worship in a church swarming with builders led by a raven-haired village girl with a pachydermal behind playing the eponymous Bob in a yellow hard hat and her father's farm overalls.

As is typical of anything associated with the twins, of course, there are more extras involved than a Cecil B DeMille Biblical epic, and, yes, Rhona has dirt on everyone of them, but when it comes to a call for volunteers to actually help with the physical redecoration of the trailer, enthusiasm wanes and I arrive with my mural paints to find Rhona and Shona, clad like vintage land girls in matching farm overalls and bright yellow headscarves, as my sole crew.

However, we quickly hose all the old straw and chicken shit out of the rusty old trailer and get to work slapping a base coat onto the malodorous bogey, but after only half an hour's labour Rhona's mobile trills 'It's Raining Men' and someone called Frank the Mechanic says that Shona's car is now fully functional and ready for collection.

It's after seven in the evening and I assume that the twins' pet grease monkey means that they can pick up Shona's hot rod on their way to work the following morning, but there is obviously some imperceptible note of longing in Frank's gruff intonation or a secret subliminal code in the way he has just said "your car is ready" that really means "I'm languishing away with unrequited desire for you" that causes Orkney's answer to the

Andrews Sisters to immediately down paintbrushes and vanish in the direction of Kirkwall in a cloud of dust, hastily slapping lipstick on their mouths as they go.

This now leaves only me as a crew of one to finish painting the trailer, but although I should be vexed by their desertion, I'm secretly glad to be rid of them, and freed of their nannyish presence I get on with the task of decorating the float.

I quickly paint in the kirk's trompe l'oeil stonework and, having now created a canvass upon which to work, move onto suitably cheeky Gala Day signs like:

WOULD LADIES IN THE CHOIR PLEASE REFRAIN FROM
HANDLING THE BUILDERS' TOOLS

before starting on my magnum opus. There have been insidious whispers flying around the village over the last week that all has not been plain sailing within the closeted walls of the Kirk Session, and there are rumours of a fierce combat amongst the brethren over what shape the new church hall should take. The most popular of these exaggerated yarns is the one where one of the village elders, an aggressive lady not known for her ability to compromise, threatens to chain herself, Suffragette style, to the church railings if her own choice of plan is not unanimously approved, and, left to my own devices without Mary Poppins and her doppelganger clucking around my feet, my paintbrush takes over and I become immersed in creating a huge stained glass window that shows the martyred elder chained to the front of the building in a suitably arrow-pierced pose.

n terms of a Gala Day gag it's probably only in the vicinity of the knuckle, but, mild as my jibe is by my own terms, I am wrenched bodily out of my creative reverie by the return of the wantons who, it seems, have been unsuccessful in flinging Frank to the floor and surrendering their virtue to him, and I turn to see two blanched white faces as Rhona and her über-introvert twin survey my work of art with looks of sheer horror on their frozen faces.

*

There are about twenty assorted people in various stages of undress and the noise is louder than Bedlam when we arrive at Rhona's house on the night of the parade.

Small boys dressed as builders seem to be everywhere and the twins are sniping viciously at each other whilst attempting to 'mature' each other's hair with a can of spray-on grey.

"Rhona, will you hold still and let me get this done?" Shona is demanding as we enter. "You're all lopsided."

"You're putting too much on, Shona. Spunky's going to be here tonight, he'll never be up for it if you make me look like an auld brat."

"Well, you've made me look like an auld klok[31]."

"Really, how can you tell?" Rhona retorts, missing the irony of insulting the facial features of her identical twin, but Shona rises to the bait nevertheless.

"You cheeky wee mink!" she yells, covering her sister in spray-on senility. "I'll..."

I hastily take over the hair conversion job before one twin attempts to insert the aerosol can where it doesn't belong, and while I have them captive, I quickly affix their large Sunday hats and, thus attired, I dispatch them to keep their hands occupied aiding the remainder of the congregation with their Shilling-like millinery.

*

Later that night, after winning the competition and changing back into normal clothes, Chancery and I leave the twins in the orbit of Spunky and his buddies at the local pub and head up to the community centre. The infamous Gala Night ceilidh is supposed to be in full swing, but when we arrive we discover that the large and gloomy hall is almost deserted.

---

31 - **klok:** dung beetle

A country band called Liam and Co are cranking out old Johnny Cash numbers but no-one appears to be dancing, and most of the villagers are congregated in noisy clumps around the bar. Of the dance fraternity, however, there is no sign, but I almost trip over a furious Roberta, who's sitting tucked away in a dark corner nursing her wrath like a troll in its cave.

"Hello. Where's everyone?" I say tactlessly, and my irate friend glowers at me in disgust.

"They've all fucked off to some fucking wedding in Stromness," Roberta complains. "Some wife from Sooth needed dancers for her reception and they've all deserted us."

I start to say 'What? Henrietta too?' but think better of it, so content myself with the equally tactless: "Well, there's nothing new in that, is there?" and Roberta gives me a look that, by rights, should have had me stone dead on the floor.

"No," she storms, "but they haven't invited me."

"Oh," I say inadequately. "Why not?"

"Because this useless fucker here can't dance," Roberta fumes, indicating the hunched figure of Silent Philip who's sitting in the shadows clicking his heels together and trying to dissolve into the chair beside her.

"Surely not..." I say without hope and Roberta makes a disgusted noise which somehow conveys all her bitter disillusionment with the man she had planned to marry.

"What a useless lump of lard," she continues, warming to her subject. "Two left feet and a clod-hopping introvert."

"I'll leave you to talk to your friends, will I?" Chancery says, smiling sweetly and promptly vanishing, despite my pleading stare.

"I was the pillar of that group," Roberta asserts, her decibel level starting to rise as naked disappointment gets her soundly in its thrall. "And two

minutes after I get mixed up with this idiot they drop me like a hot coal. I'm supposed to be the bride here, not the fucking wallflower!"

"Well, come and dance with me then..." I try hopefully, trying to defuse an undefusable situation, but Roberta is a badly wounded animal and not to be so easily mollified.

"Just look at the useless bastard," she snipes, turning on Philip. "Too scared to learn a couple of dance steps in case someone looks at him. It's not even that difficult. Fucking hell, you're completely useless, Max, and even you can manage it."

People are looking, which is possibly the very worst thing that can happen to any self-respecting Orcadian, and Silent Philip turns to face her, his face flaming and almost the same colour as his unnaturally carroty hair.

"Well?" Roberta challenges him. "Is this what my life's going to be like from now on? Give me one good reason why I should go ahead with this marriage? It's certainly not going to be for the great sex."

Philip's lower lip trembles. Sweat pours down the side of his face. "My God," I think. "He's going to speak."

His lips part. His mouth opens.

"Berth," he says slowly and without intonation, as if his lips are unaccustomed to forming words. "Folk are looking. We'll talk aboot this later in the hoose."

I am quite stunned just hearing his voice, but Roberta, who may have heard the odd vocal sound from him before, is unimpressed.

"Later?" she hisses, her eyebrows arched and oblivious to the fact that the music has stopped and that there are open mouths all around her. "Later...? There'll be no later for you tonight, my lad. You'll just have to think up something else that'll take you three minutes to perform."

And, grabbing her handbag, she strides purposefully out of the hall amidst a sea of shocked expressions.

I look at the crimson Philip who looks helplessly back at me.

"Fancy a drink, mate?" I say lamely as the music quickly starts up again.

*

My Aunty Bunty, after several years of poor health, has died peacefully in her sleep, and once her affairs are put in order, her solictor dispatches us a small legacy. It's not a fortune, but it does hold the key we have been seeking to expand our very narrow universe, and we promptly go out to buy ourselves a car. There are several bone-shakers advertised in this week's Orcadian, but they either seem to be clapped-out old farm saloons or strange boy-racer contraptions with built-in coloured lights and bubble machines, so, upon the recommendation of the twins, we cycle into Kirkwall to visit the showroom of Frank the Mechanic.

Thus we arrive in the centre of "toon" some forty minutes later, and are just about to chain our bikes to a nearby railing outside Frank's emporium when we are accosted by an ebullient James and Jasper who are both clutching little red and blue paper Norwegian flags which they periodically wave at passers-by.

"Hello, you two, have you got a new job on Safeway's deli counter?" Chancery says with a perfectly straight face.

"Oh my, and you're pulling our legs, are you no'?" Jasper giggles. "You ken fine what we're doing."

"Er, actually, no, we don't," I say. "Why are you waving little flags about?"

"Oh my, well, it's an auld tradition up here for folks tae dae aboot this time o' the year..." Jasper begins when James interrupts irritatedly.

"For heaven's sake, Jasper, it's Norway Day. Can you not just say that?"

"And Norway Day is...?" I ask, still mystified, but further conversation on the subject is dashed by Jasper crying, "They're here!" and the two fey lads suddenly dash off towards the cathedral, waving their little flags as they

go.

"Shall we follow?" I ask Chancery, and she nods.

"I shudder to think about what we're going to find, but, yes, let's go and see what's going on."

As if in answer, a small procession of Scandinavian people dressed in peasant clothes come out of the cathedral doors, the men in strange knickerbockers and little monkey jackets with red lapels; the women in long embroidered skirts with starched white aprons and little red waistcoats. They are followed at a respectable distance by some bods from the local council, and they all walk down the centre of the broad main street waving to the small crowd of on-lookers.

"Is she there?" James asks his friend urgently as the procession nears. "Can you see her?"

"No' yet, no' yet," Jasper replies, still waving his flag with one hand as he shields his eyes with the other. "But she'll be here, she said she would."

"But I don't see her... No, wait, there she is!" James cries, pointing wildly into the crowd, and we follow his gaze and come face to face with the object of his affections as a small blonde girl with flowers in her hair and dressed in a long white dress skips to the front of the procession and pirouettes to the crowd.

"Arngerd! Arngerd! Over here," Jasper cries, waving his flag, as James goes crimson and tries to blend into the general mélange. "Oh my, are you no' a picture in your bonny new frock."

The little moon-faced pixie gives a piercing shriek of recognition and bounds over to our party. Throwing her arms around the taller lad, she squeals, "Oh, it is my two favorite little Orkney boys, ja, I tell my mother, for me they will certainly always come."

"Oh aye, we're here, right enough," James says, blushing, and gazing at her adoringly. "Are you still up for tonight?"

"Tonight?" Moon Face squeals. "Oh ja, tonight we study the mortar in the foundations of the Bishop's Palace. Ja, ja, I will not be missing this prized night out. We will all meet up again soon, no?" and with a hop, skip and a jump she rejoins the parade, which our two caballeros quickly follow off into the far horizon.

"I don't believe it," I say watching their departing backs. "James's finally found himself a girlfriend."

"Yes," Chancery muses. "A girlfriend who's the spitting image of Jasper. This promises to be interesting."

*

We pick up the keys for our shiny new Vauxhall a couple of days later and go off on a belated sight-seeing expedition round the island. Like text-book tourists, we drive out to the Brough of Birsay and view the Neolithic village on the tidal promontory and then the ruins of the sixteenth century castle there, built, disappointingly not by some great hairy Viking called Erik the Large Testicles, but by the dull-sounding Robert Stewart, the first Earl of Orkney in 1574. Heady with our new-found freedom, however, we push on and motor down the island's eastern side, past the modern day Totem poles in the garden of an émigré sculptor at Evie, and then down beyond Kirkwall and out towards the Southern Isles and the legendary Churchill Barriers.

During the second world war, when the British fleet was anchored at Scapa Flow, one of Hitler's U-boats carried out a sneak attack and sank the HMS Royal Oak with the loss of over eight hundred lives, and, in a typically grandiose gesture of defiance, Winston Churchill subsequently ordered huge concrete blocks to be deposited across the narrow strips of water that separated mainland Orkney and the southern isles of Burray and South Ronaldsay to protect Scapa from further attacks.

Narrow roads were then built over the top of the causeways, or "Churchill Barriers", and these have allowed easy communication between the islands in all but the most inclement of weather ever since.

Thus we stand poised at the first barrier, ready to make our maiden

crossing, and, although the locals saunter over them all the time, suddenly, as we look across the narrow strip of road only a couple of feet above an unhappy ocean, crossing the causeway becomes a little like taking a leap of faith and driving the car into the sea.

In order to protect the blockade from torpedo attacks, "block ships", old clapped-out freighters, were towed from Scapa and sunk at the mouth of the inlets, together with large quantities of submarine nets, and although, sixty years on, the fleet has long departed Orkney's waters, these ghostly relics still remain mournfully in the water to greet us as we prepare to perform our re-enactment of Moses parting the waves of the Red Sea.

It's a relatively innocuous mid-summer night, but it's well after nine when we pull up, and although the light is still good there's a definitely twilight tinge to the evening sky and the strong wind that has been picking up all day is working itself up into a mother of a summer gale. The tide is in, and, as we look out at the narrow strip of cracked tarmac that runs over a trail of haphazard concrete blocks, like some giant child's building bricks cast into the sea, I feel a lump forming in my throat.

"So, are we crossing or not?" Chancery demands, as I sit at the edge of the first causeway, indecision writ large across my features.

"I don't know," I reply, indicating a weather-beaten signpost at the side of the road. "The sign says not."

Chancery cranes her neck and reads the notice aloud. "'Do not cross the causeway in inclement weather'. So, what's the big deal?"

"Well, it just says 'inclement weather'. What is 'inclement weather'? When the waves are ten feet tall? Twenty feet? Or just five feet, like they are just now?"

"Ah, so you're scared."

"No," I reply hesitantly. "Just careful."

"Look, just drive before the next ice age comes and freezes the bloody thing over," Chancery says with more than a trace of bravado in her tone.

"Okay," I say, letting out the clutch. "Here goes."

The car noses cautiously onto the causeway and the strong wind immediately catches it and makes the front sway towards the water, but Chancery stands firm.

"Drive!" she commands, so we head out into the middle of the sea. Rusty old wrecks grin toothlessly at us from one side; grey, seasick-coloured waves crash at the other.

"I'm not quite sure I like this," Chancery says, suddenly.

"Too late," I reply, "There's no turning back now, we've got to keep going. Anyway, what's the worst that can happen?"

And, as if in answer, a huge wave crashes up ahead of us and splatters a large splodge of seaweed all over our windshield.

*

Coincidentally, a week later, Backpack Bertha's ramblers' club announces a Between-the-Barriers Walk over private land on the southern isle of Burray, and as we've now just about conquered our fear of the causeways and are desperate to explore this normally fenced-off bit of coastline, we voluntarily sign up for it.

The ramblers are scheduled to assemble their clumpy boots and knapsacks full of oaty-snacks at nine o'clock on the Sunday morning following County Show Saturday, but as there's no show this year because of the Foot and Mouth epidemic on the mainland, and more importantly, because we are definitely not going to the annual County Show Dance that's being held in a creaking marquee in Kirkwall on the Saturday night, we foresee no problems in getting there bright and early.

However, the twins, on the other hand, are passionate attendees of the Marquee Ball, and cannot understand why we are declining this particular hop, and they petition us almost hourly in an effort to get us to recant and accompany them to the annual flesh market.

We remain adamant, however, and commit to going on the walk, and when we get the last of many calls from Rhona on the Saturday night I assume that this is her eleventh hour attempt to get us to accompany Cinderella to the ball, but instead the twins suddenly seem to have accepted, if not embraced, the fact that we're not going and Rhona asks us if we'll baby-sit Sean for her that night as she's been let down at the last minute.

The fierce summer gale that's been brewing up all day is now screaming like a madwoman as we sit and try to grasp the concept of video games with Sean, and Rhona's left enough food to feed the entire NATO forces and then some, so the evening passes quickly. Sean insists on waiting up for his mum, who has promised to be home by one o'clock, but his eyes start getting heavy around eleven and he promptly passes out on the sofa half an hour later.

I'm personally sceptical of the one o'clock homecoming promise and don't expect to see the twins much before two, but as the clock slowly chimes off the hours and the storm outside gets wilder and wilder we begin to get uneasy and then downright worried, and it's nearly four in the morning before the two of them eventually roll in, dressed in identical crumpled taffeta, brimming with the news that the marquee has blown down in the gale and the dance has been cancelled.

"So where have you been," I ask, perplexed, not seeing Chancery shaking her head and making throat-cutting gestures, "that kept you in town for three hours after the dance that didn't happen was supposed to finish?"

"Been? Us?" Shona says in a strained, high voice, frantically brushing at the seat of her dress, while Rhona looks at us coyly from under heavy-lashed eyelids.

"Oh, just the burger van," she says innocently.

*

My head has barely touched the pillow when the alarm goes off the next morning after a scant four hours of slumber and it's very tempting to turn over and go back to sleep again, or even better, just die quietly, but

Chancery's already crawling towards the shower so I drag myself out of bed and attempt to dress in suitably ramble-friendly gear.

All organised ramblers' walks have an appointed leader, a sort of combined Canadian Mountie and Kindergarten Schoolmarm figure, and today's guide is to be Bob, a strange highly-strung Londoner in baggy combat pants. Bob is what you might call an Ugly Englishman, being one of the many stressed-out Southerners who can't cut it in their native environment and decamp to the islands instead, but bring their urban values and stresses with them. He's pacing up and down and chewing on the end of his titanium rambler's stick when we arrive, and he sets off on the dot of nine at a brisk pace that would be more suited for power walking or doing a morning commuter stride across Waterloo Bridge.

In retrospect I suppose we should have been grateful that he didn't insist that we did the entire walk on our bellies under barbed wire and live gun fire, and he certainly treats the whole exercise as a military assault course rather than anything remotely pleasurable. It's a fantastic ramble over rugged coastline with unbelievable seascapes at every turn, and although there's the usual sharp wind, it's a dazzling sunny day and the sea is a sparkling Cornish blue cascaded with gleaming sun pennies, but Bob's not seeing any of this.

Bob has already timed the walk and is determined to get us round it in precisely the same time as his estimate, and it wouldn't have surprised me in the least if he'd pulled a stop-watch out of his combats and clicked it when we reached the finish line. Natural beauty beyond measure flies by at a breakneck speed, verdant rock pools go unexplored and, when we unexpectedly come upon a huge colony of about two hundred seals only a score of yards away, Bob grudgingly permits a stop of five minutes to appreciate their majesty before he hauls us all off again and delivers us back at the pick-up-point by twelve noon, on the dot, and stands there preening like a prize baboon who's successfully pushed all the right buttons in his laboratory cage to earn a chocolate button.

*

Henrietta's sister arrives back on the island on three weeks leave from her ultra-macho job supervising oil derricks in the Middle East, just as the last

fleeting sunshine of August is giving way to the chill winds of early September. It's been several years since the sisters have been together on Orcadian soil, and, in order to fully bond with her estranged sibling, Siobhan, the prodigal daughter, suggests that the two of them spend some quality time together in a rented holiday cottage on the neighbouring island of Hoy, the most beautiful but inhospitable of all the Orkneys.

Whereas all the other Orkney islands are rolling and arable, Hoy's terrain is rocky and mountainous, and the island is famed for its dramatic rocky coastline where sheer red sandstone cliffs give way abruptly to turbulent water. The coast is littered with weather-beaten reminders of the last two world wars, and the west side of the isle is almost completely uninhabited with no vehicular roads, the majority of Hoy's landmass being taken up with rough hilly terrain and a huge RSPB bird reserve[32].

Nevertheless there is a respectable population on the isle, and the people of Hoy tend to crowd onto a narrow strip of land along the east coast, farming where they can or commuting to jobs on the Orkney Mainland or the oil refinery on the neighbouring isle of Flotta, but, although you would expect a tight, close-knit community, Hoy inhabitants all seem to be part of some age-old Sicilian-style vendetta where they lead a Capulet and Montague existence, with the North side pointedly ignoring the South and vice versa.

Thus, everyone shakes their heads in disbelief when they hear that the sisters are taking themselves off to such an unforgiving locale for two whole weeks, and the "Gang" quickly takes to running a book on how long Henrietta will last imprisoned with no car and no phone and only her sister for company. For myself, I reckon that they will soon be helicoptered out to the Balfour Hospital on the Orkney Mainland, suffering from grievous bodily wounds, but the first week passes without incident and I am beginning to think that all is well when the phone rings just after midnight on Friday night.

"Max, is that you?" a whispered voice hisses. "I'm dying out here."

---

32 - See the Eurhythmics 1984 video for *Here Comes the Rain Again*, shot almost exclusively on Hoy

"Henrietta?" I say. "Where are you, and why are you whispering?"

"*She's* in bed in the next room. I don't dare wake her." Her voice is desperate. "Please, Max, you've got to get me out of this."

"Wait a minute," I say. "Aren't you supposed to have no phone? I thought that was the rule?"

"For fuck's sake, Max, I smuggled my mobile with me for emergencies, alright? Now, are you going to get me out of this or not?"

"Of course I will," I say immediately. "What do you want me to do?"

"Come and stay for the weekend, and bring as many people as you can, the house'll hold ten easily, and Max..."

"Yes?" I say cautiously.

"This was all your idea. I never phoned you. I don't have a phone."

"Alright, but..." I start to reply, but all that answers me is the baleful whine of a discontinued tone.

*

I phone round everyone on Saturday morning and by noon we have a convoy ready to embark on our "surprise" visit to Chez Henrietta, and, after stocking up with provisions at the local Safeway store, we head out to a place called Houton to catch the car ferry over to Hoy. We have been to the isle a couple of times before: once on an organised walk with Backpack Bertha's band of roving ramblers, and twice in the dark to go to dances in small, dimly-lit halls, but this is the first time that we have actually driven over in broad daylight without a fixed itinerary.

Roberta and Silent Philip have decided to car-pool with us, which seemed like a good idea at eleven o'clock this morning when Roberta suggested it, but now, an hour later, the atmosphere inside Phillip's immaculately clean Peugeot has already turned decidedly frosty.

Romeo and Juliet have very obviously had yet another disagreement before setting out, and we subsequently drive up the ramp onto the ferry in frozen silence, but eventually Roberta addresses her eleven-year-old son, Sven, who appears to have been brought along to mediate.

"Sven, tell Philip to open his window, I'm stifling," she says pointedly to her uncomfortable offspring. But before the boy has time to relay the message, Silent Philip tartly replies, "Sven, tell your mother that it's too cold to have the window open. She'll have to cool herself down".

The ferry is sounding its departure horn and there are vehicles in front and behind boxing us in, but there's still the option of just diving into the harbour and swimming to shore, and I'm seriously contemplating it as Roberta says icily, "Sven, please tell Philip that he's a total cunt."

But, before a suitable retort can be conveyed, Chancery interjects, "Let's go out on deck," and we quickly evacuate and leave them to it, despite poor Sven's pleading look of desperation.

*

It's a bright but cold September day and the wind out on the deck has a nasty bite to it, but nothing can persuade us to get back into Silent Philip's car before we absolutely have to, and we stand at the rail watching the panorama of Hoy's majestic cliff faces, dotted with derelict army observation posts and the distant architecturally outstanding Martello tower at Hackness, until the boat eventually docks at the tiny village of Lyness and we have to get back inside the vehicle again.

Silent Philip drives his car like a retired hearse-driver in a slow tractor, and as the rest of the party vanish in a cloud of dust in Ewan the builder's bright red BMW, we plod sedately off the ferry and along the narrow single-track road like an ancient Morris Minor filled with blue-rinsed old ladies.

"Philip, have you any idea where you're going?" Roberta snaps, completely forgetting that she's not supposed to be addressing him directly. "He's hopeless. He thinks twenty miles away from his farm is going abroad. He even gets lost in the bedroom."

"Well, there's only one road," I say diplomatically. "We're sure to pass every house on the island eventually."

"Don't bet on it with Speedy Gonzales here behind the wheel," Roberta snorts. "We'll be lucky to reach Betty Corrigal's[33] grave before it gets dark at this rate. At least she'll appreciate the company. For *fuck's* sake, Philip, you can go a little faster than twenty bloody miles an hour."

*

Henrietta ambushes me the moment that Silent Philip's sedate sedan pulls up in front of her temporary home and entwines her arm through mine like some sci-fi succubus.

"Quick," she says, dragging me away. "Come and see the beach. I swear I'll murder her if I have to put up with her for another minute!"

"So it's been a fun week," I say, putting a friendly arm around her waist as we walk down to the sands together. "I wondered about the sanity of this venture."

"Oh, Max," Henrietta sighs, laying her head upon my shoulder. "I love my sister dearly, I just can't stand being on the same continent as her, that's all."

*

We spend a couple of hours walking along Hoy's incomparable white sands, the cold wind making us huddle together to keep warm, and we arrive back at the holiday cottage with our colour high and our clothing dishevelled from the strong breeze.

Henrietta has been bending my ear non-stop for the whole time, minutely

---

33 - **Betty Corrigall:** A Victorian farm girl from Hoy who fell pregnant to a sailor and killed herself; thus denied burial on consecrated ground, her remains were interred in an unmarked grave in the middle of nowhere, a few miles north of where we're currently heading.

dissecting her relationship with her sister, and I'm not really aware of the atmosphere that I've walked back into until I realise that everyone's in little tight-knit groups and that they've all gone very silent. Ewan nudges me in the ribs and winks lewdly, and Roberta very pointedly says: "I thought that you were going to be looking after me this weekend"; and I realise that I have just filled the winter store cupboards of island gossip to bursting point.

CHAPTER 13 – WHERE WE DECIDE TO EMULATE MADONNA AND GO HOUSE-HUNTING

A rumour that Madonna is looking for a second home in Orkney spreads like a virus and local gossip is suddenly obsessed with numerous tales of supposed sightings. In fact, the island's new Maddie-mania gets to such a height that when a blonde-haired tourist with sunglasses is having lunch in one of the seafront hotels she is shocked to find a crowd of school children standing on the pavement snapping pictures with their phones.

We, too, are seeking a new abode as we are now finding it increasingly difficult to store all the boxes of old patchwork quilts and vintage bread bins that we have bought for re-selling on eBay, not to mention all the cartons of jiffy bags and rolls of bubble-pack that mail order trading demands, and we place an "accommodation wanted" ad in the local paper to see what we can turn up.

A strange English stoner in the South Isles tries to rent us a run-down dump that is separated from his not-yet-functioning organic farm by a dilapidated chicken coop, and says, we hope in jest, that if we sign the lease today he will not charge us for either the hens or the old tractor parts that are currently in the bath. And although our hopes soar when we go to an address in the coastal parish of Orphir to see a beautiful modern bungalow, they are dashed again when the elderly Orcadian landlord leads us up a steep track behind the first house and affectionately pats the wall of a tumbledown farmhouse with four-foot-high doorways and turf roof that's being held up by spit and dried cow shit.

"Aye, I love this hoose, I was born here," he says nostalgically. "But I'd be willing to let it oot to someone who'll decorate and take care of it... and pay me a hundred and fifty pounds a week rent."

*

As the fleeting September quickly begins to fade into a chilly October one of the local stray cats delivers a batch of kittens to our doorstep, and, after our last fiasco with Clint the animal handler, we decide to billet them out ourselves, and place an ad in The Orcadian which swiftly finds homes for most of them. Seven of the original nine Minions of Satan are quickly dispatched to unsuspecting island farmsteads, but when we eventually get down to the last two inky-black specimens there appear to be no further takers on the horizon and, since our dear old cat has departed this life the previous spring, we adopt Sooty and Suki as our own.

Meanwhile, on the other side of the island, despite a lot of very public name-calling and a pyrotechnically spectacular row where the happy couple end up throwing mashed potato at each other across the dinner table at a Harvest Thanksgiving night in Holm, Roberta gets tired of thinking up excuses to her children and sells up her house and moves her brood into Cold Comfort Farm, Silent Philip's biblical abode in the wilds of South Ronaldsay.

As the long winter approaches, the pair of them slip away to the Maldives to get hitched, Philip being possessed of a morbid fear that his peers will "blacken"[34] him if the date of their nuptials becomes publicly known. The plan is that they will make the announcement when they return, safely spliced, but Roberta's Mum, a well known local drunk, blabs the news on the first night that they're away and all of Orkney knows about it before they even touch back down at the airport.

The "Gang" are exceedingly vexed that they've been done out of what they feel is their due festivities, and the silver-headed Ewan quickly calls a clandestine meeting where, after much plotting, it's decided to hold a surprise "mock wedding" for the elopers on their return, and a convoluted scenario is quickly concocted for the occasion that, surprise surprise, involves everyone dressing up in elaborate costumes.

Mock weddings, it should be noted, are fairly standard fare in the isles and are frequently organised during the long winter months when a parish feels like a party at a time when no-one's either died or is getting married.

---

34 - **blackening:** old Orkney and Shetland custom where brides and grooms to-be are covered in treacle and other gunk and paraded through the streets by their friends.

But the Dance Gestapo decide to make theirs a bit more piquant by not actually telling the hapless bride and groom what they are in for, and merely invite them to dinner in Henrietta's large Victorian farmhouse, whose thick stone walls will conceal the sound of mischief-makers setting up a faux wedding chapel in the kitchen.

*

It's a viciously cold October night with no moon and a bitter, moaning wind as we sit in our wedding costumes waiting for a call from Ewan to say that the happy couple are safely encased behind the sound-proof walls of Henrietta's living room.

I have had to strap two large cushions around Chancery's stomach for her starring role as Philip's abandoned lover, which cause her to waddle like a duck and make it difficult for her to walk properly, and we are happily indulging in tasteless pregnancy jokes when a chorus of strident mews tells us that the kittens want to be let out for the night.

They still seem too young to be out by themselves at just twelve weeks old, but both of them are already dedicated night prowlers and we just can't persuade them to change their ways and go out to play outdoors in the daylight hours like good middle-class cats.

Ewan's call comes just as the two musketeers slink soundlessly out of the open door, and we quickly grab our coats and dash along the dirt path at the side of our house to where our car's parked in the shadow of the building. Chancery is waddling like Jemima Puddleduck with half the living room sofa strapped to her middle, and I'm carrying a large tray of food for the bring-a-plate buffet, when suddenly there's a loud banshee shriek and I realise that I've inadvertently stood on Suki, the most highly-strung of our two invisible pure black kittens, and she takes a mad fit of panic and bolts towards the side of the house and vanishes under the car.

The nearest street lights are over two miles away, and the small bulb above our front door does nothing to penetrate the opacity of the bible-black October night, and, of course, the car's sitting in the house's shadow anyway and I can't see where the damned animal has got to. Chancery's convinced that she's still under the vehicle, so I go and get a powerful torch

and lie on the ground and check the car's entire under-carriage and even the engine, but I can't see Suki anywhere.

We call her name again and again, me turned-turtle on the freezing ground and Chancery flopping about like a bloated Bugs Bunny, getting snappier and snappier with each other as I search everywhere for the blasted kitten. But it's to no avail, and while I'm doing yet another bomb squad sweep of the underside of the car at Daisy Duck's insistence, we hear the phone ringing from inside the house and it's Ewan saying that everyone's waiting and wanting to know where the hell we are.

I'm convinced that the damned cat can't be under the car, but Chancery swears that she is, so I search yet again and stick my hands into all the oily crevices under the wheel arches. It's so cold that I can no longer feel my fingers so I call the irksome animal's name till I'm hoarse, but there's just no response and I cannot find hide nor hair of her rancid pelt anywhere. The ground beneath me seems to be leeching all the heat out of my body and I eventually convince my pregnant spouse that "her" cat must have high-tailed it into the undergrowth behind the garage and vanished off into the furze on the hillside, and we get into the car and quickly drive over to Ewan's mansion in the north-westerly parish of Twatt.

*

The 'wedding' is a great success with Roberta and Silent Philip being made to repeat their marriage vows to a soberly dressed Jasper playing the minister[35] and the ceremony is, of course, interrupted repeatedly by a string of belligerent ex-lovers. By eleven o'clock, however, it is all finally over, and Chancery is finally able to divest herself of her "bump" after she has clung dutifully to Silent Philip's philandering feet and the evening's skulduggery is satisfactorily concluded to everyone's satisfaction. Restless, however, we leave the party early and go out looking for Suki again, Mulder-and-Scully style with torches, and call and call without response, but, by the early dawn when her brother returns home and wakes us, there is still no sign of her.

We're sure now that we've lost her, or, even worse, inadvertently killed

---

35 - He *wanted* to be one of the bridesmaids, but that's another story!

her, and we call and search all over the place, routing through Hordun's many tumbledown sheds and going up and down every inch of our track making sure that her injured or lifeless body isn't lying there bleeding pitifully into the gutter. But there is not a sign of her anywhere and it's as if aliens have abducted her and flown her off to some secret hide-away in New Mexico.

We never stop looking, but, when a week has eventually passed without a sighting, we start to accept the fact that she's either lost or, worse, dead. However, we still continue to go through the motions of leading our busy social life, and we're at a dance practice class on the following Monday night, rehearsing our "twinkles" under the watchful gaze of a stentorian retired gym teacher, when, in one of the frequent tea breaks, I happen to overhear Ewan the builder telling someone that his mother has found a stray kitten in her garden although there are no cats with litters for miles.

"It can't be," I mutter as I whirl round to face him. "You say your mother's found a cat, Ewan," I demand, gripping him by the lapels of his safari jacket and sending his medallion flying. "Is it a kitten, and what colour is it?"

"Will you get off me," he scolds, disengaging himself purposefully from my grasp and dusting down the front of his coat. "I don't know, I think it's black, why do you care?"

"Never mind why. Give me your mother's phone number, quickly!" I bark, and Chancery hurriedly explains the situation before an ugly rumour about my unnatural predilection for older women takes flight and spreads across the island.

*

Ewan's Mum lives in a neat bungalow a couple of hundred yards behind her son's Bauhaus pile, a common enough practice in Orkney where farming families tend to build up little enclaves of houses on their own land, and, our hearts pounding with vain hope and fervoured anticipation, we phone her first thing the next morning to ask if we can come over and inspect her new arrival.

Sensing an hour's entertainment, the old lady readily agrees and we rush straight over to her bungalow. But she has obviously put her phone onto auto-dial and summoned an army of her friends, and, when we are shown into an auditorium-sized living room some twenty minutes later there is an audience of about a dozen grey-haired old dames in pastel coloured cardigans sitting in a semi-circle to witness our reunion with the intrepid wanderer.

"Oh what a shame, is it your peedie cat that you've lost, bhouy?" a frail-looking old woman asks, gripping my wrist in steely claw. "I lost an auld tom cat to a thresher once, it was like jam sandwiches in that field for weeks and weeks after."

"Away and don't tell the lad that auld story, Senga," one of her friends interrupts. "Away and see if the caddie lamb's yours, bhouy, and dinnae think aboot her lying dead by the roadside." I've been telling myself not to hope and that this can't be our kitten, many miles away from where we had last sighted her, but I have to admit that Henrietta's farm is just a quarter of a mile over the rise from here. I can feel my heart beating anxiously as we're led through the spacious living room and out to a sunny porch, accompanied by the soft creaking of Zimmer frames as the aged audience follows at a respectful distance, and there, with a solitary open tin of kitten food for company, is our sorry-looking Suki.

Her fur is matted and she looks lost and woebegone, but she lets out a howl that could be heard in New York as soon as she sees us and leaps up joyfully into Chancery's arms.

"Oh my, my," one of the old ladies sighs. "It's your peedie darling after all. I really love a happy ending, so I do."

"But how did she get away over here from Finstoon?" another pastel cardigan asks and I shake my head in reply.

"I wish I knew," I say, looking at the wretched bundle of black fur that's happily chewing the hem of Chancery's jumper, and I swear that the damn cat looks back up at me and winks.

*

After the chilly October we sink into another dark and bitterly cold November and the days get shorter and shorter with the dusk creeping in well before half past two in the afternoon. The glacial winds howl all day; sailings and flights from the mainland are constantly cancelled resulting in no post or national newspapers; and everyone is walking around looking depressed and generally miserable. There's a momentary respite, however, when a couple called Billy and Lana announce that they're holding a huge party for their silver wedding anniversary in a small church that sits neatly tucked away behind the St Magnus Cathedral, locally referred to as the Peedie Kirk.

We go out in search of the venue in question and find it is a suitably Calvinist stone shoe box with austere and disapproving architecture, but we then discover that the celebration party is to be held not in the kirk but in the adjoining "sma[36] hall" and that this is an even smaller minster, with blank featureless walls clad in dark brown hardboard.

The "gang" are busy hatching a plot to smuggle in party bombs when a strange reedy voice suddenly pipes up, "We could all dress up to make it brighter," and there's a moment of stunned silence as everyone looks around them for the identity of the mysterious stranger.

"Fuck me, he spoke!" Ewan inadvertently blurts out, his face flushed by his own unaccustomed profanity, and all eyes quickly follow his gaze to a rapidly crimsoning Silent Philip.

"It would be fun..." Philip repeats, his face beetroot and his eyes firmly on the floor as his voice tails away, and Henrietta whispers impishly in my ear, "Wow. Two sentences in one evening. Roberta's going to be really hot for him tonight."

*

To cut a long story short, Orkney's love of drag quickly rears its ugly head, and as soon as an evening of cross-dressing is suggested all other ideas fall by the wayside. The girls quickly raid the Salvation Army shop for old

36 - **sma:** small

suits for Roberta and Henrietta to shoehorn themselves into; while Silent Philip and I opt for more of a panto dame look, and there is much hilarity when we all show up at Philip's farm, the designated pre-party rendezvous point of the evening, in shapeless dresses and hideous joke-shop wigs.

Everyone is laughing and pointing and being generally frivolous, and even Silent Philip allows himself the luxury of an audible chuckle or two, when a dark shadow suddenly falls ominously across the worn lino of the old farmhouse kitchen as two muffled figures slink into the room on towering stilettoed feet.

"Who the...?" Ewan starts to utter from under his cerise feather boa, then, suddenly recognising the intruders, exclaims, "Oh my Lord, it's James and Jasper!"

Everyone stands there staring open-mouthed at the two, apparently, elegant old ladies who stand before us, immaculate in vintage dresses and furs, their meticulously pancaked faces flawless and porcelain in the dim yellow light of the kitchen, and, other than James's slightly too broad shoulders, there is very little on display to indicate that there are men beneath the costumes.

Until Jasper speaks. "Oh my, here we are, and whit a sight. Roberta, I've not got enough boob here, can you maybe lend me a bra?"

*

The official festivity is set to conclude at midnight as it's a church hall and we're not allowed to party on into the Sabbath, and while most of the older people go home those of us who still want to boogie are invited back to the hosts' home for phase two of the party. We all have a change of clothes with us and I, for one, am desperate to get out of the very scratchy woollen tights I'm wearing, and I'm standing by the hall door at quarter to twelve taking a break from dancing backwards' when Jasper sidles up to me with a gleam in his eye.

"Oh my, well, Max, are we not all a sight for sore eyes?" he gushes. "Are you and Chancery taking the car over to the party? Would it not be a right laugh if we were all to walk to Billy and Lana's through the Toon with all

those modern folk and see what happens? We might even get a boyfriend!"

"I don't think even the most short-sighted drunk's going to go for my hairy legs in this get-up," I laugh, trying desperately to keep the conversation away from the dark side where it's rapidly heading.

"No, maybe not," he muses, hitching up his false boobs with an easy movement. "But some of us might have better luck."

*

Our accommodation problem is finally solved when we're out in the car one melancholy windswept day in early December and we happen to pass a spacious old farmhouse that we have noticed earlier in the year in the rural West Mainland parish of Quoyloo, a few miles west of the unfortunately named coastal parish of Twatt.

As is typical on Orkney farms, the main house has been replaced by a modern bungalow and appears to be vacant, so we drive into the muddy farmyard and locate Kevan, the owner, with his arm elbow-deep up the rear end of a cow. Kevan is a small, blonde man in his mid thirties, clad in the ubiquitous farmer's boiler suit and a padded fur hat with ear-flaps, and resplendent in his winter garb he bears a striking resemblance to Elmer Fudd.

"That auld hoose? Oh aye, we rented it oot once before. It's no' locked, have a walk round and see if it'll suit you," Elmer tells us when we explain the nature of our errand, and we have to admit that it's certainly a nice roomy villa. There are four bedrooms, a huge, if scruffy, kitchen, and proper coal fires and clanky oil-fired central heating. Outside, there's plenty of grass and the remnants of a garden to separate it from most of the farm, but, unlike our present house at Finstown, there's no view to speak of, although some of the most beautiful coastline in the northern hemisphere is only five minutes away and, in fact, the sound of breakers hitting the steep rock cliffs can be clearly heard from where we stand.

I look over at Chancery and nod, and we decide to take it there and then. We stroll back to the byre at the other side of the yard to talk terms with the

wabbit- killer, and, after negotiating a mutually agreeable rent and deposit with him, agree to take the house from the first of March on the condition that we can have access to clean up and decorate over the ensuing weeks. This is cheerfully granted and we are about to depart with the keys in our hands, astounded that we finally have a decent space to live and work in, when Elmer calls us back.

"That front grass," he says with a farmer's sense of the practical. "It'll need cutting in the summer. Do you want to do it or will I just put in a couple of sheep?"

*

December gets colder and darker and it snows heavily after Christmas and then freezes over making the roads impassable. All the narrow country lanes around us have been covered with deeply rutted snow before the freeze and are now really only fit for tractors, so the natives dig out their old wooden sledges and take to the fields to ferry sacks of provisions from the village store to their homes.

There's no sign of a thaw as Hogmanay comes and goes, with first-footing being limited to getting shit-faced with only your immediate neighbours, and, tired of being imprisoned in the house for days on end, we decide to walk out to visit our friend Lorna, who directed the pantomime the previous year. There's absolutely no question of taking the car, and, wrapping up like Eskimos, we don our wellie boots and start out overland on the four mile trudge to Lorna's house on the other side of the village. It's a bitter but clear night with a strong moon reflecting on the frozen snow, and we make good speed along the glittering lanes, passing no-one other than some frozen sheep, and the lights of Lorna's palatial residence eventually appear on the distant horizon after about three quarters of an hour's brisk walk.

The frosty fields are deathly quiet, with only the gentle moaning of the ever-present wind and the odd snatch of accordion music from a party in a distant yellow-windowed farmhouse, but Chancery suddenly pauses mid-stride and says, "Did you hear that?"

"Hear what?" I reply irritatingly.

"That," Chancery says, and we both distinctly hear a ghostly woman's voice lilting out across the empty snowbound fields.

It's a sad and unearthly sound that chills me to my very bones, like the melancholy aria of some long dead soul wandering listlessly through eternity, and I grip Chancery's arm like a tourniquet.

"Oh bloody-fucking hell, the God-dammed place is haunted," I shriek like a girl. "We're about to meet fucking Betty Corrigall's ghost[37]!"

"Yeah, a ghost that's singing an S Club Seven song," Chancery snorts, and, as she speaks, the distinct sound of someone crooning "Reach for the sky..." comes floating across the frozen wastes to us.

"That's Lorna," I say in a bemused tone.

"It is. But where *is* she?" Chancery wonders aloud. "It's at least another mile to her house."

"It's coming from that field over there," I reply, following the sound along the deep drainage ditch at the side of the road.

"What would Lorna be doing in a field in the middle of the night?" Chancery demands, and I'm about to answer when the icy grass at my feet gives way to nothingness and I plunge headlong into the blackness of the ditch.

I expect to hit the bottom of the frozen ditch with a crump that will knock the breath out of me, but instead I land on something soft and, actually, quite warm, with a delicate aroma like night-scented flowers on a summer's evening. I am convinced that I must be severely concussed, when an arm encircles me and a woman's voice slurs, "Fuck me, it's my lucky night. Have a drink," and I hear Chancery's voice from above me shouting "Will you get out of there and pull Lorna out of the ditch before

---

37 - **Betty Corrigall:** In case you've forgotten, a Victorian farm girl from Hoy who fell pregnant to a sailor and killed herself, and whose remains were interred in an unmarked grave in the middle of nowhere. Keep up.

she freezes to death. She must have fallen in there on her way back home."

*

January is dark and cold and the howling gales never let up, but the kittens keep us fully occupied and their antics help to prevent us from falling headlong into the deep pit of depression that Orkney's long, lightless winters can invoke. Suki has fully recovered from her Indiana Jones journey on the underside of our car and plots more commando-style raids on our kitchen worktops with her brother, Sooty, who proves to be a more-than-willing accomplice, and we are always losing frozen meat left out to defrost.

Like all of their kind, however, they have already mastered the art of looking endearing when caught red-handed perpetrating some misdemeanour, and one of Sooty's favourite habits is to come and sit on my knee while I'm working at my new iMac[38]and then, when he gets too warm, climb up onto my desk and curl up and go to sleep on the mouse mat. This is fine when he's tiny, as there's room for me to keep working round him, but, as he starts to grow it soon becomes a battle of wills as to who'll crack first, and, of course, the cat always wins, despite my attempts at running the mouse over his back or clicking his tail, and I often find myself stopping work for an hour rather than moving him when he gets too comfortable.

Not that I'm spending too much time creating artwork at my desk these days. With the combination of being unable to get down to London to drum-up new business plus eBay dealing and decorating the new house, most of our days are spent peeling off mouldy old wallpaper from crumbling walls and illustration projects seem but a hazy memory, a state of affairs I constantly tell myself not to think about.

What has started out as a simple strip and paint operation has quickly turned into a full-scale renovation project, and we make up great buckets full of plaster each morning and try to get it to adhere to the walls in something remotely resembling smoothness. However, it's a craft that neither of us appears to possess any talent for, and both of us seem to end

---

38 - Another by-product of eBay money!

each day looking like low budget extras from Frosty the Snowman with no corresponding improvement to the general appearance of our new abode.

Nevertheless, the work progresses slowly and the living room is habitable by the time moving day looms on the horizon, but although we have been impersonating itinerant farm labourers from the Great Depression and heading over to the new place with boxes of books weighing down the boot and Triffid-like house plants flapping out of the back window, we have to face the fact that the combination of our own personal chattels plus all the stuff we have purchased for resale means we are over-burdened with paraphernalia which we will be unable to shift in one day without assistance.

We have always guarded our independence fiercely when it comes to such stressing and potentially inflammatory ventures as moving house, but it is clear that even if we could rent a truck – which we can't as there aren't any for hire on Orkney – there is no way that we are going to shift all our moveable stuff plus the additional sofas and chairs we have bought to accommodate our now frequent guests. And so, after much debate, we decide that we need the assistance of an organised and one hundred and one per cent reliable person, so ask the indomitable Roberta if she will assist us.

*

Moving day has started out badly and gets steadily worse as the afternoon progresses, and we are running two hours behind schedule when the reliable Roberta arrives on the dot of six. However, just as I'm about to heave a sigh of relief and welcome the cavalry a fury storms out of Philip's immaculate Peugeot, slamming the door violently behind her.

"He's a cunt, he's just a fucking cunt!" a distraught Roberta rages, throwing her arms around me. "Chancery, will you swap Max for him if I throw in my youngest and fifty pounds?"

"There, there, I'm sure it's not as bad as all that," I say, patting her back and disentangling myself from the sticky Octopus Woman that has crept into Roberta's bed and taken over her body during the night. "And who

are you, by the way, and what have you done with Roberta?"

"You're right," she fumes. "Living with fucking Philip's not that bad, it's fucking worse than bad. Why am I putting up with it? Why? Fuck, you pair have got plenty of spare rooms, I'll just go and get my stuff and move in with you!"

"Tell me she's joking," Chancery hisses through gritted teeth. "Philip, don't just stand there, come on up to the house."

Silent Philip has been cowering behind his car, waiting for an opportunity to dash for cover, and he quickly zigzags across the strip of no man's land to the safety of Chancery's orbit while Roberta continues to hurl abuse at him.

"That's right, run, you fucking cunt!" Roberta yells. "You're not so fucking brave now I've got my friends to help me, are you? And just wait till Henrietta gets here and she hears what you're really like, you'll not be fucking laughing then."

Chancery shoots me a venomous glance and whispers "You didn't ask bloody Henrietta to help as well, did you?" and I shake my head emphatically.

"I might be an idiot but I'm not stupid," I whisper back. "Roberta must have told her. But she'll probably not come, she doesn't usually show up if there's work involved."

"Pah!" Chancery spits. "She'll be here. Your little girlfriend won't miss the chance to make doe's eyes at you. Roberta, will you help me pack? And Philip, go over with Max in the van and start unloading."

*

Glad to be escaping, Silent Philip and I climb into the rusty old hire-van and drive over to the new house at Quoyloo in deeper than normal silence. There's something vaguely different about Philip's normally blank expression tonight that I can't quite put a finger on, but with a house-load of possessions still to be moved it's the last thing I want to be worried

about, and I'm, quite frankly, happy for the break from human interaction that the half hour drive affords.

A fine rain has started and it's being quickly whipped up into a downpour by the strong north-wester that's blowing in over the coast at Yesnaby, and by the time we reach Quoyloo the farmyard is already a sea of mud. Chancery and I have packed the van to the roof with furniture, including a heavy antique sideboard bought from the local auction mart, and Philip and I squelch through the quagmire in a strange sort of quadrille as the weight of the hefty dresser pulls us this way and that in the wind. It's only half past six in the evening, but it's already almost dark, and we lurch to and fro, crab-like, towards the house, guided only by a dim and flickering bulb above the back door, me walking in reverse and Philip's expressionless face a macabre death mask in the greeny-yellow light.

The sideboard weighs a ton, and there's nowhere clean or dry to lay it down for a moment's respite between the farmyard and the house, but we're almost at the door with our arms dropping off when something strange comes over Philip and he pushes heavily on his end and pins me against the house wall.

"You're no better than me," he declares in a peculiar toneless voice, his eyes glassy and not seeing me. "Just because you talk more, that doesn't make you my superior."

'Oh shit,' I think. 'He's flipped. I'm going to be murdered by a psychotic sideboard- wielding farmer in the middle of nowhere and they'll feed my body to the cattle in the morning to dispose of the evidence.'

It's as if Philip's suddenly making up for a lifetime of swallowed feelings, and I wonder just what Roberta could have said to him on the journey over to stir up the murky waters of his soul so violently.

"Philip, old friend," I say placatingly, an ornately carved acorn digging viciously into my gut, the weight of half a ton of solid oak crushing my ribs and making breathing difficult. "You're a great guy, everybody thinks so. Roberta's just goading you, don't take it to heart."

"You're damn right," he grunts, addressing not me but some procession of

long-dead family and probably the whole blood-line of Banquo's heirs for all I know. "I am a great person and don't you forget it."

"Right on," I croak. "Now let's move the sideboard a little to the left and we'll get it in the door, that's right, gosh you're a dab hand at the old removal game."

*

We arrive back in Finstown some three-quarters of an hour later, more-or-less intact, and Chancery greets me at the door, her face a mask of annoyance.

"Well, you were wrong, Mr Know-It-All," she says in the special low voice that she reserves for stressed-out occasions such as these. "Your little girlfriend just couldn't stay away," and I can hear the sound of Henrietta's dulcet tones listing a long litany of woes as I stagger down the hall towards the kitchen.

Roberta, her on-going row with Silent Philip now completely forgotten when faced with a logistics problem to solve, is not hearing her, however, and has become wholly absorbed in the task of organising our move like a military campaign. She has already constructed a neat row of packing cases, all colour-coded and stacked in precise order, but Henrietta, rather than pitching in to assist, is seated at the kitchen table with a mug of coffee in her hands, her big eyes on the brink of tears.

It's a sight that's normally guaranteed to have me rushing to her side to commiserate, but with the clock ticking and mountains of packing cases still to be shifted the novelty of playing the role of Prince Charming has palled.

"Hello, Darling," I say in as warm a tone as I can muster in the given circumstances. "You here to help?"

"If I can..." she replies, weakly, and I know immediately that we'll get nothing out of her all night. "It's just been such a difficult week"

"I know the feeling," I grunt, hefting up two neatly packed cartons. "Do you think you can manage a box or two?"

"Of course, I'm not crippled," she replies with some of her normal spirit, rising from the table. "Oh damn, I've forgotten my mover's gloves. Philip, give me a lift home to pick them up and we'll meet you at the new place, Max."

*

I pack the van single-handed and drive over to Quoyloo to find Henrietta and Silent Philip already installed, but, thankfully, the kettle's still at the old house so they haven't got too comfortable. Philip, however, is still wrestling with his inner demons after his row with Roberta and stands by the unlit kitchen range, his eyes blank and his jaw slack, his general stance resembling a pickled frog in formaldehyde, while Henrietta is surveying our progress with the décor like a between-the-wars English tourist examining Grecian ruins in the Mediterranean sun.

"Hi Guys!" I yell in a forced cheerful tone, keeping my hands behind my back to prevent me from slapping my own forehead. "Everyone ready to unload?"

"Sure thing," Henrietta calls back enthusiastically, apparently having experienced a complete volte face of mood, and follows me back to the van while Silent Philip continues to stand staring into space.

"Okay," I cry, burrowing into the back of the loaded vehicle in the pitch dark. "I'll dig the stuff out and you ferry it across to Philip..." when I become aware of muffled sobs coming out of the blackness of the farmyard.

"I'm sorry, I'm sorry," Henrietta sniffs. "I've just had such a shitty week..."

"There, there," I soothe robotically, trying not to mentally calculate how many van loads still remain at the old house. "Tell me all about it."

"Life's just so fucking shitty," Henrietta keens, falling into my arms and pinning me to the side of the vehicle as the full force of her eighteen stone impacts and knocks the breath out of me. "I'm such a fucking failure..."

"There, there," I say, kissing goodbye to any hope of getting finished before dawn next year. "You know that's not true, you're a highly successful business woman."

"A successful business woman who's thirty-nine and single," she sobs, a new torrent of tears soaking the last small dry area at the collar of my jacket that the rain's managed to miss. "Oh Max, why can't I just marry you?"

"There, there," I say again, leading her back into the house and sitting her at the kitchen table. "You need a drink. I think there's some alcohol in one of these boxes. Philip can you pass that one over to me?"

"I don't take orders from you," Silent Philip replies petulantly. "I'm a worthwhile person in my own right."

"Yes, yes, you are, you both are," I sigh, silently adding, "and, fuck me, this is going to be a *very* long night!"

CHAPTER 14 – WHERE I DECIDE TO RE-ENACT THE ATTACK OF THE FIFTY-FOOT BUG PEOPLE

In an effort to liberate more time for my creative work, I decide to apply for a high-paying job advertised in the local paper as a part-time Marketing Officer for something called the Biodiversity Records Office, and am duly summoned to the dusty corridors of a converted grey-stone schoolhouse in Kirkwall for an interview.

As I have no clue what biodiversity is I do extensive research for the interview in the form of a hasty Google-search fifteen minutes before going out to the appointment, and I cheerfully face my interview panel with nothing more than my winning smile and an exceptionally classy Hugo Boss tie in my arsenal.

However my sartorial prowess appears to fall on stony ground as the panel consists of two grey-haired, pragmatic-natured, tweed-clad Orcadian men in their mid-fifties, and a soft-spoken florid-faced English woman dressed in an exceptionally tatty old fleece and wellies, and I reckon it's a safe bet to assume that none of them have ever heard of the aforementioned Mr Boss.

With the tie out on the substitute's bench I become aware that all I have is my winning smile, and ten minutes into the fiasco I realise that even that's no good as I have absolutely no clue what anyone's talking about. The panel's sole female interrogator, when not talking in Latin, makes constant references to her "Raptor Records" – and I'm sure she's not a fan of Jurassic Park– while the other two earnestly discuss their "baps"[39]. However, although I am totally out of my depth, and am convinced that there is no way in hell that they will actually give me this job, I continue to waffle on regardless, and the meeting seems to stretch out for its allotted hour without trouble.

---

39 - Hindsight tells me that these are Biodiversity Action Plans and not burger buns!

I leave, mopping my brow and never expecting to hear from them again, unless, of course, they decide to take out a restraining order to prevent my coterie of designer ties from ever darkening their doors again, and I forget all about the position until the phone rings some three weeks later, just a few days after we've moved to Quoyloo.

"Hello," says a well-spoken Orcadian voice. "This is Alan from the Islands Council. I'd like to offer you the position of Marketing Officer for the Biodiversity Records Office."

*

A week later me and a very garish Versace tie show up suitably suited and booted at the council offices for my first day and I meet with Alan to determine how I will approach the project. The Biodiversity Records Office turns out to be a large archive of botanical and biological records dating back to the nineteenth century.

These have been in the possession of the Orkney Field Club but have now been transferred to a computer database and are being stored in the Library and funded by the Islands Council, who are seeking to recoup some of their outlay by selling data and reports to local businesses seeking planning applications. By culling money from various environmental bodies, the Council have found a handsome salary to pay me to work for them two days a week on a one year contract, and my job is to give an organisation that nobody's ever heard of a public profile.

The niceties dispensed with, the meeting breaks up and Alan, one of the men from my original interview, takes me over to the old Kirkwall library where I'm to be based. Now, ever since they first rang to say that I had got the job, I have been fantasising about what my office would look like[40], and I've already planned the décor in my head and catalogued the executive toys that I want to stand on my desk next to the high-powered matt black Apple Mac that they're sure to allocate me.

Needless to say I haven't really looked at my surroundings or taken in the fact that Kirkwall's library at this point in time is housed in one of the

---

40 - You're right, I need to get out more.

oldest public library buildings in Britain, and one look at its historic but exceedingly cramped bookshelves should have told me that being allotted a cupboard will be a major concession.

Alan, meanwhile, is leading me through dark, musty-smelling carrels and up some winding stone stairs to a museum-like mezzanine, and then up yet another twisty staircase to a dimly lit attic room that smells of damp and old paper, and which is filled to the roof with precarious towers of old school books, plastic anatomical skeletons and working models of Roman war machines.

"This is the educational resources library," Alan explains when he sees the look of total bewilderment on my face. "The Records Office is just through here."

"Ah-ha", I think smugly, "I'm getting a penthouse office up in an ivory tower where I can look down at the scurrying citizens of Kirkwall while I sit at my Power Mac and compose erudite marketing campaigns." And I'm still expecting Alan to open the door to my cosy den at any moment, although by this time I'm beginning to think that the entrance must be via the back of a magic wardrobe.

However we're still amongst the towering Hogwart-like stacks of academe when Alan comes to a halt at a rickety old desk, which is bare save for two out-of-the-ark grey computers, and says expansively, "This is it."

*

The trouble with local authority departments who don't have their own budget is that they're like orphan children in Victorian novels who have to take their relatives' hand-me-downs and be grateful. Thus it is with the Biodiversity Records Office, whose meagre budget has already been spent on a suite of highly temperamental database software and all its furniture and computers are all cast-offs from other – richer – departments in the council.

Alan, who's skilfully avoiding meeting my eye, ferrets busily under the desk for something that some long dead resident of the dark, badly-heated room has secreted many centuries before, and eventually pulls out a grey cardboard storage box and hands it gravely to me.

"Here," he says in the hearty avuncular tone of a genial old boy handing out prizes at his former Alma Mater. "I've kitted you out."

Stung with gratitude, I murmur my heartfelt thanks and take a cautious peek into the box, expecting a stuffed otter at the very least, but the carton merely contains a standard council staff survival kit, and although I have not been granted an office of my own, I at least now have my own stapler and hole-puncher.

"Well, I'll leave you to it," Alan says quickly, sensing imminent awkward questions, and with the practiced ease of one who has done this many, many times before, he slips between the musty book stacks and vanishes into the gloom of the old library.

*

With typical Orcadian friendliness, various members of the library staff come up to introduce themselves to me, but the person I'm really anxious to meet is a guy called Stanley who is the biodiversity technician and will be my partner for the year that I'm to be here. He's due at noon, and as the hour strikes sonorously on the cathedral clock outside, he appears out of the gloom, sniffing his way around his environment to see what I've disturbed, and eyes me warily.

"Hi, you must be Stanley," I say extending a hand in what I hope is a warm and friendly tone, and he inclines his head reservedly.

"Aye, and you'll be Max," he replies cautiously, ignoring my outstretched mitt. "That's my computer you're sitting at."

He's a tall thin man in his late forties with close-cropped thinning hair, a serious face and a suspicious demeanour; a farmer of few words but a passionate lepidopterist[41] who would probably do his job here for free if they ran out of wages to pay him.

---

41 - Lepidopterist: a butterfly and moth fanatic

Aware that our meeting is going pretty disastrously, I resolve that I'd better make the first overture, and I ask Stanley to show me the famed database, which is, after all, what he has been waiting for me to do, and after some token grumbling, he warms to his subject and opens the temperamental recording software that he has been having an illicit love-hate relationship with for the last two years.

There are, Stanley lectures, hundreds of different species of insect and plant life on the islands and the Recorders are the grubby old men who have been lying face down in muddy ditches dedicatedly cataloguing them for the past hundred years.

All their raw information has now been in-putted into Stanley's computer and the software, on its good days, is able to analyse the data and produce reports for either the whole island or specific map grid squares.
However, Stanley says, keeping his favourite party trick up his sleeve for his finale, the database can also generate species maps of the islands, and he prints out an outline drawing of the area covered in hundreds of little coloured dots indicating the spas and watering-holes of various dormice and other furry-footed miscellany.

"Wow," I say, clutching the still-wet document and hoping that I sound suitably impressed. "This is great... But why are there so many dots around here, is it a special environment?"

Stanley glances at the area I have indicated and laughs humourlessly. "Oh no," he says dryly. "That's where the Arachnid Recorder lives. He's old and he doesn't get very far from home these days."

*

I have been instructed to go and kiss the Papal rings of various members of the Orkney Field Club, a strange cognoscenti of environmentally-friendly retired science teachers from Buckinghamshire, whose sole claim to fame is that they seem to make up the entirety of Orkney's official Recorders – local people, it would appear, being incapable of documenting their own ecology. Thus, I spend the next few days driving up rutted farm tracks to out-of-the-way locations and calling on various Landrover-driving men in chunky Judith Glue sweaters who stare at me open-mouthed as if a fruit bat in a suit has walked into their offices.

I'm already reconciled to it being a very long year as I plod dutifully through the next few weeks, slowly learning the quirks and oddities of Biodiversity Recording before going out to pitch local businessmen on the benefits to the environment – and, of course, their pockets – in them obtaining a report from our department before embarking on any new development.

The locals are all curious about this strange Ferry Louper with the loud ties who's trying to gain access to their normally quiet citadels, and I am received warmly with cups of tea and typical Orcadian friendliness in most of the local construction companies' Portacabins as I flannel my way through elaborate sales pitches on the superior data we can supply.

However, I also discover that there are a surprisingly large number of "environmental companies" on the islands, and although I never quite work out what it is they actually do, I track these down by following the power leads from their windmills back to their eco-houses and try to persuade them all to incorporate a Records Office report into the packages they provide for their clients, but my receptions here are more mixed.

Most of these esoteric firms are run by fidgety incomers and, as well as being totally incurious about who I am, they are not nearly as polite or as well-balanced as their Orcadian counterparts, and I meet a lot more eccentrics behind these recycled storm-wood desks.

Some companies stonewall me completely and refuse to let me over their transoms or listen to their whale song CDs. A strapping six-foot redhead who works for the local branch of FWAG[42] snorts contemptuously at my suggestion that she would need a report and says that she can collect any information that she needs herself, and probably with one hand while she arm-wrestles the likes of me and my spiv suits with the other. And a haunted-eyed guy working from his fortified house up a two mile dirt track grasps my wrist maniacally while he tells me all about the gangs of thieves who are out to steal his enzymes.

---

42 - **FWAG**, officially the Farming and Wildlife Advisory Group but better known in the locale as "Farmers Without A Girlfriend"

However, all these rubicund specimens are only the kindergarten class and I finally celebrate my biological bar mitzvah when the good weather comes around and I'm introduced to the inner sanctum of hardcore Bugland – an immense, swarthy-skinned lady called Freida who resides deep within a damp, book-lined office in Stromness where she holds court over a quivering coterie of oceanography undergraduates like a bloated queen bee lording it over her pimply drones.

Stanley has mumbled something about publicising the annual Summer Classes and it appears that Freida's mission in life is the seeking out of tame academics and persuading them to come up to the islands to teach "field courses", and part of my duties as head marketing guy include getting saturation media coverage for these awesome gigs.

Obtaining mega-publicity will, of course, be a breeze, as this year's star-studded syllabus includes courses on "Know Your Pond Weed", "How to Identify Grasses by Their Seeds" – be still my beating heart – *and* Freida tells me in a breathless voice, they've actually managed to secure The Otter Detective this year and he'll be coming up to organise a two-day search for "spraints".

Now my imagination is already conjuring up pictures of great furry otters in deer-stalkers carrying magnifying glasses, but I quickly put a curb on this flight of fancy and ask politely for more details. However, I learn, disappointingly, that the great otter detective is neither an anthropomorphic mammal nor an infamous hard-boiled sleuth, but, in fact, just one of Freida's usual Landrover-driving men, only this one specialises in tracking otters by their spraints.

"Spraints?" I ask, still perplexed, and Freida nods vigorously.

"You mean otter shit?" I say baldly.

"Er... droppings, yes. It's the most reliable way to find an otter," Freida replies, a deep blush spreading over her multitude of chins.

"Well, there you go," I say, wondering if I can use her very blunt ornamental paper knife to deftly slit my writs and end it all quickly.

174

"Orkney won't know what's hit it. There's pond weed to study and otter crap to find. This is going to be the most sensational press release that I've ever submitted to The Orcadian," but my sarcasm's wasted on her and she just looks worried.

"Be careful what you say," she says anxiously. "We wouldn't want the courses to become over-subscribed."

*

Henrietta, who runs her own book-keeping and accountancy firm from her nineteenth-century farmhouse, rings me at work to ask if I can help with some graphic design ideas for a local company she is trying to woo, and she picks me up from home in her rusty old car the next day to go and make our combined pitch.

Although most major Orkney businesses are situated in Kirkwall, there are scores of independent companies dotted all over the island in old barns and sheds, and we chug away from the beaten track and along a twisty back lane in search of Henrietta's current prospect.

"You do realise that we're fanning the flames of incipient gossip here," I say as a couple of wellie-booted women in headscarves standing by a farm gate see us together and immediately furnish their own lurid back-story.

"God knows what they're going to have us out here doing."

"Do you care?" Henrietta asks as the narrow lane divides up in two even narrower tracks. "Shit, is it this road, or this one?"

"Don't ask me," I say. "I'm just a Ferry Louper. You're a born and bred Orcadian."

"I've only been here once before, and it was in winter and it looked different," she says, biting her lip. "No, it's this one... I think."

"You think?" I say as the little car noses its way down the very narrow track. "Don't you know?"

"Relax, Max, what do you think's going to happen? We're not going to get mugged by a gang of voles."

"Oh, I don't know, I've met some pretty belligerent voles in my time..." I start to retort when Henrietta's countenance suddenly goes a deathly white.

"Oh shit!" she exclaims. "We're at The Stone Caravan."

*

Much as I adore Henrietta I am well aware of her tendency to over-dramatise things, and I am, thus, not unduly worried that we have blundered into the wrong field, and wonder quite why my companion is so obviously put out.

The "Stone Caravan" in question is an old mobile home that looks as though it's been sitting in its field since about 1957, and some enterprising soul, in the days before rural planning permission, has thoughtfully encased it in an outer shell of breeze blocks to protect it from the winter gales. There is the usual Orkney spoil heap behind the structure; a pile of old tyres and a couple of abandoned motor vehicles to the front; and, more unusually, several weird and wonderful sculptures made from scrap metal, old toilet bowls, bits of driftwood and the ubiquitous Orkney baler twine.

Henrietta is exclaiming, "Oh shit, oh shit, oh shit!" as she searches desperately for a turning space on the narrow track, and when I ask her which particular island serial killer resides in the shanty she looks at me with wide, saucer-like eyes.

"The Hermit," she hisses, employing a delivery that should have Guy Madden[43] hopping on the next plane from Winnipeg to sign her up. "Have you never heard the stories about him?"

"Obviously not," I reply. "What's so terrible about him?"

---

43 - **Guy Madden:** Canadian art film-maker who emulates silent melodramas.

"Oh my God," Henrietta cries. "You've never heard of The Hermit? He's... well, he's... I mean, he's... Fuck it, he's just plain weird."

"Henrietta, half the island's weird, why are you singling this poor guy out?"

"Because he's *weird*, not engagingly eccentric. Oh fuck, fuck, fucketty fuck, there *has* to be somewhere to turn before he sees us."

"Up there," I say, pointing to a flattened out piece of ground ahead. "We can turn there."

"Oh thank God," Henrietta breathes, reversing deftly into the cramped space, then suddenly turning pale again as she beholds the adjoining rough grazing field.

"What?" I say, but she can only point, so I follow her gaze as the car rapidly turns around and starts to head back up onto the track, and I see, in the middle of the unkempt grassland, a tall elderly man with long straggly grey hair, playing the bagpipes. His dishevelled clothing furls out in the strong wind behind him like a banner, but his eyes appear to be closed, lost in his plaintive melody.

We should, of course, be on our way by now, but Henrietta's old car finds the muddy grass difficult to handle and the back wheels spin ineffectively, fighting for enough grip to propel us back onto the track. The Hermit obviously hears the sound of the labouring engine, however, as his eyes suddenly snap open and he begins to stride over towards us.

"Oh no, no, no, no, no!" Henrietta almost screams. "He's seen us. He's coming over."

"He probably just wants to lend us a hand," I say, trying to restore a sense of reality to the proceedings. "Hang on, I'll get out and push."

"No!" Henrietta yells, snapping all the locks shut. "No-one's going out there!"

"But..." I start to say, but she silences me with a stern yell of *"No-one!"*

The Hermit has reached the drystone dyke that separates the field from the track by now, just as the car's tyres find their grip and we begin to move again, and I can see him raise his hand in a sarcastic parody of a friendly wave as the car pulls away, and, winding down my window I hear him yelling to our departing backs,

"Yes, that's fine, use my private road to turn your environment-polluting petroleum-guzzler on. I don't mind at all while you consume all our natural resources. Never mind that this is against me and everything I stand for. I know you, and I know that that's what you and your like are all for doing..."

*

Elsewhere on the island a fish farm that's refused point blank to let me past their portals has a major disaster and their piscine cages burst and release thousands of tame salmon into the local waters. The whole place turns into an old Compton Mackenzie movie and all along the coast there seems to be people literally lifting five-pound salmon out of the water, and scare and counter-scare stories about the safety of eating or not eating the free fish abound.

As the weather improves we can actually sit on our porch and listen to the sea crashing against the Marwick cliffs on the cold but beautiful summer evenings. Our new house at Quoyloo is within easy walking distance of the scenic Bay of Skaill and a fifteen minute cycle to the Cornwall-like Brough of Birsay, and, when we have wind-free days, we go out and walk along some of Orkney's most magnificent coastline.

Kevan has made good his promise and delivered a fragrant old ram called Megabyte to keep our grass cut, but unfortunately the hungry herbivore also eats all the rose bushes in the lumpy garden before finding the rhubarb patch and making short work of that too. So we relegate him to the large grass area at the side of the house and buy a lawn mower to take care of anything that might reasonably be described as cultivated.

The cats, too, like their new home and tend to head out for the great outdoors as soon as it's twilight and we don't really see them again till the small hours when, like little vampires, they return with the light and wake me at five in the morning howling on our bedroom windowsill. Sooty quickly learns that he can get in by simply clambering up to the open top window, and although the squeal of cat paws down the glass tends to break our sleep it's not a major inconvenience, but Suki, on the other hand, will tolerate no such neglect of correct feline protocol and howls doggedly on the windowsill until I stumble, usually naked, out to the porch door to let her in properly.

Both of them, of course, insist on walking all over our bed and greeting us formally on their return, which is bad enough, but if they've been prowling in the nearby byres they smell strongly of cattle and there's nothing to compete with the sensation a manure-scented feline flopping down on your pillow and licking your face at half past five in the morning.

*

Back in Biodiversityworld the fleeting summer quickly runs its course as I put on slide presentations for businesses and become Uncle Peter's Nature Notes and contribute numerous articles on everything from seagulls to pond weed to The Orcadian. I am also frequently heard talking about the environment, usually through a hole in my head, on Radio Orkney and sounding, to my mind, like a complete dork, but it all has the desired effect and the name of the Records Office slowly finds its way into the island's vocabulary; and we are even rushed in like the bomb disposal squad when the local supermarket finds an exotic beetle in one of their banana boxes.

However, as the all-too-brief August draws to its conclusion I find that I'm now expected to host part of a Biodiversity Day at Orkney's annual Science Festival in September, and I decide to promote a one hour "practical workshop" on biological recording and round up various tame bug-people and persuade them all to bring glass tanks full of their pet dung beetles.

The response to this idea is extremely positive, however, and nearly everyone I approach seems more than willing to flaunt their pets in public, so, confident that I have a huge and varied dramatis personae for my gig, I duly show up at the venue on the day in question and find a cast of absolutely nobody assembled at our appointed meeting place.

Petrified that I will have to perform the show alone and flannel to a room of scientists for a full hour, I go off in frantic search of my fleet of missing bugophiles, and, when my exhaustive investigation yields a blank, I collar one of the festival stewards in the hope of finding my lost recorders safely tucked away on a shelf somewhere.

"So, sonny, you say you've lost *twelve* people?" the sandy-bearded man says with a withering stare and a deliberate slowness calculated to irk me beyond belief. "Is it your mother and all your aunties that are missing, or just someone completely unrelated to you?"

"It's a group of biologists," I snap back, trying my hardest to remain calm while horrible pictures of angry people in white lab coats throwing petri dishes full of rancid bacteria at me flash through my mind. "They shouldn't be too hard to find, they're a bunch of fat old guys in anoraks carrying tanks full of slime."

"Uh-huh," the steward says slowly, surveying a roomful of fat men in anoraks bustling around with jars full of creepy-crawlies. "Could you maybe be a bit more specific in your description?"

"Sorely tempted as I am..." I say through gritted teeth, "I clearly need to send for Spiderman," and frantically punching numbers into my mobile, I heave a sigh of relief when I hear Stanley's flat tones at the other end of the line.

"Hello, it's me, are you here?" I gasp.

"Aye, weel," he replies evasively. "That'll depend on who you are and where you might be."

"Oh don't fuck me around, Stanley," I snap. "I'm at the hall and there's not a bugger in sight – including you!"

"Aye, that's right. We're having a coffee."

"You're having coffee?" I almost yell. "Where? The Seattle Starbucks?"

"No, we're at the St Magnus canteen," Stanley says with unflappable farmer calm; "Don't worry, we'll all be there in time," and then summarily hangs up on me.

Spiderman's got it all under control then?" the ginger steward enquires scathingly.

"I don't know that I can stand another four months of this," I reply to no-one in particular, and go off to find a secluded corner to bang my head quietly against a wall.

CHAPTER 15 - WHERE STORM CLOUDS BEGIN TO GATHER ON THE HORIZON

On the bitterly cold St Valentine's day of February 2003 I jubilantly leave the dusty carrels of the Biodiversity Records Office for what I think is the last time. Hoping never to have to use another acronym again, I head for home content to finally finish decorating the upper floor of the house and maybe even pick up a pencil and do some artwork, neglecting, in my euphoria, to change all the locks on our doors and procure a new phone number.

Thus I have barely shaken the scent of musty specimen-cases off my clothes when I get a call from a bouncy and ever-so-slightly-hyper lady called Nadine, a displaced Canadian who is the school biodiversity officer for Orkney. I'm standing there mystified, with a dripping paint roller in one hand, wondering why in hell this woman has decided to pick up a phone and contact me when I no longer work for the council, when Nadine finally gets to the reason for her call.

It would appear that the Department of Education has discovered a budget surplus which they are desperate to spend before the conclusion of the financial year, six weeks from now, and the wily Iroquoian proposes to splurge all her superfluous bucks on a biodiversity super-website complete with detailed species tables and records of all known Orkney habitats and plant groupings. I'm thinking 'Fuck me, that's a brain-numbing job-and-a-half for some poor rube', when I hear that good- old people-pleasing part of myself saying, "Golly. That sounds like a really exciting project. Yes, of course I'll be your webmaster."

*

I'm sitting in Chancery's half-decorated study five minutes later with my head in my hands, pulling out what little hair I have left and wailing, "Why can't I learn to just say no to people?" when there's the sound of heavy footsteps at our front door and Roberta's voice booms up the stairwell, yelling, "Hello! Are you up there? It's just me. I need a favour."

Chancery pointedly drops her paint roller into the paint tray, covering me

in a fine spray of white emulsion and hisses, "Time to practice saying no!" as she hurries down the stairs to greet Roberta, whose cloudy countenance does little to support my desperate wish that she wants a hand moving some furniture, and my vain hopes are quickly dashed to pieces when tea is poured and Roberta intimates the nature of her request.

"You know that me and him ben the hoose[44]aren't getting along too well," Roberta begins, in what must be the understatement of the century, since her and Silent Philip's public rows have already become legend. "And I think it's time that I did something about it."

"Sure," I commiserate. "Do you want us to suss out a good divorce lawyer for you?"

"No," Roberta says baldly. "I want the two of you to come to marriage guidance with me."

I gape like a goldfish and Chancery drops her cup to the floor with a deafening crash, wet liquid and shards of bone china going everywhere, and she darts through to the kitchen to get a cloth.

"You want us to what?" I say, aghast.

"Come to marriage guidance," Roberta says again, slowly and bleakly. "There's no councillor here so we're getting a video link to one in Inverness, and they said we could each have a support buddy, and Henrietta says she's not up to the task, so..."

Chancery returns with a bucket and a roll of kitchen towel, the latter of which she drops pointedly in my lap, and I can read the hastily scrawled words "No, no, NO!" on it, and, I must admit, four root canals without anaesthetic sound infinitely more appealing than wading into this particular swamp right now, but poor Roberta looks so miserable and woebegone that all my resolve melts and I hear myself saying, "Of course we'll come. When's your meeting?"

*

---

44 - **him ben the hoose:** him indoors

The Orkney counselling centre is housed in a small grey stone terraced house in a back street of Kirkwall, and the room we are shown into has two armchairs arranged around a TV set at one end for the real clients, and a neat row of hard, cast-plastic bucket chairs for the support teams at the other. A video camera with a big mike sits on top of the television, and there's a mega-size box of paper tissues on the floor by the chairs, making me wonder if they use the room as a sperm bank during the day.

Roberta and Silent Philip are already installed in the armchairs when we arrive, and an iron-haired old lady, Philip's auntie, we later discover, sits rigidly in the support area, her arms tightly crossed and her countenance frosty.

"I suppose this is better than writing a Dear Margie letter to Woman's Own," Chancery whispers. "But only just."

I nod my agreement, just as the television comes on and the councillor appears, a strange old woman with harshly dyed hair wearing a 1980s' jacket with shoulder pads, and Roberta immediately begins to talk, the video camera somewhat disconcertingly detecting her voice and swivelling over to her.

The councillor smiles beneficently, dings a Tibetan brass bowl and makes a quietening gesture which stops Roberta mid-flow, then proceeds to put the couple through fifteen minutes of breathing exercises which irritate Roberta intensely and mortify Silent Philip beyond belief.

"Now, dears," she says in the voice that the mail order company who provided her diploma told her was caring. "Why can't you two lovely people get along?"

"Because he's cold, unloving, uncaring, selfish, inconsiderate and a bully," Roberta blurts out in a voice raw with naked hurt. "And he loves his fucking cats more than me!"

"My my," tuts the councillor. "Philip, dear, how many pussy cats do you have?"

Philip makes a strangulated sound and the camera swivels round to him expectantly, which causes him to blush furiously.

"What was that, dear?" the old woman asks.

"Two," Philip mutters into his socks and Roberta makes a derisive snorting noise.

"Well, dear," she asks, "why do you think Roberta feels threatened by your little pussy cats?" But Philip seems unable to answer this one and simply shrugs his shoulders.

"Because he'd tuck them into bed with him at night if I fucking let him," Roberta blurts. "After an evening of treating me like I'm invisible."

"Oh dear, you poor thing," the councillor coos. "But not to worry, I've got the perfect solution for you both."

"Fuck me, that was quick," Chancery whispers and gets a glare from Philip's auntie.

"Philip, dear, you've two pussy cats," she goes on. "Why don't you get one of the wee darlings re-homed, that way you can devote some more of your time to Roberta. How does that sound to the two of you?"

Both parties begin speaking at once, which really confuses the camera, with Philip adamantly shaking his head and saying that he's not parting with either of his cats and Roberta yelling, "What? That's it? You're fucking kidding me." And pandemonium reigns until the councillor strikes her brass bowl again, a tad more stridently than the first time.

"Well, I've tried. So help me, I've tried, dears," she says in her hurt-but-not-angry voice. "But it's no use, you're irreconcilable, and there's nothing more I can do for you," and, without so much as another ding of her Tibetan bowl, she makes a dismissive gesture and her image fades from the screen.

"Guess they should have bought Divorce for Dummies after all," Chancery says quietly.

The drab and gale-swept March is now almost over, but this year's interminable winter just doesn't want to go away, and we pace our rooms like caged animals, desperate for a break in the punishing weather so that we can stretch our legs and go out and walk along the beach. My proposed illustration come-back has been postponed yet again as designing Nadine's wonder-website keeps me exceptionally busy, and my days are spent grumbling in my studio, transcribing pages and pages of exceedingly dry data into readable content and graphics, while the chirpy Canadian seems grimly determined to become my new best friend.

I have always worked to a strict ethic of not mixing my clients with my social life and I'm really not a hundred per cent sure about this, but after six weeks of lengthy meetings and innumerable cups of coffee in Kirkwall restaurants, Nadine decides that it's high time we met each other's spouses, and invites Chancery and I to dinner back at her flat to meet her husband, Malcolm, a professional magician whose career has taken an understandable nose-dive since he was dragged, screaming, up to Orkney in her wake.

A strangely child-like young man, dressed in a checked shirt, gaudy braces and trousers that are too short for him, answers our ring on the night in question and ushers us inside with slightly forced bonhomie.

"Hello, Hello," he gushes in a strange Anglo-American accent, offering an outstretched hand. "You must be Max and Chancery. I'm Malcolm, Nadine's hubby. Whoops. What's this? There was a coin behind your ear, Chancery. Oh no, it's turned into a flower. Help. Oh no, now it's in Max's pocket..."

"Malcolm!" Nadine's voice bellows from the kitchen, "Would you stop doing those God-damned magic tricks."

"Sure, Honey," he calls back, showing me to a chair, and almost collapsing with laughter when a loud farting sound rings out.

"Whoopee cushion!" he roars, "It works every time."

"Gosh, you are a prankster," I say dryly, "You must be a big hit at kiddies' parties."

Malcolm's rubbery-smiley face clouds. "I'm a close-up magic professional," he says very slowly, "I don't do 'kiddies' parties',"

"Of course you don't," I say, swallowing hastily. "Gosh, Nadine, what *are* you cooking? That does smell good!"

*

Meanwhile, twenty-first century Orkney is finally catching up with 1950s America and the island's first bowling alley opens in a converted industrial unit on the outskirts of Kirkwall, and when I'm creating more gossip by dancing cheek-to-cheek with Henrietta at yet another traditional dance ceilidh, she suggests that we all have a change of culture and organise a group outing to go and check it out.

I've been expecting some sort of Rockwell retro joint with a milkshake bar and Thelma Ritter-style waitresses on roller skates, but am quickly disillusioned when we thread our way through lanes of parked fish trucks and enter the palace of pleasure, only to discover an austere aeroplane hanger on the outer edge of Kirkwall's lorry park. The attraction has only been open for a few weeks, but its ascetic decorations are already scruffy and, although licensing laws govern the amount of unaccompanied children inside, the dimly-lit foyer areas are packed with amusement machines and, subsequently, are teeming with Kirkwall's spotty disaffected youth.

It should be emphatically stated at this point that in Orkney it's still possible to shell out £5 for a dance ticket and be served up half a cow and a stone of potatoes, plus get your evening's entertainment without any further delving into your purse, so when the girl in the little ticket booth asks us for fifteen pounds a head and then tells us there will be an additional fee to hire shoes, a cold shudder runs through our merry band of would-be bowlers. Henrietta's face takes on a pinched expression as she hisses "Stall them" into my ear and dashes quickly over to the cash machine; and James and Jasper, who have made parsimony into a religion,

are haunted-eyed with shock.

*

"So what do we actually *do* here," I ask, tying the laces on my strange teal and white bowling shoes. "Form teams or what?"

"Oh my, is it teams we're doing?" Jasper pipes up in his high falsetto. "James can go up against me if he likes. As hard as he wants."

"Jasper!" James admonishes, scarlet-faced. "You're going too far."

"Shut up the pair of you," Roberta snaps, taking control. "Max, Chancery, Henrietta, you're with me; James and Jasper, you can have this useless bastard here. Come on, team, let's go get ready."

*

I'm really never going to enjoy sporty pursuits, so the fact that I cannot fathom what the Americans see in this amusement is no surprise, but tonight's extra-marital tensions give the game an added piquancy that it would probably otherwise lack, and things start badly and just get generally worse and worse.

Jasper is apparently in the frisky phase of his lunar cycle and spends the entire evening flirting shamelessly with the blushing James, and Roberta and Silent Philip, who have very obviously had a row on the way here, seem determined to turn the entire evening into a sniping match, and Roberta promptly gets her team into a huddle where she makes an ostentatious show of groping my behind in full view of Philip as she instructs us all in our tactics.

"Okay," she commands, with no trace of humour in her tone. "James and Jasper are a pair of girls and Philip's got it coming, so let's publicly humiliate these fuckers and make them wish they'd never been born. Philip, are you tossing for the boys?"

Silent Philip snorts derisively and flips a coin into the air and Roberta shouts, "Head, something you wouldn't know anything about." But the

coin falls tails up and Philip bowls first, demonstrating an unexpected skill for the game and scoring a strike on his first bowl.

"Gosh, everything lying down flat," Roberta says nastily. "No surprises there then. Go on, Max, you're next, you're sure to have something upstanding after a session with me."

Chancery casts her eyes heavenwards as I heft one of the large fluorescent pink plastic balls towards the runway.

"The trick is to push your finger really deep into the hole," Roberta says in a perfectly audible whisper, glaring at Silent Philip. "Some people can't seem to manage even that."

"Okay, now what?" I say, ignoring her jibe and swinging the heavy bowling ball experimentally, making a party of diminutive farm-wives in the next lane look exceedingly nervous.

"Just roll it down the lane," Henrietta hastily interjects before Roberta can think up any more barbs. "Try to knock down as many skittles as you can."

"Right," I say, setting my face in what I hope is a suitably butch bowling expression. "I can do that. I think. Here goes nothing," and I swing the ball towards the end of the alley, but unfortunately forget to let go and fall flat on my face.

"Out!" Philip calls with a satisfied smirk.

CHAPTER 16 – WHERE WE ADMIT THAT WE MAY WANT TO LOOK BEYOND OUR PRESENT HORIZONS

Nadine and Malcolm, our Canadian friends, arrived in Orkney via a long stay in Japan and then a position in Poland, which they journeyed to by train across Russia and then through Estonia, Latvia and Lithuania to spend a year in volatile Warsaw – and their story makes our own epic journey to the isles up the length of the United Kingdom suddenly feel like a kindergarten day out.

Thus, on a grey and windswept April morning, Chancery turns to me and says, quite simply, "We've been here almost five years now, I think it's time we thought about moving on..." and I reply equally tonelessly, "Yes it is," before we both say in unison, "But where on earth do we go?"

There is a long moment's pause that Harold Pinter would be proud of, and then, as the wind blows sleety rain against the windows, Chancery speaks again.

"I think we need to talk," she says quietly, and I nod.

"Where?" I ask.

"I think you know," Chancery replies.

*

The Pomona Café in Kirkwall is a cramped little cheese-and-chips bistro with rickety old Art Deco tables and ancient grease-stained frescos of Orcadian Scenes on its grimy walls, and is one of the cheapest places to eat on the island. It's one of the few cafes left in the locale that still permits smoking, and entering its oily bower is like venturing into a thick fug of smoke and chip fat, but, on a cold and rainy day in pre-tourist April, it is almost deserted and the perfect place to sit and talk without distraction.

A group of scary old ladies known locally as "The Coven" occupy their

customary top table where they are snorting black tea and chain-smoking for Europe, and a couple of early Twitchers are huddled by the fire eating gigantic mince rolls, so we arm ourselves with enormous rock buns and decamp to the furthermost corner of the restaurant to decide our future fate.

"I really can't go back to living in another flat in yet another industrial city," I start, unpromisingly. "I can't stand all that crime and neighbour noise again."

"So did you have some other plan in mind?" Chancery asks quietly.

"Yes," I say, taking a deep breath and swallowing uncomfortably as I finally give voice to the life-plan that has been buried deep within me for several months now. "I want to try living in Mexico. I think that we could be happy there."

With the M-word out in the open now and unretractable, I look across at Chancery, expecting to hear the same string of objections from her that I have been providing for myself since I first fell in love with the notion of a life spent devoted to my painting in a land of flame-red bougainvillea and Frieda-Kahlo-blue adobe houses.

However, instead of the expected litany of 'How would we get there?'; 'What would we do for money?'; 'How would we communicate, we can't speak Spanish?'; Chancery simply nods and says, "Yes, that would be worth checking out, wouldn't it."

*

Chancery is sitting by the fire with a stack of books on Mexico for Your Golden Years at half past eight on a chilly evening in late April when headlights sweep round the farm gate and Rhona's Volkswagen threads its way through the muddy yard and comes to rest outside our house. I've been quietly doing a jigsaw puzzle Constable's The Hay Wain, ostensibly to de-stress and relax, but, after over an hour of trying to make sense of some eight hundred pieces of miscellaneous sky and water my mood is closer to foul than Zen. Chancery, likewise, is in an equally irate frame of mind after trying to decipher an impenetrable book on Mexican visas, so

we both welcome the interruption and Chancery goes out to the kitchen door to receive the twins.

"Aye-aye, whit like?" Shona chirrups as she bustles into the room, dressed in a heavy monogrammed sweater and denims, "Are you pair busy or do you feel like a peedie jaunt?"

"Aye, Shona's got a new love in her life and she needs some new skimpy knickers," a similarly clad Rhona interrupts, receiving a well-aimed kick in the ankle from her twin. "So we're off to the fifty-fifty shop. Do you two want to come along?"

"It's nearly nine o'clock, Rhona," I say from behind my jigsaw puzzle, like somebody's fuddy-duddy old dad in his button-up cardie hinting that such an activity is surely unsuitable for a school night. "Will the shop not be shut by now?"

The twins, however, just laugh as it seems that the emporium in question opens whenever there are customers at its door, and so we quickly grab our jackets and bundle into Rhona's car, where a strange hunched figure sits crouched in the back seat, almost invisible in the twilight gloom, his face lit eerily by the greenish light from his Gameboy.

"Aye-aye, Sean," I say in the local patois, squeezing in beside him. "How's you?"

"You wouldn't ask," he says glumly, his face weary and long-suffering, "if you knew where we were going."

"I do know where we're going," I say, a little of my self-confidence already beginning to evaporate. "The fifty-fifty shop."

Sean shakes his head. "Be afraid," he says portentously. "Be very afraid."

*

Darkness is beginning to fall as Rhona's loaded car creeps down a narrow country lane and then turns sharply up a rutted farm track and eventually pulls up at a large, jerry-built structure that looks like a cross between a

medieval tithe-barn and the Witch-Finder General's castle. I'm still naively looking for a shop, but the twins, with the knowledge of those who have been here many times before, simply stride confidently up to the unlocked door and walk in.

It's pitch dark inside and smells like something crawled in to die two centuries previously, but Rhona reaches for a hidden switch with an experienced hand and a dim strip light flickers into being, illuminating a large, low-ceilinged shed that's piled up to the roof with twenty tons of old clothing and shoes. There are homemade hanging racks made out of old electric lamp-flex along all the walls, groaning under the weight of suits and dresses, and the floor and shelves are stacked with hundreds of crates and boxes overflowing with everything from old wellie boots to ancient wedding dresses.

The Dickensian hovel is deserted, however, and there doesn't appear to be a shopkeeper anywhere in sight, and I have never been able to get comfortable with the Orkney custom of just walking into people's houses unannounced, so I ask Rhona if we should ring a bell or something, but she just gives me one of her cognoscenti smiles and says that "they" will know that we're here.

Sure enough, a secret panel slides silently back on oiled wheels from behind one of the many coat racks, and a pair of hausfraus straight out of a pre-Bowdler Grimm's fairy tale sidle through the fabric minefield and take their place behind a battered glass counter, apparently unperturbed at being called away from their supper of small children's barbequed body parts.

"Well, is it no' Rhona and Peedie Shona?" the older of the two ogresses intones in a voice as ancient and cracked as hundred-year-old Scapa whisky being poured over sand and gravel. "How's you mother and your Uncle Howie? Is he still getting that trouble from the piles now that he's had that new ointment?"

"Aye, tell him we'll easy distil him some hen's blood," the younger of the two interjects. "It'll clear it up faster than anything the doctor'll give him." The older woman shushes her daughter and glances in our direction. "Hush, Ola," she says. "Rhona, who's this you've brought with you

tonight?"

'Oh fuck,' I think. 'This is it, the twins have only pretended to be friends with us so that we could be fattened up to be eaten by this cannibal coven. The place is full of the discarded clothing of all their previous victims, I'll uncover the bones at any moment,' and I almost flinch as Shona pulls me gently into the pool of dim light around the old glass counter, which I now see holds long-forgotten children's toys from the 1980s and earlier, still nestled in their crumpled cardboard cartons.

"This is Max and Chancery," Rhona says by way of introduction. "They're good friends of ours."

"Hmmm, Soothies," the older woman mutters.

"And have you been in Orkney long?" the daughter asks, looking me up and down like a crooked mortician sizing up a poor-house corpse, but her countenance brightens when she hears just how many years we have actually resided in the locality.

"Aye, weel, I've known Rhona and Peedie Shona since they were both squalling bairns," the mother says grudgingly. "Have a look aboot the place. There's lots to choose from."

She sweeps a ham-shank hand expansively across the vista of her universe, and I look at the unappetising acres of mouldering fabric spread out before me with a creeping sense of dread.

"Where do they buy all this crap from?" I whisper to Shona as she steers me through the swamp of dead people's effects with a practiced hand.

"Oh they don't buy it," Shona replies in the explaining-things-to-the-idiot voice that she reserves especially for me. "Folk bring it in for them and they go fifty-fifty on the sale price. That's why it's called a fifty-fifty shop. There are lots of fifty-fifty places here."

"Oh," I say. "But judging by the age of some of this stuff the original owners must be long dead and unlikely to ever claim their portion of the profits."

"Oh no," Shona replies matter-of-factly. "It's all written down in the book, their families can still collect their money."

*

Even though the weather's improving outside, the shop is exceedingly damp and the smell of mould is overpowering, and after fifteen minutes I'm in dire need of fresh air and about to suggest leaving when the twins, who are just ahead of us, appear to lean against a rack of fusty old coats and suddenly vanish.

"Oh holy fuck! My instincts were right," I whisper panic-strickenly to Chancery. "They've fallen down a trapdoor to the dungeon."

"You really need to get out more," Chancery says dryly, pushing ahead through the fabric jungle to where the twins were last sighted and promptly vanishes as well.

*

I plough quickly through the undergrowth to the abduction point and find Sean, pecking disconsolately at the controls of his Gameboy, seated on a large tea-chest full of old sticking-plaster-coloured corsetry.

"Where *is* everyone?" I demand, but he merely inclines his head laconically towards the aforementioned rack of overcoats.

I part the malodorous sealskin wraps gingerly and discover a narrow hatch beneath, and, hearing voices, crawl quickly inside to the shop's inner sanctum, a narrow, low-ceilinged wood-plank lean-to with no windows and a single bare bulb hanging from a tacked-on wire. This room, like the outer atrium, is also piled to the roof with aged Gortex, and Rhona and Shona have found an old seaman's chest full of boots dating back to some previous decade's Great Universal Catalogue, and they are eagerly fighting over their spoils like Dracula's brides dismembering a still-warm corpse in some ancient Hammer blood-letting extravaganza.

"Oh look, Max's come through to see if we're trying on knickers," Rhona

giggles as my head appears through the trapdoor in full hero mode, my countenance wearing its ready-to-take-on-all-alien abductors expression. "Do you go for peedie thongs or full-leg, Max?"

Chancery shakes her head and the twins dissolve into fits of giggles at their own humour, and I decide that the best thing I can do is finally admit defeat and beat a retreat.

"I think I'll go and sit with Sean," I say, and leaving Narnia behind, disappear back into the main body of the store where Sean sits with a glum patience that's unique to small boys.

"I told you to be afraid," he says wearily.

*

Orkney's grumbling ex-pat community are thrown into an unprecedented fervour of panic in early May when it is suddenly announced that Kirkwall's oldest grocers, Cumming and Spence, have been put up for sale. And the following Thursday's Orcadian then proceeds to run a scare story saying that a buyer for the business has not been forthcoming and hints at the ancient retailer's possible closure.

This is devastating news for all the Ferry Louper Townships, as all city refugees inevitably find themselves involved in an intense relationship with this dimly-lit, quaintly Edwardian emporium that stocks all the products that ex-patriot émigrés wantonly crave, making Cumming and Spence the outsider's premier port of call when the thrill of getting away from it all first begins to pall, and the store's possible closure sends a wave of dread rippling through our ranks.

Being myself disinclined to drink the conventional Typhoo tea that the local supermarket stocks, I throw the predictable tantrum and then proceed to drive poor Chancery to distraction by pacing from room to room loudly despairing of ever finding another packet of Rooibos tea on "this Godforsaken island" ever again, but it is our Canadian cousin, Nadine, of all people, who puts forward a more practical solution to the problem the next day.

I go into her office for our normal Friday morning meeting, expecting to be given yet another exciting fifty-page file on seagull's wingspans, but instead find her hopping up and down with excitement, and, after quickly getting the boring work out of the way, she proudly unveils her new business plan to me.

Nadine proposes to buy the moribund Cumming and Spence and convert it into a whole-food supermarket and provide a marketplace for the rapidly growing numbers of Orkney's organic farmers. On paper, it's a really great scheme and something that's much needed in the community, but the cost of her proposal is about one and a half million pounds and I'm curious to know how someone of her resources plans to lay hold of a sum of this magnitude.

Nadine, however, is well ahead of me and, using her credit card, has already employed a lawyer to investigate grants on her behalf, plus a special accountant to help her prepare a business plan for her enterprise.

*

The phone wakes me just before seven on Monday morning and I answer to some unfamiliar person who seems to be demanding my presence at Kirkwall Airport. I shake my head violently to de-grog myself and ask the caller to start again from the beginning, slowly, and, as the mists clear, I suddenly recognise Nadine's dulcet tones at the other end of the wire.

"Nadine, what the fuck are you doing calling me at this hour?" I grumble. "You know I don't do mornings."

"Max, you're not listening to me," she remonstrates. "I told you, I need you."

"Sorry?" I mutter. "Start again."

Nadine sighs. "I've hired a retail consultant to come and view the store and approve my business plan before it goes to the bank, and he gets in at eight-fifteen this morning. Malcolm's going to be at the Brough of Birsay[45]all day, and he can't come with me, so I need you to be my Back Up Guy."

"Hold on," I say blearily. "I'm still not getting this. What's Malcolm doing at the Brough of Birsay at this hour of the morning?"

"I told you, he's working there for the summer."

"He's doing a magic show at eight in the morning? Won't the tide be in?" I ask stupidly.

"No, dummkopf, he's not doing a show. He's the summer custodian of the Neolithic village."

"Christ. That's the job from hell. Why's he doing that?"

"Oh, he loves it. He spends the time he's cut off by the tide doing magic and perfecting his meditation," Nadine explains proudly, as if justifying the eccentricity of her five-year-old child. "Anyway, I'll brief you later. Get your butt down to the airport for eight and I'll fill you in. And Max..."

"Yeah, what?"

"This is major league stuff, wear a suit."

*

We make a slightly incongruous pair, standing in the tiny arrivals lounge watching the early morning passengers filing off the miniature aeroplane that sits silver and gleaming on the tarmac in the early morning sun. Nadine is in her customary bright orange designer anorak that is rumoured to have cost her several hundred pounds in a Stockholm boutique, while I am resplendent in the best Armani copy my wardrobe can boast, both of us anxious to make a good impression on the extremely costly consultant from England who is, even unseen, burning a hole in Nadine's credit card at an alarming rate.

"Just how much is this guy costing you?" I ask as we survey the stream of

---

45 - **Brough of Birsay:** a tiny promontory on the West Mainland which is cut off by the tide for approximately half of each day

scruffy denim-clad oil men headed for the refinery at Flotta.

"A thousand pounds a day. Plus expenses."

"Fucking hell," I splutter. "What's his pedigree? Harrods?"

"Not quite," Nadine replies, slightly uncomfortably. "Asda."

"Fucking hell," I splutter again. "Are you sure he's on this flight? I'm not seeing any thousand quid suits here."

"I sure as hell hope so," Nadine says. "I paid for his God-damned ticket."

As if in answer, a runtish oik in a baggy-arsed £59.99 suit with a cheap anorak slung over it walks up to my companion and extends a bony hand.

"Nadine? I'm George, from Retail-dot-com. Pleased to meet you."

*

Introductions have barely been made when Asda George looks sideways at Nadine's jacket and casts his eyes heavenwards, and when we walk over to her bright yellow Skoda in the car park outside he snickers loudly into his £2.99 anorak and sneers, "I thought you had to be one of them with all this pinko organic stuff. The car says it all, doesn't it."

Nadine flashes him a look while I raise my eyebrows at her in the mirror from the back seat, and we're barely into the new-build estates on the outskirts of Kirkwall when George sees fit to share his opinions with us again.

"Flippin' heck, they've got houses," he observes. "That's progressive."

"What were you expecting?" I enquire in my most civil tone. "Mud huts?"

Asda George laughs. "No pulling my leg, lad, I know there's no mud huts up here."

"But you're surprised at houses," Nadine says. "What *were* you

expecting?"

"Wood shacks," George replies, puffing up his shoulders and trying to fill-out his jerkin. "Right proper shacks with creosote walls and fishing nets on the roofs."

"Oh yes," I say dryly. "They have those at Stromness."

"Aye, right proper," he replies, gazing out at the newly opened library and space-agey sports centre. "This is good stuff for Scotland, this. Did they bring in German labour to show them how it's done?"

*

We pull up in the small car park behind Cumming and Spence and George gets out and stretches his legs, gazing unbelievingly at the old grocers' original eighteenth century stone façade and Edwardian carved-wood doorway.

"Is this it?" he asks incredulously. "That'll all have to come down, that will, get some glass in there, and rack lighting and a polymer floor..."

Nadine and I look at each other as Asda George goes into a dreamlike state, visualising a glittering steel and glass structure towering above Kirkwall's eighteenth century flag-paved high street.

"Do you want to see the business plan before you visit the site?" Nadine asks eventually, fiddling with her briefcase, to break the silence.

"Aye, let's see what you've got, duck," George says, coming back to reality and flicking abstractedly through Nadine's immaculately researched and prepared plan.

"No, no, this is no good."

"What?" Nadine asks, stunned. "How can you tell so quickly?"

"This isn't a profitable plan, sweetheart," George says briskly. "Forget all this organic nonsense. That's just a flash in the pan, that. People want

good cheap beans and bananas. And tomato sauce. And proper bread too. You go this organic route and all you're going to get are queers and pinkos, there's no money to be made out of them."

"But there's a huge organic farm movement here," Nadine says, her voice high with sheer incredulity. "They're desperate for a marketplace for their produce."

"Farmers? Flippin' heck, you can't trust bloody farmers!"George brays, oblivious to the many red-faced wellie-booted characters milling about the street. "First government subsidy they get they'll be back to spraying chemicals again and you'll be left with nothing to sell your pansy customers."

"Let's go inside and meet the management," I say before some passing agriculturalist lynches the little Yorkshireman. "They're sure to love you, George."

*

The day, which has begun badly, gets steadily worse, and by four o'clock we are both ready to take George to the end of the pier and throw him off. Malcolm is due to finish work in half an hour when the tide turns, and having more than done my duty, I gratefully slink off home with the promise that I'll be back with Chancery for dinner at Nadine's house later that evening.

Malcolm, still dressed in his custodian's blue trousers and red tartan waistcoat, greets me anxiously at the door at seven and shakes my hand violently with nary an electric shock buzzer anywhere in sight, and, drawing his face close to my ear, whispers, "Thank God you're here. I can't stand another minute of talking to Mr Wanky-Poo-Head in there," and I wonder what Asda George can have done to have produced such a violent reaction in Mr Magic so quickly.

I'm not kept in the dark for long, however, and when I take the bottle of wine we have brought through to Nadine in the kitchen she clasps my hand and sobs, "Oh it's going so badly, Max, and he's sneered at Malcolm's magic tricks."

*

We have never stayed in one place for more than five or six years at a stretch, but as we get older and accrue more possessions and responsibilities, this feat seems to be becoming more and more difficult to accomplish, and the prospect of picking up sticks and leaving Orkney for a foreign destination is a path strewn with pitfalls, the top item on our long list being the transporting of our cats to our proposed destination.

We have been reading numerous horror stories in our immigration guides about people's pets dying of asphyxiation in the holds of aeroplanes or being crushed by careless baggage handlers at South American airports, and we are petrified at the prospect of Suki and Sooty being hurt as a result of being taken on our proposed transcontinental trek with us.

Several of the books that we have studied advise that it is, in fact, kinder to pets to re-home them rather than subject them to the risks and rigours of lengthy air travel, and this throws us into a severe dilemma of indecision. I am not really the best person to reach a sane conclusion on a sore point like this one, as I come from an old colonial family who were regularly doing the Liverpool to Bombay runs by ocean liner in the 1960s, and I grew up in a world where pets were simply given away rather than face the draconian quarantine laws governing the transporting of animals at that time.

This, then, leaves Chancery with the majority vote for choosing if the fiends from hell should accompany us to South America or not, and we reluctantly conclude one miserable windswept morning that perhaps it will be "for the best" to place an advert in the paper and see if we can find someone who will foster our two devil's disciples with a view to taking them on permanently.

*

I go down to the newspaper office and place the ad, my feet feeling as if they're encased in old-fashioned lead divers' boots, and I toss and turn through several sleepless nights, dreading Thursday and the publication of this week's miscellany of cheerful island news and views – and our Judas

advertisement offering our two precious pets up to the highest bidder. However, the cock eventually crows thrice and Black Thursday comes around, but the phone remains mute all day, and I'm wiping cold sweat off my brow when it rings ominously on Friday morning, and, despite my fervent prayers for it to be someone looking for volunteers for the church bazaar, a cold and sinister voice says that it's come to claim the souls of our two beloved cats in exchange for the freedom for us to travel to more colourful climes.

*

Feeling far worse than any Nazi guard rounding up Jews into trains bound for Auschwitz, we put the cats in their basket and drive out to "Toon" to let them have a trial fortnight with their prospective stepmother, pausing at every leaf along the thoroughfare in a effort to find some excuse to find the road blocked and have to turn around and head homewards again, but our prayers go unanswered and we pull up outside the address that we have been given.

I've got my fingers tightly crossed and am hoping fervently that we will discover a vivisectionist's laboratory with the screams of tortured pets ringing out from hidden chambers, but instead all I can hear is the distant sound of synthesised angel chimes as we approach the doorway to be greeted by Amber, a fat forty-something new-ager dressed in a knee-length sweater and garishly-coloured leggings.

The lady ushers us into a small and cosy living room where incense burns pleasantly from little Indian brass holders and there are numerous books on Gaia, white magic and women's menstrual celebration on the shelves, and although on the surface we couldn't have found a more devoted person to look after our cats, I have to be brutally honest and say that I dislike her instantly.

*

Our trial separation fortnight from our cats drags on and we don't miss them any less as each excruciating day slowly passes, and I'm taking a shower one morning seven days later when I hear the phone ring and Chancery answer it. Our shower is old and clunky and makes quite a din,

so I can't quite make out all that's being said but from what I can glean it's Amber of the multi-coloured trousers and that there seems to be a problem with the cats. I'm only catching every second or third word, but when I hear Chancery say the words "we'll come over and get..." my heart takes a leap.

It hasn't worked out and the cats are coming home.

I grab a towel and go skidding out into the hall with water flying off me to celebrate the good news, but Chancery's face immediately tells me that it's not as good as I'd been expecting. It turns out that although Suki is not taking to her new home and she is refusing to eat and has even peed in Amber's wardrobe –nice one, Suki! – the baggy-trousered one still wants to keep Sooty "on trial" for a further fortnight while unburdening herself of his much-harder-to-please sister, and Chancery has insanely agreed to this.

*

The electronic angel chimes are still plinky-plinking away when we arrive at Amber's transcendental pad, and we find poor Suki wedged into a small space behind the TV, her eyes wide and traumatised, and while she doesn't appear to even recognise us, she lets me lift her up and put her in her basket without protest.

Meanwhile, Sooty is seated disinterestedly on the window ledge, laconically watching all these proceedings without the least flicker of reaction or emotion, which is his nature and also his tragedy, and as we are still locked into our it's-for-the-best-even-if-it-hurts mind set, he lets us content ourselves with just taking his sister home and leaving him behind to his fate.

*

Henrietta is turning forty in late May and has decided to mark the occasion by throwing a pyjama party in her draughty old farmhouse, and Chancery and I are charged with the task of creating a programme of party games to involve lots of running around to keep her guests from contracting frostbite. We are missing little Sooty terribly and are really far too miserable to contemplate getting involved in someone else's celebrations, but decide that the project might be a good distraction and duly make up the required amusements then don our jim-jams and go over.

However the extra heat is not really required as the party is already a hotbed of sizzling gossip when we arrive, as the bespectacled James has finally hooked up with a real live woman under sixty. It seems that he has pledged his troth to the gawky moon-faced Scandinavian who we met on Norway Day, and made the union official at a druidical circle-dancing event at the ancient standing stones at Brodgar the previous week.

*

I'm formally introduced to the pigtailed Rhine Maiden, and she giggles childishly and blushes when I shake her hand and ask if she has been back in Orkney long.

"I come only three weeks now," she grins to me in halting English. "James, he wants me earlier but I am in a play in my homeland where I am a... how you say? A booney?"

She makes a strange gesture putting both hands to her temples, waggling her fingers and hopping, but her charade doesn't produce the desired result and she stamps her foot in child-like frustration.

"What is that word in the English?" she cries, her small freckly features scrunched into a tight ball. "In the burrow, on the field, eating the lettuce?"

"Rabbit?" I venture hesitantly.

"Ja, rabbit!" Moon Face exclaims, jumping up and down. "I am a rabbit, so I cannot be here for James to announce our wedding when he wants to. But all is well now, no?".

*

Poor little Jasper has had his nose put well and truly out of joint by his life-partner's sudden announcement of forthcoming nuptials with a bona fide member of the opposite sex, and to make matters worse, Peer Gynt and

Solveig have begun teasing him unceasingly about his own single status, which is pretty rich coming from a confirmed old bachelor like James. But Jasper still rises to the bait every time and is suddenly more or less sniffing the behinds of every available woman on the island in his desperation to find himself a matching girlfriend.

He has, however, taken the pyjama brief very much to heart tonight and has come wearing a vintage woman's chemise, crotchless antique bloomers and, for his fin touché, two water-filled balloons nestling comfortably in a 1920's silk brassiere.

Thus we find him standing by the fire in Henrietta's living room, holding forth on old Orkney building techniques to a straight-laced architect from Stromness – who, it must be noted, has *not* come in his pyjamas – unaware of the look of sheer panic on the poor man's countenance, or the way his eyes are darting hither and thither in search of an escape route, and we quickly release the helpless victim and take Jasper into our safekeeping.

I leave him by the fire talking to Chancery while I go through to the kitchen, and midway down the long dark hall, I find the buxom Roberta nestled into a shadowy alcove known to Henrietta's friends as The Priest Hole.

"Fucking hell, Roberta, you scared the bejasus out of me!" I exclaim. "What are you doing out here. You must be frozen."

"I'm hiding from his nibs," she replies, her normally confident eyes on the brink of tears. "Is the bastard still in there?"

"If you mean Philip, he's in the living room hogging the fire," I reply. "Backpack Bertha's pouring him tea and feeding him shortbread."

Roberta snorts derisively. "Oh well, he'll be in his element playing Mummies and Daddies with her then," she says, a subtle change slipping into her tone. "He'll be so busy suckling at the teat he won't even notice I'm gone."

"Well, come through to the kitchen with me," I say, made slightly uncomfortable by the way the conversation seems to be going. "You'll

catch your death out here."

"Yes, I am a bit cold," she says, not moving. "Give me a hug to warm me up before we go through."

I hesitate, thrown by the strangeness of her request, as Roberta melts into my arms, her body hot and vibrant under the thin cotton of her nightdress and not the least bit cold, and although I am well used to her ostentatious flirting in crowded rooms, here, alone in the dark, dressed only in flimsy nightwear, I can feel waves of panic engulfing me.

"Shouldn't we go through?" I ask in as close to a normal voice as I can muster as Roberta's grip tightens.

"In a minute," Roberta replies in a thick, husky voice that I have never heard before. "God, you're lovely, Max. Wouldn't you like to come and live with me?"

I am, for probably the first time in my life, completely lost for words, and am only rescued by someone unexpectedly opening the kitchen door and filling the dark hall with light.

Muttering something completely indecipherable I make a bolt back to the living room and run straight into the crestfallen Jasper who runs a cold hand over the fabric of my pyjama jacket.

"I'm really going to miss James when he gets married," he sighs. "Maybe you and I could spend some time together, Max?"

*

We don't have a television and are mystified to see a banner in the post office window the next day bearing the somewhat inexplicable slogan "Go Cameron" and, as the days pass, more and more of these Maoist standards begin to appear in household windows and shop doorways, and one even flutters brazenly at the gate of a neighbouring field.

Eventually, curiosity getting the better of us, I ring Rhona to ascertain his identity, but the twin finds it difficult to conceal her disbelief.

207

"Cameron?" she says in astonishment. "You're telling me you don't know who *Cameron* is?"

"Apparently not," I reply. "Are you going to put me out of my misery or let me go to my grave ignorant?"

Rhona laughs. "Come round tonight, the pair of you. It's time you were both educated."

"Oh no, please don't educate us, Rhona," I beg. "Couldn't you just be irresponsible and tell me?"

"Nope," Rhona replies firmly. "You need to come round and learn who your true gods are."

*

We sit in Rhona's lounge later that evening, while both the twins shake their heads and try to get us to admit that we really do know who the mysterious Cameron is, but, eventually convinced that we really are as pig-shit-thick as they think we are, Rhona concedes defeat and turns on the television set.

"This is Cameron," she says as the old set hums into being and a dog food commercial appears on the screen.

"Cameron's a dog?" I say, but Shona gives me her sternest school teacher look and holds up her hand for silence.

The commercial fades as the Big Brother theme music fills the room and the credits quickly lap-dissolve to a pan of the "House" and finally ends up at a young man in an oatmeal-coloured sweater seated at a table quietly reading his Bible.

"Watch and learn," Shona says in her teacher's voice. "*This* is Cameron Stout. He's from Harray and he's gone on Big Brother to put Orkney on the map."

"No shit," I say. "You mean he's not interested in the fame or the money?"

"Cameron's no' like that," Shona says firmly, and there seems to be absolutely no point in arguing.

*

We finally decide that a life without Sooty is just too unbearable to tolerate and, on a cold but sunny Wednesday evening, we agree that, travel risks or not, we will phone Amber the following morning and bring him home, and we go to bed early filled full of resolve to set matters to rights.

It's about half past ten on a bright late-May night, and though it has been a raw, bitter day it is still sunny outside and golden shafts of light speckled with dancing flakes of dust are projecting through chinks in our heavy velvet bedroom curtains, threatening to keep us awake. But, exhausted from the last few highly stressful weeks, we soon fall into a fitful slumber nevertheless.

However, we have only been asleep for about fifteen minutes when the phone suddenly rings shrilly and wakes us, but we are both too groggy to answer and I let the ansafone take it, but the message that is left jolts us both wide awake in an instant.

The machine is on speaker and through the open bedroom door we can hear an unfamiliar English voice saying, "Hello. My name's Nicky. You don't know me. I've got your cat, Sooty, here. He seems to have eaten something poisonous and he's having a seizure. I think he's going to die."

CHAPTER 17 – WHERE WE SUDDENLY FIND OURSELVES CAST INTO FOUR MONTHS OF PURGATORY

It's normally about a forty-minute drive to "Toon" over the twisty, narrow roads from our rural homestead in Quoyloo, but I get us there in twenty-eight minutes flat tonight, and we quickly find Nicky's address in the only suburb of Kirkwall and hammer loudly on her door like a pair of mad things.

A nervous-looking young girl swiftly takes us round to the back garden where, in the reflected glow of the porch lamp, a brown-haired, forty-something woman is sitting holding a very sick-looking Sooty, who's foaming at the mouth and convulsing like an epileptic. I gently take him from her and hold onto his shaking little body until the vet she has summoned eventually ordains to show up and gives him an injection which finally stops the seizure.

The medic we have previously used and trusted has left Orkney the preceding summer, complaining vociferously about bloody islanders who leave their bloody bills unpaid as he goes, and the guy who comes out tonight is from a firm who are better known for their work with livestock rather than domestic pets, and, to be honest, he's not the best feline veterinarian in the world, but he's here and it's a case of any port in a storm.

Donny – the vet – a fat red-faced man who's, quite honestly, more at home on a bar stool than a clinic, has no real clue about what's happened to Sooty and is pessimistically vague about what his chances of survival are, but says, skilfully tacking on those magic vet words 'if you're willing to pay the bill', that he'd like to take him into the surgery and keep him there so that he can be monitored at all times.

We agree straight away and tell him to give Sooty all the care he needs, and before we know what's happened our beloved little cat is packed into a regulation white metal cage and driven off in the back of Donny's mud-splattered four-wheel-drive.

*

I phone Amber the next morning to tell her what's happened and she immediately goes into extreme remorse overdrive and starts trying to perform multiple penances to make amends.

"Oh my God," she wails, "I've let you both down so badly. And Sooty too. I just let him out for a minute, only a minute, and he went over the fence, and I thought, well he's a cat, he'll be back, but he didn't come back, and I thought, well, he's a cat, a tom cat, he'll be back, but now he's not coming back, and, oh, I've let you both down. But I'll make it all up. I will. I'll really, truly make it up.

"I'll pay the vet's bills. And your petrol. You must have had to use petrol to come and get him. Oh, you poor dears, and finding him like that, what a shock, I'll make it up. What do you want me to do? Tell me and I'll do it. I'll pay all the fees. I'll pay for his funeral if he dies. Oh, God, I feel so guilty. Max, what can I do?"

"There's nothing you can do, Amber," I say, being burned up with my own personal guilt for blithely handing over the care of my precious little buddy to this batshit old hippy. "Just keep your fingers crossed and hope that he's strong enough to pull through this, that's all."

"Oh yes, I can do that. I'm a witch, you know. A white witch, mind you, I only do good. I'll make a health spell for him. Oh, now did I sweep? I'll need some of his hair for the spell, there'll be some in his basket. Okay, I have to go, there's no time to lose, I have to cast the recovery spell to give him strength. I'm going now. I'm so, so sorry. Honestly I am. But I'm making it up to you all now..."

"Yes, alright," I say, a little too sharply. "But don't go and do anything stupid, Amber."

But my only reply is the mournful howl of the disconnected tone, and Amber has already hung up and departed to her Gaia spell book to find the right incantation to bring our little cat back from the abyss.

211

*

Later that day we get a blustery call from the vet saying that Sooty is still very ill but that he's picking up, and we're just getting optimistic when he calls the next morning to say that he's now not so good. However, the next day's report is more cheerful and we're just about to start hoping again when the phone rings at about four o'clock on the fourth day and Donny delivers the following piece of news.

"Hello, Donny here," he says in his veterinarian's school you're-not-going-to-like-this voice. "Sooty's much worse today and Amber's decided to have him put down."

"WHAT?" I say, totally gobsmacked. "Amber's decided what, and what's bloody Amber got to do with any of this anyway?"

"Well," he says uncomfortably, "Amber's come in and agreed to pay all the bills, so it's her call."

*

No-one is killing any cat of ours and we speed over to the surgery to rescue Sooty and bring him home, but, when we arrive at the antiseptic-scented veterinary practice we are physically shocked by the sight of our little friend. When we had last seen Sooty he had been in a sorry state, it is true, but he had been just a sick version of himself. Today, however, he's like one of those 'customised' teddy bears that they sell in shopping malls, before they put the stuffing in, and his fur looks like a limp, boneless rag and he weighs next to nothing when I pick him up and lay him gently in his basket.

We pay the vet's bill and quickly take our pet home, but he has no clue where he is and his sister takes one look at him and vanishes off to another room, as though seeing the angel of death already by his shoulder and getting quickly out of the way.

The idea that the pompous Donny could have been even remotely right is completely odious to me, but much as I hate to admit it, I'm beginning to wonder if there is anything that can be done for Sooty by either medicine

or love, and it seems like it's only going to be a matter of time before our poor little cat just slips quietly from this life to the next.

Tears are streaming down our cheeks just at the very sight of him and we are left with only a crumb of solace from reminding ourselves that Sooty is alive and that where there's life there's hope.

We fetch his basket from his favourite spot under the living room coffee table and make him as comfortable as we can by the fire, hoping that being amongst the familiar scents of his own bed will help him to rally-round better than the alien aroma of the vet's surgery, and at eight that evening, he suddenly seems to recognise Chancery's voice and the film lifts from his eyes as he gets up and takes a few halting steps towards her across the carpet.

We are still in the market for miracles at this point, but our joy is exceedingly short-lived, for the effort exhausts him and he just flops down again, and the awareness of where he was quickly passes away from his eyes.

*

We make up a bed for him in our room and he goes to sleep almost straight away, but we pass a fitful night afraid to really go to sleep in case he needs us, and we're jerked into wakefulness just before four in the morning to find him in the grip of another seizure. We know in our heart of hearts that putting him out of his misery is now the kindest thing that we can do for him and we call the surgery's emergency night number and are told that the duty veterinarian will be with us soon.

The vet who comes out is a soft-spoken, considerate man who seems trustworthy, and he has obviously been out on call at a neighbouring farm as his clothes smell strongly of cattle and antiseptic soap. It's already starting to get light outside and the sky is a grey-streaked blood red as he looks at Sooty and asks about his history, and when he's learned the details, slowly shakes his head and asks us if we're prepared to let our little cat go.

It's the decision that we've been dreading but we can't stand the thought of putting poor Sooty through any more pain and, the words sticking in my

throat, I give consent and sign the death warrant for the little piece of trembling fur that's convulsing on my lap.

The vet goes out to his van for his medical bag and returns as we're saying goodbye to Sooty, then I wrap my beloved little cat in my arms to ease his shaking and the veterinarian gently puts a needle in his paw and a few seconds later his pain-racked body goes limp and his horrible ordeal is finally over.

*

Meanwhile, the dreaded Cameron-mania is still sweeping the length and breadth of Orkney and the whole place begins to resemble a totalitarian dictatorship with businesses and households everywhere displaying banners ordering people to vote. Social functions almost grind to a halt as islanders glue themselves to their television sets and The Orcadian reports that they have been snowed down with letters from women all over the country proposing marriage – and worse – to Comrade Stout.

I personally think that this latter is an exercise in poetic licence on the part of the island's drama-starved journalists, as who in their right minds would be lusting after this stocky little Bible-basher from Harray. But as I'm sitting at my computer one day there's a sound like a doorbell and a little window pops up bearing the single word "Hi".

"Chancery!" I yell. "There's a window on my screen saying "Hi". Do you think my computer's talking to me?"

"What garbage are you talking now?" my beloved grumbles, coming over to my desk to look. "Let me see."

At that moment the little doorbell noise sounds again and below the word "Hi" appears "RU there?"

Chancery laughs. "Someone's messaging you," she says, explaining modern technology to an aged relative. "They want to talk."

"Oh," I say, not really having a clue what's really happening. "What do I do?"

"You could try answering back," Chancery suggests. So I tentatively type in the word "Hello?"

"Whoa! Don't get carried away there now," Chancery smirks.

The little bell noise dings again, almost immediately, and the words "RU in Orkney?" appear.

I hunt and peck "yes".

"Do u no CAMERON?" asks the correspondent.

"NO," I reply.

"Do U have an address 4 him?"

"No, but you could just write to Cameron Stout, Orkney," I reply, getting into the swing of this. "That would get to him."

The letters "OMG, really :-)" appear on the screen and I look over at Chancery quizzically.

"No, it's not hieroglyphics, before you ask," my better half explains. "She says, 'Oh My God, really,' and then she smiles at you."

"Ohhh," I say, suddenly comprehending, then I type in, "the local post office will know where he lives. Why do you want to contact him?"

"OMG!" says Lol_Girl_304. "I just am so in luv with him, he's the most totally perfect man in the world 4 me, lol!"

"Bloody hell," I mutter, "I've met my first Cameron stalker."

*

Things reach an emotional watershed for me a couple of weeks after Sooty's death when I receive a message from Henrietta asking me if I can drop by her house, alone, as there's something that she wishes to discuss privately with me. I query the "alone" and she reiterates that this is strictly for my ears only, so, half an hour later, I find myself dutifully sitting in her large farm kitchen on a grey, windswept Friday in mid-June.

Henrietta is well-known for hedging her bets and talking round issues, but today she is unaccustomedly direct and comes straight to the point within seconds of me sitting down.

"You know how old I am, Max," she begins, dabbing tastefully at the corner of her eye. "And I'd always hoped to have had children and started a family by now."

This is news to me but I nod vigorously anyway, looking for all the world like one of those flock-covered figures of Churchill the bulldog that car insurance companies give you for the rear shelf of your vehicle.

"Well, I've had an offer. And it's not ideal. But it's a chance to start a relationship, and maybe a family. But it's not ideal..."

Her voice trails away into the gloom of the draughty old kitchen and I look at her incredulously.

"You're not telling me Jasper?" I say.

Henrietta nods, her eyes downcast. "It's not ideal," she repeats.

'Not ideal' has to be the understatement of the decade, if not the century, as it's a well-known fact throughout Orkney that Jasper has been chasing every unattached woman he can think of like a heat-seeking missile in a desperate attempt to procure a partner before he has to face the ordeal of still being single at his fast-approaching thirtieth birthday. James and his Norwegian bimbo have threatened to present their friend with a Bachelor's Pepper Pot[46], and thus everyone blessed with a vagina, from eighteen-year-old school girls to elderly eighty-year-old spinsters, are all desperately being considered by the fey lad for temporary matrimony.

"You do know that this will be a huge mistake, don't you?" I say, flatly.

---

46 - Apparently a *Really Bad Thing* in Scandinavia

"In what way?" Henrietta asks back, just as flatly.

"I can't believe I'm having this conversation," I breathe. "Are we talking about the same Jasper? High voice. Likes to wear women's clothes. In love with James. How many more potential disaster scenarios do you want me to list?"

Henrietta shakes her head.

"The clock's ticking," she says pointedly. "I want kids and I'm not hearing any other offers."

Realisation slowly begins to penetrate my thick skull as to why I've been asked to come here alone.

"And do you have anyone else in mind?" I ask, very quietly.

Henrietta nods and says nothing, but looks at me expectantly with a definite rising and falling of her more than ample bosom, her long-lashed eyes big and beseeching.

'Oh... my... God,' I think.

I tentatively put my hand on her left hand and she immediately covers it with her right and clasps it there in a vise-like grip, holding it so firmly that the circulation stops and my fingers turn blue.

Her face is very close to mine and I can feel her breath, hot and rapid, on my cheek, her countenance expectant as she waits for me to make her a better offer than the one she has just received from the panicking Jasper.
'
Oh... my... God,' I think again.

Henrietta's house is well-known for being cold and dark and, sitting here by the feeble heat of the old cast iron range with a small lamp on the scullery table providing the only light, it's like suddenly being cast in some provincial rep theatre's production of a turgid kitchen-sink drama by Eugene O'Neil, and, really, Backpack Bertha should enter at any moment,

coked up to the gills and carrying her own wedding dress.

However, I'm not saved from the consequences of the tangled web I have thoughtlessly been weaving over the last three years by the somnambulistic perambulations of any of Henrietta's relatives, living or dead, and like the Day of Judgement, I stand alone to face my demons.

"Henrietta, I think you're really great..." I start to say, but she silences me with a sideways movement of her head.

"Max," she says, very slowly and deliberately, a sudden chilly metallic tone making her words resonate like a funeral bell on a grey, frosty morning. "Be very careful what you say here. Be very, very careful."

A lump forms in my throat and stays there, unmoving, like an accidentally swallowed plum stone, and I realise just how much I have come to rely on Henrietta's enabling over the last three years. I see, spread out before me like a drowning man's life flashing before his eyes, all the things that I had set out to achieve in our island retreat and I suddenly find myself thinking about what my life used to be before I came to live on this godforsaken rock, what it was supposed to have been and the hollow sham that it has now become.

The lump finally moves and let's me speak.

"I think that there's no harm trying out how things will go with Jasper," I say in a low, small voice.

Thus the official Jasper and Henrietta fit-up duly takes place the following evening round a campfire with James and Moon Face at a Native American Chanting Session in a Red Indian tepee in James's mother's back garden. This is followed by a ritual bar mitzvah the following weekend, where the three who are now four decamp to a cold, stone-bedded hostel in Hoy to celebrate Jasper's final ascent to manhood and sing ancient Valhalla Ballads well into the small hours while the Old Man of Hoy clutches his ears in torment.

*

The summer, which has rapidly been turning into a complete social and emotional disaster, reaches its final crescendo on a fragile Saturday night in mid-July when the annual Ploughboy's Dance is announced at St Andrew's parish hall just outside Kirkwall in the East Mainland.

Already well-tired of the social scene, neither of us wants to go and play gooseberries at yet another emotionally tense ceilidh, but we have previously agreed to attend this particular festivity with Roberta, so we reluctantly trail along with our happy faces shoved shoddily into place.

However, despite our dedication to the cause the organisers have little faith in the rest of the population tearing themselves away from Big Brother, and are painfully aware that a poor turnout is imminent. To try to fill their hall they announce a two-tiered ticket system, whereby the admission price after nine o'clock is to be double the cost of a pre-nine entrance, and we duly make a point of being there for half past eight sharp.

Roberta and Silent Philip are already installed and looking like the occupants of a dentist's waiting room on their way to a funeral when we arrive, and one look at their tightly-drawn faces tells us that this is to be yet another fun-filled evening.

Roberta looks like a despondent Myra Hindley, her face white with dark grey shadows under her eyes from frequent crying, her mouth a thin white line of suppressed rage; while Silent Philip makes a convincing agricultural Ian Brady, having drawn himself into a small, tight shell, his brows lowered and his normally blank countenance thunderous, and the two of them look like escapees from Madame Tussaudes' Hall of Murderers.

They are, however, totally self-absorbed in their own misery and haven't seen us, and, hoping that we can still get out of yet another evening behind the barbed wire of no-man's-land, impersonating a UN peace-keeping corps, we're in the process of quietly tip-toeing backwards out of the hall again. However, Roberta spots us and feigns waving animatedly, and with the weary tread of those doing "a far, far better thing" we trudge over and take our seats beside the happy couple.

Tonight, of course, is to be Henrietta and Jasper's official Coming Out Cotillion and they eventually drift into the hall at twenty minutes to ten.

This evening sees Henrietta clad far from her normal depressive colour palette of mud brown and sea green and, instead, resplendent in an unprecedented shade of glowing cerise, her pupils dilated and her normally level mood transformed to a near-hysterical plane of frantic party spirit as she grips her hesitant beau's arm, lest he elude her and slip away back to his happy bachelor haunts.

Little Jasper, on the other hand, is looking decidedly green around the gills, as no-one has ever broken it to him that having a girlfriend actually entails paying for her dance ticket, and his first one-on-one brush with Henrietta's time-keeping skills has just cost him double the entry price. The poor man is already hyperventilating and breathing into a paper bag, but worse is in store for him when he discovers that being part of a tight, three couple group means that he can't conveniently duck his round as has been his custom in the past, and he's a gibbering wreck by the time Henrietta has blithely ordered drinks for the entire company and left him to settle the bill.

*

Most of the parish have stayed home to watch Cameron turn the page of his Old Testament from Genesis to Exodus and the band are a rather pedestrian trio who only know songs for about four different dances. Add to the mix that the half-empty hall is doing nothing for all those introverted Orcadians who are still fuelling up at the bar, and you can see why our own little party soon rapidly becomes decidedly Beckettesque in its tone.

To break the almost deafening silence, Henrietta launches into a one-woman monologue, talking rapidly with a hollow joie de vivre about her evening, so far, with Jasper, who sits white-faced beside her like a Mexican mummy, his jaw slack and mouth wide. Roberta is on the brink of tears, Silent Philip is more silent than usual, and I surreptitiously tap out text messages of desperation to the Samaritans, while the atmosphere in our tight little group just gets worse and worse.

The band eventually announces a Strip the Willow, a lively and exhilarating jig, and in desperation I take Chancery up to the dance floor to try and lighten the mood, and Jasper also quickly escapes our impromptu production of Waiting for Godot and follows suit with Henrietta. However, Silent Philip point blank refuses to dance even this simple two-step with his livid spouse and slopes off to a dark corner to talk about lamb gelding with some gingery farmer types, and we are all very painfully aware of the deserted Roberta glowering in her corner.

It's a situation destined for certain disaster, so, when the dance is over and the North Ronaldsay Kazoo Collective stops for their mid evening break, Chancery and I seize the moment to go under the wire and slip quietly away.

*

However, the fat lady has not yet sung and Henrietta, who is possessed with a narrative style similar to that of The Castle of Otranto, rings me from Cold Comfort Farm[47] early the next morning and proceeds to treat me to a purple account of the previous evening's shenanigans which reads like a treatment for a cadenza episode of Peyton Place.

"It was awful, Max, just awful," she begins, commencing her account with a relish similar to the dying Mimi preparing to launch into her last great aria, and I fancy I can hear violins tuning up in the background. "After you left, Roberta got really angry and went to the bar and downed three double rums in a row and started screaming at Philip across the dance floor. He went to get her to be quiet and she tried to shove him away, but the floor was covered in Slipperene, so she just went down like a sack of flour. Are you alright, Max?"

"Oh fine, tip-top," I say painfully, the sleeve of my heavy-duty fleece shirt clamped firmly between my teeth to ensure no hint of laughter becomes audible. "Go on. Please."

"Well, I asked Jasper to go and sort it out but he wouldn't, so I had to try and do something, but it just got me upset and Jasper was no help at all. And Roberta was sitting in the middle of the floor crying and Philip just ran away and hid in the toilet, and they couldn't get the dance started again

---

47 - **Cold Comfort Farm:** the name employed by Roberta's friends for Silent Philip's ancestral home

because she was right in the middle of the floor, so they found Philip and told him to take her home. But Roberta just kept crying and wouldn't move so the hall people called the police, and they told Philip to take his wife home or they'd arrest her. So then there was this mad scramble trying to get her into the car, and she was screaming and calling everybody cunts, and Jasper just ran away and left me to deal with it and I was just so embarrassed I started to cry. Are you sure you're alright?"

"Never better," I wheeze, tears running down my cheeks. "Go on."

"Well, Philip eventually got her home and they were both screaming at each other and upsetting all the kai in the byre, and then the dogs all started howling and woke everyone up, and Aaron[48] tried to punch Philip, so Roberta stormed up to her bedroom and locked the door, and Philip had to spend the night on the sofa. And, oh Max, it gets worse..."

"Oh, I'm sure it does," I say painfully. "Go on."

"Well, in the morning Philip had to do the milking and his byre clothes were in the en suite bathroom, so he started banging on their bedroom door and telling Roberta that she was a bad wife and he was throwing her and all her bastard children out of his house for good. So she told him to go fuck himself since it was the only sex he was ever likely to get, and he totally lost it and broke the bedroom lock and tried to pick her up and throw her down the stairs, but she punched him in the face and he fell over and went headfirst down the staircase himself, but the kids thought he was trying to murder her and called the police. And, when Philip found out, he just panicked and got into his car and drove away."

"And where is he now?" I manage to ask, using super-human powers of will to keep the mirth out of my voice.

"We don't know. Roberta's charging him with assault and they've got an APB out on his car now. The police are here and they're interviewing Roberta just now. Hang on... Mum's just come out to tell me something."

I can hear Backpack Bertha earnestly whispering something in Henrietta's

---

48 - **Aaron:** Roberta's fifteen-year-old son

ear, whilst in the background, through the open door, I can just discern Roberta saying, "And he promised before we were married that we would go dancing and then he wouldn't ever go. He just bullied me and treated me like shit..." And a weary constable uttering, "And is this still leading up to the assault?"

"Max, it's all just a fucking mess," Henrietta suddenly wails into my ear, cutting out the sounds from the main room. "Now she won't have Mum in the room with her to give her statement and I'm no good at this kind of thing. Can you come down? Max......? Max, are you *laughing*?"

*

Jasper's dreaded thirtieth birthday has arrived, and he phones one chilly summer evening, probably at Henrietta's behest, to invite us to a party at the home of the two elderly aunts whom he lodges with, but tells us to "keep it dark" as he's "not inviting everybody", and when we show up on the night the "party" consists only of ourselves, Henrietta, James and Moon Face.

It has been a summer of excruciatingly uncomfortable social evenings, but tonight very definitely gets the coconut for Worst Soirée Ever and makes the previous week's disastrous dance at St Andrew's seem like the Rio Carnival.

We're all seated elbow to elbow on hard chairs, wearing gaudy paper hats, their bright colours in direct contrast to the Presbyterian-fundamentalist décor of Jasper's twin maiden aunts' tiny living room on the summit of one of the island's highest hills, and tonight the tiny wood frame house is engulfed in a thick low cloud.

From the inside all the windows look as if they've been covered with dense grey cotton wool, and they project a dull greenish light into the room and onto the framed correctional texts that adorn the otherwise bare walls, turning us all into over-made-up characters from Polish expressionist theatre and, as a fitting coincidence, the entire evening's dialogue seems to have been scripted by an unholy partnership of Ibsen and Harold Pinter.

"Oh my, well, is this not grand?" Jasper gibbers to no-one in particular.

"James, is this not grand? I've not had such a grand party since I was peedie."

"Ja, we also have many parties like this in my homeland," Moon Face chips in. "I had thought that we study the arch construction of the cathedral this night, but James, he say, we need to let our hair out now that Jasper is finally a man." She glances over at Henrietta and exchanges a knowing glance. "So we have the party to celebrate the union, no?"

"Aye, we're grand modern people tonight, right enough, so we are," Jasper trills neurotically. "And I never thought that I'd be having this birthday with Henrietta by my..."

He halts abruptly as his two elderly aunts enter the room handing out jelly and ice cream in bear-shaped waxed-paper bowls that look as though they've been in their cupboard since 1947.

"I was just saying, Auntie Morag..." he falters. "That I've never had a party as grand and fine as this since I was peedie."

"Aye, weel," his aunt replies. "You've still your presents to open, shall I bring them through?"

"Presents, ja, please bring, Tante," Moon Face squeals, clapping her hands together in childish delight. "Jasper, we have got you something so very special!"

"Aye, and it's no' a pepper pot either," James jibes as Aunty Morag goes out of the door. "You just saved him and no more, Henrietta."

"Maybe he saved me." Henrietta says, looking meaningfully in my direction as Auntie Morag comes back into the room laden with crepe-paper-wrapped parcels.

"Open ours first," Moon Face urges, grasping a large box with a card stuck to the top of it and thrusting it into Jasper's hands, and I can just see that the flimsy wrapping paper is covered in her childish scrawl and personal baby-talk, citing copious references that only she, Jasper and James will understand.

"I told you that this wasn't ideal," Henrietta says quietly from behind me, reading my mind. "He blatantly prefers their company to mine, and I only see him on Friday nights when his aunties go to bingo. He thinks they don't know what he comes to do."

"Why are you telling me?" I ask through tightly closed lips.

"Because I'm still open to offers..." she says expressionlessly, leaving her unfinished sentence hanging like a stairway to nothingness in the oppressive, airless little room.

*

At the end of July Cameron wins Big Brother and returns triumphantly to the island, and, as all of Orkney gets ready to gather at Stromness harbour for a hero's welcome and ticker-tape parade, Chancery and I decide that it's time to face a few hard truths and accept the fact that the dream we set out to achieve here bears no resemblance to the life that we now lead. We also realise that there have to be some very major changes to our lives, and as we walk for miles in the rain along the deserted Skaill beach, we talk frankly for the first time about our feelings of personal isolation and frustration with our island life. Chancery finally tells me of the profound sense of abandonment that my addictive flirtations with Henrietta are causing her, and I realise with a deep and overwhelming sense of shame that I really have to terminate my liaison with her post haste.

I go round to Henrietta's farmhouse to make a clean split and, a few days later, just as I'm beginning to start thinking about my first tentative steps towards building a new life for myself, I run smack into Backpack Bertha, Henrietta's mother, in the middle of Kirkwall's main street, just in front of the now-closed Cumming and Spence.

Bertha's weather-beaten features look a bit like a cliff face on a particularly grey and stormy winter dawn, and I really don't want to have a conversation with her this morning, but there's no way I can pretend that I haven't seen her so bite the bullet and greet her.

Bertha looks at me coldly, examining me like I'm a piece of particularly

rancid dog shit that's got itself smeared in the sole of her clumpy hiking boot, and, in completely non-Orcadian style, addresses me loudly in a voice that echoes up and down the length of the busy street.

"So, you've had your fun with my daughter and now you're just throwing her aside like so much bruck[49]," she begins, effectively silencing every conversation on the street as the whole thoroughfare stops what they're doing to listen. "You can't just treat a person that way, Max, you can't make them promises and then cast them aside and leave them depressed and alone when you've had your fun. Shame on you."

"But I didn't *make* any promises. And Henrietta's not alone, she's going out with Jasper..." I start to bleat, but neither Bertha nor the rest of the street are paying the slightest bit of attention to me.

"You're just like all the rest of the men on this island, with one thing on your mind and your mind driven by your thing," the same motherly woman who had been feeding me tea and home-made cake a fortnight before declaims in a loud foghorn voice. "You've treated my daughter deplorably, Max Scratchmann, *shame* on you."

And the rest of the street nod their heads in agreement.

49 - **bruck:** rubbish, garbage

CHAPTER 18 – WHERE WE DISCOVER JUST HOW DIFFICULT IT IS TO GET OFF THE DARK ISLANDS

Self-help books all assure us that when we make a definite commitment to change the forces of the universe step in and scatter bounteous opportunities at our feet. Having finally conceded that we need to make a significant alteration to our lifestyles if we are to really live our dream, we are surprised and delighted when an artist friend rings us out of the blue and offers to rent us her house near Thurso, on the Scottish mainland, for the winter.

It's a beautiful old Arts & Crafts cottage in a small village by the coast, with twisty staircases and little mullioned windows looking out over the sea – in fact, a painter's paradise – but, faced with the reality of actually getting on a boat and leaving the security of Orkney and the network of friends, or perhaps enablers, that we have so carefully built up, we are suddenly filled with an unnatural sense of terror.

Beautiful as it is, it is not really what we need, but instead of simply getting ourselves over the Pentland and taking the tenancy for six months as a first step to sorting out our priorities, we have a fit of blind panic and turn our disappointed buddy down, deciding to stay where we are until "the right place" turns up. Enraged by our cowardice, the Forces of Change promptly desert us, and, as if sent by Satan's minions to confuse our already confused minds, a week later the local enterprise company invites us to a seductive showing of a suitably propagandist film called Live Local, Work Global. After forty minutes of watching multinational ventures being master-minded from derelict lighthouses in the middle of the Hebrides, we go home inspired to fill the huge void in our artistic careers by bringing Los Angeles to Orkney, and set about borrowing several thousand pounds to form an independent publishing company which will have its nerve centre in our Quoyloo living room.

In order to keep our already escalating borrowing to a minimum, I go back into part-time employment when I spot an advert in The Orcadian for someone to create and run a "computer learning centre" in the community

centre at the village of Dounby – a barren windswept crossroads in the middle of nowhere, with flat unbroken farmland to one side and rough peat country to the other.

There's an old co-op that's now a private store, plus a hairdressers' and a pub, and it's hard to see who in this Amish-like settlement would be in such dire need of adult education, but, hero that I am, I plunge straight into the breach and have the new centre up and running by late August.

*

Elsewhere, life goes on as normal. The rotund Rodeo Raymond surrenders his role as head of the Orkney dance community and leaves the island for the distant shores of Bognor Regis, of all places, to marry his internet lover as the mellow August fades into a chilly September. September, in turn, quickly gives way to a gale-wracked October with etched steel skies and scudding clouds as I spend two days a week teaching herds of apron-clad farmers' wives how to send emails to the members of their families who have made it under the wire and escaped to the Scottish mainland, and employ the rest of my time administrating the set-up of our publishing venture.

It's pitch black well before three each afternoon and we abandon the now decidedly- palled social scene and keep ourselves to ourselves, only really venturing out during the daytimes when we drive out to the distant South Isles to walk for miles along remote pebbly beaches, bouncing endless ideas to and fro about where our life should be going.

We buy ourselves a tiny portable television set and set up the small windowless box room on our upper floor as a secret sitting room so that we can lock ourselves in and be "out" to passing potential visitors, and we are sitting locked in our hidey-hole at about nine one freezing Sunday night when there's a loud hammering at the locked door.

A harsh wind is howling like a dying Wagnerian diva and the house is like an icebox from the draught, so I'm understandably loath to leave the warmth of our cosy room, but it's like the post murder scene in Macbeth with the insistent knocking at the south entry, and whoever's there is just not taking no for an answer. It's still very tempting to just ignore them,

but our car's parked by the gate so they can see it and know that we're in, so I reluctantly go down to see what all the fuss is about, hoping with all my heart that it's only the Jehovah's Witnesses[50].

I tiptoe through the dark kitchen and open the door, which, in a grotesque parody of an old film, flies inward with the force of the strong gale as the storm blows sleet and hail into the house and there, in the glow of the outside light, are an icy James and Jasper in a perfect tableau of Grant Wood's American Gothic. Other than, perhaps, the Grim Reaper, they are probably the last people that I want to see tonight, but like all good Orcadians I turn no-one away from my door in inclement weather without offering a hot drink and some refreshment first, and I bring the two of them indoors and install them by the living room fire where they happily settle down and accept our offer of a cup of tea.

Chancery keeps the pair of them entertained while I busy myself in the kitchen, and there's a definite feeling of something being afoot with the gruesome twosome tonight, and as I heave more coal on the fire and clank teacups and biscuit tins, I wonder what it could be that has brought the Thompson Twins so far from home on a bitter stormy night like this. However, I'm not kept in suspense for long, and Flanagan and Allen have barely accepted their teacups and "oohed" and "ahhhhed" over our vintage china plates before Jasper eagerly comes out with the news that's been dying to burst out of his chest like an agricultural version of the creature from Alien.

"Aye, it's been a strange summer, has it no'?" he says, his high soprano voice still sharp and discordant despite the eerie background chorus of the shrieking wind. "James getting married and me having a grand time with Henrietta..."

His voice trails away and I look up sharply. "You're not getting married too, are you?" I ask, and the fey lad colours brightly in the reflected firelight.

"Married? Me? Oh my, no," he splutters in his best outraged old granny voice. "Oh my, no, not at all. The very thought of it. That's what we came

---

50 - Yep, they have them in Orkney too!

over to tell you."

"Well, what are you doing then?" Chancery asks bluntly and Jasper colours again.

"Oh my, well it's about me and Henrietta," he says, in an almost normal tenor, his eyes downcast. "She's a bonny lass, right enough, but things between me and her were never quite right..."

"Oh my, *whatever's* happened?" I ask.

"Oh my, well," Jasper says, flustered. "We had some laughs, the two of us, so we did, but she didn't really enjoy the antiques, and we could never just go to the Auction Mart together because she got so bored and was always wanting to go up to the canteen..."

"He took her up there once and she ate three doughnuts," James interjects. "That hit the auld meanie right in his wallet."

"James," Jasper admonishes. "What a thing to say."

"Aye, but true nevertheless," his friend retorts. "And a doughnut's no' exactly dear, either, three would only have cost you aboot one-fifty. You couldn't have got much for *that* doon at Stromness harbour on a Saturday night."

"James!" Jasper cries, like an insulted Mrs Slocombe sans the blue rinse. "How could you even imagine me doing such a thing?" and an argument is just about to break out between the two of them when I intercede to enquire about the whereabouts of the notably absent Moon Face.

However, it seems that, by some strange coincidence, she has recently packed her bunny ears and been shipped off back to the fatherland for the long Nordic winter.

"So the boys are back together again?" I ask facetiously.

"Aye, I suppose so," Jasper replies as James turns a deep guilty red.

*

The long Orkney winter is unrelenting but we take advantage of the occasional breaks in the gales to go walking as much as we can. Although the fiasco with our cats means that our enthusiasm for an ambitious destination like Mexico has well and truly waned, we are now more than ever resolved to broaden our horizons and leave Alcatraz, and we have endless discussions on the subject as we trek for miles along the breathtaking coastline of Orkney's West Mainland, seabirds swooping and diving above our heads. But with such an awe-inspiring backdrop it seems difficult to work up enthusiasm for urban destinations, despite the fact that the isolation of Orkney has been slowly driving us to distraction over the past few years. Spring, however, eventually drags its leaden feet into being, and June gives way to a rainy July as our new publishing company gets off to a great start with a glitzy launch and exceptionally healthy sales figures for its first month, but by mid August we have already exhausted the potential of our geographical region and, unable to afford the cost of a stand at the Frankfurt book fair or some other sane promotional activity, we do what we perceive to be the next best thing and reserve a pitch at the County Agricultural Show in Kirkwall instead.

We have purchased a neat green and white garden gazebo from the local branch of Woolworth's, which we meticulously kit out with Letrasign in our company livery, but the delicate tubular steel structure has been designed for suburban gardens in Surrey and is no match for Orkney's summer gales, and when we try it out in our back garden two days before the show, it quickly inflates and flies up into the air and vanishes over the nearby cliffs into the sea, never to be seen again.

We borrow a saggy-roofed old tombola stall, but when we set up at the show are forced to admit that it doesn't fit our image of a cool, cutting edge publishing firm; but, we ask ourselves, should a cool, cutting edge publishing firm really be sandwiched in-between the Orkney Cheese Shop and mass-produced Celtic jewellery at an agricultural event on some distant island?

However, despite our village-fete shabby-chic look we do manage to shift a fair amount of books, especially Chancery's controversial novel about abuse and incest that has had island tongues wagging from day one, and

late in the day when tired farmers are beginning to sheath their prize cocks and shoo their cattle towards waiting trailers, a flotilla of drunk girls who have been propping up the beer tent all afternoon come over and adopt Orkney's most shocking author as their guru.

"Wow, I've never met a real writer before," a curvaceous brunette slurs adoringly, but the compliment is somewhat spoiled by another drunken princess sharply enquiring "Is this that sick book that's got nothing about Orkney in it?"

*

The brief summer is soon over and by the time another November has blown in with its four hours of daylight and unremitting gales we realise that nothing significant has changed in our lives in over a year. Driven to desperation by boredom, frustration and unfulfilled ambition,we go to see our bank to ask if there's any way at all that we can qualify for a mortgage to buy something off Riker's Island, and, to our surprise, the girl punches numbers into her computer, smiles, and says, yes, of course, and prints us out a loan guarantee on the spot. It's not for a huge amount of money but it's enough to enable us to set our sights on the other side of the Pentland Firth, and although we have not been off the island since we visited my dad several years ago, we decide to try our luck on the north east coast of Scotland where, at the time, it's still possible to pick up a modest property without having to pawn all your vital organs to cover the deposit.

*

When they hear our price range and finish laughing, most of the estate agents we contact immediately try to get us to look at run-down flats in the moribund grey granite port of Fraserburgh, once the centre of Scotland's white fish industry and now the last bastion of Scottish Protestant Fundamentalism – a bleak Calvinist town of derelict fish-packing plants and litter-strewn streets, where the local record store prominently displays audio tapes of the Sermons of the Reverend Ian Paisley in its main window.

We are, however, unwilling to move to such a depressed settlement, but two or three interesting domiciles do come up in the neighbouring municipality of Peterhead, and although it's not our ideal location of

choice, we decide to have a look and make arrangements to go over to the mainland to view a couple of houses.

*

Peterhead is a bleak nineteenth-century town in the far north with austere streets and granite weather-worn Presbyterian architecture, and we eventually find the "holiday flat" that we've rented in a shadowy back alley off the town's main thoroughfare. The place is in total darkness, with no sign of the landlady, when we arrive, and we stand shivering in the doorway, impatiently waiting for her to show up.

It is beyond freezing cold and, being a Saturday night, there are already a few belligerent drunks weaving around the lane singing football songs, and after trying unsuccessfully to attract the imbibers' attention, a pair of shivering Eastern European girls in short skirts and bustiers spot us and come down to our dark doorway to suss us out.

"It is a cold night, no?" the first, an emaciated peroxide blonde clad in two miniscule straps of fabric chances. "You want, maybe, to make warm?"

"He'll be fine," Chancery interjects, and both the girls laugh at her protectiveness.

"Is okay," the second says. "We not forget you also. All Estonian girls AC-DC. Make you both warm on cold night."

"Scottish boy unfortunately has no money," I say, and their interest level visibly wanes.

"Have good night," they say, winking lewdly, and they teeter back on their spike-like heels up the cobbled alleyway towards the lights of the pub doors, just as a battered old Mercedes pulls up and a bent bird-woman gets out with keys jangling in her claw-like hand.

"You'll be the *holiday* folk," she says, looking us over shrewdly with her gimlet eye. "You best come upstairs."

We follow her through a cold and musty hall and up some shadowy stairs

that have been thickly carpeted in something dark and cheap, and she rifles through her large ring of keys like a jailor just as the light goes out and we are plunged into inky darkness.

"Timer," our jailor mutters. "You need to be fast."

She opens the door with the practiced hand of an underworld creature who doesn't often walk in the light of day and deftly switches on the inner light. A dim, unshaded, low-watt tube flickers weakly into life and we're led into a small and dingy bed-sitter that's been decorated with unmatching wallpaper remnants.

There's a lumpy double bed, an antique Baird television and a couple of jumble sale ornaments on the fireplace, but not much else. To one side there's a kitchen with an ancient electric cooker and a disgusting old fridge that's gone brown with age and neglect; and to the other, a bathroom with a prehistoric suite that's been gloss painted.

The landlady surveys her kingdom proudly and points out the electricity meter under the kitchen sink. "I put fifty pence in there for you," she says beneficently. "Make sure that there's plenty of credit in it when you leave."

We nod dumbly, our eyes darting this way and that looking for the escape hatch, but the landlady's still standing in front of the door barring the way like a bellhop in an old detective movie who's waiting for his tip. Are we supposed to tip her?

She looks at us and shakes her head wearily. "You pay me now," she prompts patiently.

Surprise must have been writ large on our faces at the thought of actually being asked to pay upfront for this dump, but the scary lady misreads it.

"Problem?" she asks sharply, and I hastily make some feeble excuse about not having been to the cash machine yet. She looks dubious but sighs again and says that, since we look honest, it's okay, but that she'll be round in the morning to collect
her money.

"And that's first thing in the morning," she warns as she disappears out of the door and into the gloom of the haunted staircase.

*

Late on a sleety Saturday night in winter is never a good way to get an introduction to any town, particularly one in the far north of Scotland, but what we see of Peterhead that evening we really don't like, and there seems to be an overall feeling of desolation to the place. The twisty old streets are grey and unwelcoming, the shops boarded-up and graffiti-daubed, and the bitter December wind is creating little mini tornados and swirling dust and litter around the feet of shabby Saturday night revellers who are dashing quickly from pub to pub.

However, we go out, street map in hand, to preview the properties that we've selected, but as the hours pass and we cross one fixer-upper after another off our rapidly diminishing list, Chancery eventually voices what we've both been thinking when she flatly declares, "I'm sorry, I can't live here," and we decide to promptly pick up sticks and go home.

It's well after three in the morning by now, so we go back to our seedy flat to spend a restless night, being woken time and time again by noisy street fights, homeward- bound drunks and, as the night's final crescendo, a Russian couple who have a fight in the doorway below our apartment and then appear to settle their differences by having noisy make-up sex.

After a raucous chorus of "Da, da, da!" sleep is now quite out of the question, and we rise bleary-eyed at half past five, and, leaving the landlady enough money to cover one night in her fleapit, quickly bundle all our possessions into the car and away as fast as we can before the old bloodsucker catches us and demands her full week's rental.

*

The sky is the colour of lead and it snows unceasingly the next day as we speed back through the imposing glory of the Cairngorms to catch the ferry back to the safety of Mother Orkney, the companionship of our friends, and the relative sanity of island life. Our brief time away has shown us, to our horror, that we have become exceptionally countrified after almost

235

seven years away from the real world, and we have found other drivers' intolerance to strangers who hesitate for a quarter of a nanosecond at road signs unendurable – and the psychotic Christmas crowds of haunted-eyed people intent on mugging each other in shops inexplicable – and we despair of ever finding somewhere where we can finally feel at home.

It's an exceedingly rough crossing back, with screaming gale-force winds churning up the black and angry sea, and the deserted ferry contains only the few hardy souls who are desperate enough to want to spend December in Orkney, but we find ourselves glad to be passing the dark silhouette of the Old Man of Hoy once again and there's a certain spring of relief in our step when we eventually disembark at Stromness that night.

Orkney, it would seem, has become like a pair of worn-out shoes for us, that trusty old pair of plimsolls that we wore all summer but which now let the rain in and are really no longer capable of performing the task that they were made for. But there's nothing in the shops that's quite as comfortable and we cling desperately on to them in spite of our better judgment.

*

Life drags on as usual and we find ourselves living an almost hermit-like existence, seeing only our best friends and going nowhere; desperate to leave and paralysed by fear at the same time. Roberta and Silent Philip establish an uneasy peace in their marriage; James weds his chirpy Norwegian Rhine Maiden and goes off to live in Oslo; and little Jasper wanders around Orkney like an unquiet spirit without him.

The year already seems to be unravelling with fantastic rapidity but it is on my fiftieth birthday on a melancholy Saturday in late May that I finally receive the cathartic impetus to strike out afresh.

I have spent the grey and sunless morning disconsolately reviewing my life so far, as so many of us do when we celebrate the anniversary of a major birth-decade, and I have to be honest and say that my achievements on attaining my half-century are nothing like the picture I had imagined for myself on reaching this ripe old age.

Although I had been struggling to get by financially prior to our move to Orkney, I was spending most of my working hours illustrating and painting and slowly developing the artistic career of my dreams. However, today, seven years later and installed in our "creative laboratory", I am still poor and lucky if I am producing one or two images a year, and if I'm really honest with myself, am really just a part-time computer teacher instructing middle-aged women in the basics of Microsoft Word, stuck on an isolated thirty-square-mile landmass with eight months of darkness and a climate to rival Alaska.

However, today appears to be the day that the scales are finally set to tip us into the realms of action, and it is a small and insignificant thing that finally inspires me to make the long-needed commitment to change all the things that are wrong in my life.

We have invited some of our dearest friends round for dinner, to mark the auspicious occasion, and as I usher everyone into the house, they all, for some reason, mark the juncture of my formally attaining official old-git-status by presenting me with an assortment of bland china mugs.

It's a small thing, I know, and it is no problem for me to feign gratitude for the haphazard pieces of insipid porcelain with their carelessly affixed wishy-washy transfers, but I am suddenly hit by the stark realisation that we have been grimly hanging on here because we do not wish to part from our friends. Yet, for almost seven years now, I have sat here religiously drinking Rooibos tea out of a glass cup and never once putting a china vessel to my lips - and not one of them has ever noticed.

Worse, now that I'm fifty and with middle-age no longer approaching but laughing hysterically at my last seven year's worth of life-choices, I suddenly realise that we must make a move now or we'll be stuck trying to manoeuvre our Zimmer-frames around Voodoo Island forever.

The Computer Centre is due to close for six weeks over the summer and, finally galvanised into action after two years with a fence post impaled up my arse, I bite the bullet and quietly hand in my resignation, while up in heaven God slaps a weary hand to his forehead and sighs, "Oy vey, *now* they get it," and, two weeks later, in recognition of us finally making a definite gesture, The Fates send us an offer of housing on the British

mainland and we sign the lease on our new life.

Thus, on a bright sunny day at the end of August, almost seven years after first setting foot on the islands, we stand at the rail of the new MV Hamnavoe and wave goodbye to Orkney for the last time. There's a certain feeling of melancholy as the sedate stone buildings of Stromness fade slowly out of sight and the ferry picks up speed as it leaves the sheltered waters of the Hoy Sound. But as we sail sedately past the impassive Old Man of Hoy for the last time and I whisper "Goodbye, I'll maybe be back again some day," he seems to reply, "No, you won't," and we sail boldly off into a glassy Pentland Firth, our hearts brimming up with the forgotten feelings of adventure and excitement as we *finally* embark on the next chapter in our lives, after almost seven years of being well and truly downshafted.

EPILOGUE - WHERE WE EXPERIENCE A SURREAL MOMENT IN AN ALL-NIGHT TESCO SUPERSTORE

It is two months after our departure from Orkney and, sleepless, we are walking the aisles of a twenty-four-hour Tesco superstore, disconsolately flicking through DVDs at half past three in the morning. It's the hour when all decent humans are in their beds asleep, and, aside from the night packing crew, the shop is deserted, and there's an unnatural and ghostly feel to this gigantic land-locked ocean liner as it sits, only half-lit, softly humming, in the black and velvet night.

"So, how many months away now?" a soft Orcadian voice asks from behind me, and I turn to see a small, sandy-haired boy, dressed in a Tesco packer's uniform, who possesses a vaguely familiar cast to his features.

"I'm sorry?" I say, wondering if we've known each other in some previous life, and he laughs softly at my confusion.

"No, we've never met," he says quietly, reading my thoughts. "It's just that I remind you of so many folk you once knew."

Chancery has wandered off to the next aisle and is looking at CDs, and there is no-one else here but the phantom and me as I rub my eyes blearily, wondering if this foundling boy is real or the result of something that crawled up from the black waters of the North Sea to take temporary human form, and he reads my mind once again.

"No, I am real," he says with a grin. "I just know who you are because you're displaying all the signs."

"The signs?" I ask, and he continues with his impromptu tarot reading, glancing into my trolley as he does so.

"Let's see, it's four o'clock in the morning and you're out buying DVDs, leaf oregano and fresh wholemeal pasta. And you can't sleep because it's too hot, and the noise of traffic wakes you in the night, and you have to

239

come out to check that all this cornucopia is still here, and that it's not all been a dream and you're back to no boat and two kinds of tinned soup in Jimmo Baikie's store. How am I doing so far?"

"Like you're in my head," I say, amazed. "Are you sure you're real?"

"It'll take a peedie while," he says softly as he disappears round a corner into the gloom of the giant store. "But you'll acclimatise eventually."

"Who were you speaking to?" Chancery asks, reappearing, and I shake my head ruefully as the glittering world around me comes back into focus.

"I really wish I knew," I say.

Smiling.

If you have
enjoyed this book
please post a review
to your favourite
online
bookstore
today

ANOTHER HILARIOUS MAVERICK GUIDE

How to Write the
PERFECT NOVEL

Chancery Stone

ISBN 978-0-9546115-7-6

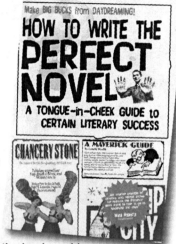

There are hundreds of conventional writers' guides on the market, but none so scathing, cynical and downright cantankerous as this one.

Forget toadying to publishers or obsessing over return postage; in this insider exposé veteran author, Chancery Stone, spares no-one's blushes as she strips the book world bare and reveals the true natures of publishers and authors alike.

Packed with laugh-out-loud parodies of best-selling thrillers, romances, crime, science fiction, erotica, and even the Booker Prize, **How to Write the Perfect Novel** names names and shows no mercy to the perpetrators, submerging you in such brain-numbing brilliance that you may never browse through a book shop in quite the same way again....

"This is the kind of book that you read for the humour, the scathing remarks and the blatant flaunting of all the rules. Yet it is so cleverly written that you find yourself learning things that, quite frankly, none of the other how-to books teach you."
W H Smith

"The perfect antidote to the thousands of well-meaning, hefty writers' guides that currently flood the market."
Essential Writers

"A bitter look at how to succeed."
Writers' Forum

"Chicken soup for the jaded writer's soul."
Good Reads

**Available from all good book stores or direct from
www.poisonpixie.com**

978-0-9567154-8-7

978-0-9567154-1-8

978-0-9567154-2-5

POISON PIXIE
FICTION

Available in Paper and/or Digital Editions

Digital E-Book

Digital E-Book

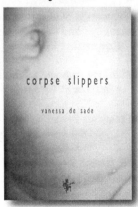

Digital E-Book

978-0-9567154-3-2

978-0-9567154-4-9

978-0-9546115-3-8

POISON PIXIE FICTION

Available in Paper and/or Digital Editions

978-0-9546115-4-5 | 978-0-9546115-5-2 | 978-0-9571920-0-3

available 2012

available 2012

Chancery Stone

CPSIA information can be obtained at www.ICGtesting.com
Printed in the USA
BVOW02s0103161113

336476BV00017B/554/P